Baseball's Iconic 1-0 Games

WARREN N. WILBERT

THE SCARECROW PRESS, INC.

Lanham • Toronto • Plymouth, UK

2013

Published by Scarecrow Press, Inc.
A wholly owned subsidary of The Rowman & Littlefield Publishing Group, Inc.
4501 Forbes Boulevard, Suite 200, Lanham, Maryland 20706
www.rowman.com

10 Thornbury Road, Plymouth PL6 7PP, United Kingdom

British Library Cataloguing in Publication Information Available

Library of Congress Cataloging-in-Publication Data

Wilbert, Warren N.
  Baseball's iconic 1-0 games / Warren N. Wilbert.
      pages cm.
  Includes bibliographical references and index.
  ISBN 978-0-8108-8578-3 (cloth : alk. paper) — ISBN 978-0-8108-8579-0 (ebook)
(print)
1. Baseball—United States—History—Miscellanea. 2. Shutouts (Sports)—United States—
History. I. Title.
  GV873.W54   2013
  796.357'64—dc23   2012034024

Printed in the United States of America

Respectfully dedicated to
Jim Juergensen
and
Roger Schmidt

Contents

List of Abbreviations

These terms and designations will help you read the various columns, figures, and tables used in this book. The more obvious and oft-used terms are not included here since they are a part of the common lexicon of the game of baseball. Legends often precede tables, so further explanation in those instances is not presented here.

League Designations

AA	American Association
AL	American League
FL	Federal League
NA	National Association of Professional Base Ball Players
NL	National League
PL	Players League
UA	Union Association

Playoff Designations

ALDS	American League Division Series
ALCS	American League Championship Series
NLCS	National League Championship Series
NLDS	National League Division Series
WS	World Series

Team Designations

Most team designations will be readily recognizable: NY for New York, Clv for Cleveland, Phl for Philadelphia, etc. In cities where there are two teams (e.g., New

York, Chicago), the abbreviations AL or NL follow the city name to indicate which team is meant.

| WOR | Worcester (NL, 19th century) |
| Brk | Brooklyn Dodgers |

General Terms

Note that these abbreviations are often expressed in lowercase in tables and statistics. For example, 3bh indicates three base hits.

1B	First Base
2B	Second Base
3B	Third Base
A	Assist
AB	At Bats
B	Bases (2B = double, 3B = triple)
BB	Bases on Balls (walks)
BF	Batters Faced
BH	Base Hits
C	Catcher
CF	Center Field
CG	Complete Games
DP	Double Play
E	Errors
ER	Earned Runs
ERA	Earned Run Average
HOF	Hall-of-Famer
HPB	Batter Hit by Pitched Ball
IP	Innings Pitched
K	Strike Out
L	Losses
LF	Left Field
Lg	League
LOB	Left on Base
LP	Losing Pitcher
ML/MLB	Major League/Major League Baseball
MLBA	Major League Batting Average
OF	Outfielder
PH	Pinch Hitter
PO	Putouts
RBI	Runs Batted In
Rec	Record

RF	Right Field
RP	Relief Pitcher
SB	Stolen Bases
SF	Sacrifice Fly
SH	Sacrifice Hit
SHO	Shutout
SO	Strikeouts
SS	Shortstop
W	Wins
WP	Winning Pitcher or Wild Pitch (context governs meaning)

Acknowledgments

I'd like to extend my sincere thanks to those who have been so very helpful in putting the 1-0 story between covers. The list is short but sweet. These people graciously stepped up to lend their help with timely information and support.

This is my list of Hall of Fame aides:

1. Fellow SABR members: Bill Deane, Scott Longert, Pete Palmer, Walt Wilson
2. Editorial assistance: Christen Karniski, Jessica McCleary
3. Correspondence and personal support: Virgil Trucks
4. Family: Daughters Karen and Ellen, all my grandchildren

To Begin With . . .

On April 16, 1940, Bob Feller fired a no-hitter to open a new baseball season at Comiskey Park, defeating the White Sox, 1-0. Ever since, he has been *el maestro* of baseball history's opening day. No one since has been able to match that extraordinary feat, and it will take a perfect game to surpass it. Feller's one-run victory that day enables us to tie both no-hitters and 1-0 scores into a neat little bundle as we concentrate exclusively on baseball's most minimal victory margin, 1-0. Although there have been many 0-0 ties throughout the years, that score does not produce a winner. Indeed, 1-0 is the one and only topic of discussion in these pages.

A review of that singular part of baseball history can be accomplished in a number of ways. We're going to begin on opening day, that very auspicious and ceremonial day that begins each season with pomp—waving flags, parades, presentations, the "first ball," new uniforms, and the great expectations of fans and franchises alike. The opening day review in chapter 1 covers some 39 ball games, including the only three that took place in the 19th century.

Following our opening day review, the best of the regular season 1-0s take center stage in chapter 2. Here you will find the most entertaining, longest, most exceptionally well played and intriguing among the 2.5 percent of major league ball games that wind up with a 1-0 score. Did I say 2.5 percent? That's right. The 1-0 score is but a smidgen of the number of games played each season. And that alone makes it worthy of special consideration, to say nothing of the fascinating stories embedded in each of those taut, spine-tingling contests.

Beyond the regular season 1-0 games, there are other areas of interest. Championship play, from the first inning of playoffs to the final out of World Series drama, has its own treasure store of tense, 1-0 contests. Those captivating ball games take center stage in chapter 3. Other areas include some of the more exceptional and extraordinary games: the no-hitters (chapter 4), games featuring Hall-of-Famers and their exploits through careers that included upwards of 20 and more 1-0 games (chapter 5), and the marathons, those extra-inning games that stretch into the evening hours or well into the night as the case may be (chapter 6).

Not all care that much about the tight, suspense-laden 1-0 ball game. Some fans would rather see a parade of pitchers and home runs that pile up the runs. They can rest securely in the fact that in only two to three games out of a hundred will there be only a run or two scored. They have not been denied, especially during entire eras that featured the "big sticks." But for those who revel in a run being scored in the bottom of the ninth with two away that wins one for the homestanding nine 1-0, here's a collection of stories that will, hopefully, not disappoint you.

CHAPTER 1

Opening Day

Restricting our review of opening day to 1-0 encounters necessarily reduces their number, but it also brings into the limelight those games whose outcomes are in doubt from beginning to end, calling for premier effort on the very first day of the long season ahead. And the mystery thus involved makes each pitch, each play, and each call from behind the plate critical, as well as demanding, as far as the game's outcome is concerned. For many baseball buffs, that's exactly what they come to see.

A total of 57 games with a 1-0 score made their way into opening day headlines between 1876 and 2005, when the Chicago White Sox got off to an impressive start in their World Championship season behind Mark Buehrle, defeating the Cleveland Indians before 38,141 Sox fans in a masterful two-hitter. Interestingly, there were but three 1-0 openers in the 19th century, the first of which came during the National League's inaugural season, 1876, when George Bradley led his St. Louis team to victory over the Al Spalding–led Chicago White Stockings. That game is featured later in this chapter.

Debuting 1-0 games in the 20th century was left to the Pittsburgh Pirates, who edged the St. Louis Cardinals on a beautiful spring day in 1902. The 1902 Pittsburgh team was one of baseball's very best of all time, winning the pennant by a whopping 27½ games over second-place Brooklyn, running up a 103-36 season record. Led by the immortal Hans Wagner, the Pirates fielded a strong defensive ball club and an even stronger offense. The pitching staff, led by 20-win Deacon Phillippe, also included two other 20-game winners, Jack Chesbro and Jesse Tannehill, plus Sam Leever (15-7) and Eddie Doheny (16-4). Those five won 99 of the team's 103, an incredible number.

Phillippe's 1-0 outing on April 17, 1902, was the first of five shutouts in a 20-9 season featuring a career low 2.05 ERA. His '02 log showcased 29 complete games in 31 starts while issuing but 29 bases on balls in 272 innings of work for the year. In the Deacon's opening game win, Wee Tommy Leach scored a third-inning run that the Pirate ace made do, countering a fine effort by St. Louis' Stan Yerkes. Many great 1-0 games were to follow. The following games are among the best of these very special encounters.

Bradley and Spalding, May 5, 1876

St. Louis	100	000	000	1-7-3
Chicago	000	000	000	0-2-6

WP, Bradley; LP, Spalding

This remarkable game was played at the western outpost of professional baseball in the year of the great Centennial Exhibition at Philadelphia, 1876. The year and its major events, such as Bell's telephone patent, the bitterly contested election of Rutherford Hayes as president, Custer's Last Stand on June 25, and the admission of Colorado as the 38th state, also happened to be the inaugural year of the fledgling National League, founded on February 2 in Chicago.

Mound City baseball enthusiasts had taken to baseball in a big way, fielding teams that rivaled Chicago entries in various sandlot and traveling leagues. Consequently, diamonds sprung up in St. Louis fields and parks, some of them, like the ball diamond known as Sportsmans Park, were on a par with venues like the New York, Brooklyn, and Philadelphia ballparks in the East. And it was at Sportsmans Park that the St. Louis entry into the new league won its first game of the season, a closely matched 1-0 affair won in the first inning on a throwing error by Chicago's Al Spalding that enabled the Cardinals catcher John Clapp to ultimately score on a pair of singles, the latter by early baseball stalwart Lipman Pike. It was all the run support the very able George Bradley needed, as he thwarted Chicago's forces on a two-hitter, setting St. Louis aflame with pride over its conquest of archrival Chicago. The St. Louisan George Bradley was the pitcher of record, incidentally, for every game his team played during the 1876 season, a record unmatched in baseball annals. This same George Bradley also recorded the National League's first no-hit game, the sparkling event taking place, also in St. Louis, as the final of a shutout trifecta against the Hartford Dark Blues and Tommy Bond on July 15, 2-0.

The next in our series of outstanding season opening 1-0 games took place almost two-score years later. A pair of opening 1-0 games in the 19th century and six of them prior to the April 9, 1913, tilt had taken place, highlighted by Phillippe's 1902 victory over the Cardinals in Pittsburgh.

Seaton and Rucker, April 9, 1913

Philadelphia	100	000	000	1-7-0
Brooklyn	000	000	000	0-6-3

WP, Seaton; LP, Rucker

In 1913 Philadelphia's baseball fans looked forward to a World Series between the Phillies and the Athletics. It almost came to pass. At season's end the Athletics were World Series bound, but the Phillies wound up in second place behind McGraw's Giants, having slid from the top rung to a 12-½ game deficit, far behind the league-leading New Yorkers. From opening day forward, the Phillies played at a commanding pace, winding up the month of May with a 22-11 record behind the incomparable Pete Alexander, Ab Brennan, and a sophomore right-hander who specialized in knuckleballs and scuffed ball pitches. His name was Tom Seaton, a tall, tough Nebraskan. During his 1912 rookie campaign he had appeared in 44 games, pitching 255 innings, while compiling a 16 and 12 mark. Because the Phillies experienced a raw, windy, and cold spring training camp in North Carolina, manager Red Dooin gave Seaton, Brennan, and George Chalmers extra work, saving the big guns on his staff—Grover Cleveland "Old Pete" Alexander, Chalmers, and Eppa Rixey—for more favorable weather.

Apparently Red Dooin liked what he saw when Tom Seaton took the hill, and he named him the Phils' opening day pitcher to face young Nap Rucker, whose quick one, along with an arsenal of breaking pitches as good as Seaton's, marked him as one of the top pitchers in the circuit. In Brooklyn, Superba fans were eagerly anticipating the official opening of the 1913 season, and the first National League game to be played in Charlie Ebbets' new baseball arena.

The game was a magnificently pitched thriller. A capacity crowd in the new $750,000 stadium saw Seaton and Rucker match strike for strike, the Phillies pushing across the only run they needed right off the bat. Leadoff hitter "Dode" Paskert punched a line drive past Bobby Fisher, the Brooklyn shortstop. It was Nap Rucker's first pitch of the day, followed by another seasonal and stadium first, as Paskert was rubbed out on a fine throw by leftfielder Zack Wheat. Then Otto Knabe doubled and held at second while Hans Lobert flied out. With two outs Sherry Magee lofted a lazy flyball for the apparent third out that would get Rucker out of the inning. Benny Meyer, Brooklyn right fielder, got under the fly ball but let it slither through his gloved hand, enabling the game's only run to score. The next day the teams traded playing sites, opening the Philadelphia home season. Brooklyn avenged its loss by stomping the Phils 11 to 3.

In its next ten games the Phils took three more by a 1-0 count, Seaton beating Rucker again, Brennan defeating Brooklyn again in the fourth game of the season, and Grover Alexander nudging the Giants on May Day. Eight shutouts dotted the Philadelphia ledger before May was over, as well as a number of 2-1 and 3-1 contests. They had permitted an average of slightly less than three runs per game. No wonder Phillies' fans were excited about World Series prospects.

Tom Seaton went on to a better season than Pete Alexander had, posting a fine 27-12 mark while leading National League pitchers in strikeouts (168), wins (27), and innings pitched (322.1). He finished the season with five shutouts, four fewer than Alexander's league-leading nine. That was good for a second-place ranking among the NL's shutout pitchers.

Tom Seaton also had the honor of opening the Federal League's initial season in 1914 with a 2-0 victory, this time for the Brooklyn FL team. He defeated Elmer Knetzer in that season opener on April 14 at Pittsburgh. His days at or near the top of the list of big league pitchers, however, were soon to come to a halt under pain of arm troubles due to overwork and less-than-helpful treatment. That sad story, often the lot of deadball era pitchers, and many others for that matter is, unfortunately, a familiar one.

Johnson and Perry, April 23, 1919

Philadelphia	000	000	000	000	0	0-10-1
Washington	000	000	000	000	1	1-7-1

WP, Johnson; LP, Perry

Walter Johnson was involved in more 1-0 games than any other pitcher in baseball history, a total of 64. He won 38 of them, including a no-hitter against Boston and two extra-inning thrillers, one of which remains the longest 1-0 game in opening day history. His victory over Eddie Rommel and the Athletics opened the 1926 season. That 16-inning marathon, crafted at age 39, was listed in Henry Thomas' definitive review of the famous hurler's life as number one on his list of Johnson's 15 best games. Thomas wrote this capsule about the 1926 opener:

> This is the game Johnson believed to be his masterpiece, and who's to argue with the master himself? Well into his 39th year and starting

1-0 king Walter Johnson.

his 20th season in the major leagues, the Big Train thrilled a capacity Opening Day crowd in Washington by blanking their 1925 pennant rivals until the home team could score in the bottom of the 15th. The powerful A's managed just six hits, nine of them going down on strikes (five times called), and not one saw second base all day. Knuckleballer Eddie Rommel also went the distance in this classic pitching duel.[1]

There was still another 1-0 season opener authored by Walter Johnson, occurring some seasons earlier, on April 23, 1919. That year he was a 20-game winner for the 10th consecutive season and Johnson had 1-0 victories over Cleveland, New York, and Philadelphia, twice. The first of those 1-0 games was his opening day victory, a tense, 13-inning affair, over Philadelphia's Mackmen, who were led by Scott Perry, a fidgety Texan who went by the nickname "Jittery Joe." During the prior AL campaign Perry had been a 20-game winner, which included a one-hitter against pennant-winning Chicago on May 11 at Shibe Park in Philadelphia. Winning one out of every five Athletic victories (the team finished a dismal last with a 52-76 record in the shortened, 130-game season), in 1918 Connie Mack gave him the ball 36 times, enabling him to record a league-high 30 complete games, 332.1 innings pitched, and a 1.98 ERA. This, despite 19 losses and an insufferable ball club behind him. However, those A's were not quite so insufferable on the two occasions that Perry and Johnson met early in the 1918 season. On April 22 the Fidgety One bested Johnson 5-1 and again in early May at Philadelphia, when Perry won an 11-inning heart-stopper, winning 1-0 and edging Johnson, who had come on for a 5.1-inning relief stint.

After his 1918 heroics Perry was an odds-on pick to open the Philadelphia season in Washington in 1919. With President Wilson attending to some international affairs following World War I, the Army Chief of Staff, General Peyton C. March, was dispatched to Griffith Stadium to do the opening day honors. Parades, ceremonies, and Gen. March's first ball all went off without a hitch, and the game soon followed the same flawless pattern with neither team able to muster a score through 12 innings of play. The Athletics managed to get to Johnson for 10 singles but constantly beat his offerings into the ground for infield outs, two of which were double plays that frustrated Philadelphia's attack.

Finally, with one out in the bottom of the 13th, Eddie Foster singled home pinch runner Mike Menosky with the winning run. The victory put Washington into first place for at least a day, and sent the A's to the bottom of the standings where they remained for the rest of the season. Clark Griffith's 1919 Senators didn't fare much better, winding up in seventh place, with a lackluster 56-84 record. Almost 40 percent of the Senators' victories came when Walter Johnson was on the mound. In 1919 his 1.49 ERA led the league as he fashioned 20 wins for the 10th consecutive time. All that notwithstanding, the peerless one's salad days were about over as he struggled the next several seasons before reaching back for the extra it took to bring his Senators in with a winner in 1924. He won 23 that year and another 20 during the 1925 AL championship season.

After his career was over there were those who claimed he never really lost his fast one; he just didn't throw it as often. In his Johnson biography[2] Thomas quotes Grantland Rice in this witty comment: "Johnson seems to have slowed up in the same way John D. (Rockefeller) has gone broke—both have lost something, but they still have enough."

The story is told that during the 1930s, long after his last blinding fast one was thrown, Johnson was visiting the Senators' spring training camp. Standing behind the batting cage with "Goose" Goslin, his old teammate and friend, he chatted amiably about the pitchers and hitters he was watching in the warm Florida sun. A young prospect stepped into the cage and promptly blistered a few to the distant reaches of Washington's training facility. After some cajoling, Johnson was persuaded, mostly by Goslin, to take the mound and show the young one what a real fastball looked like. And so the big fellow ambled out to the mound and tossed a few softies the young slugger's way. Then, as if out of the blue, came a whoosh, followed by the crack of the ball in the catcher's mitt. A few more followed with the same result, and Big Walter left the mound, stating, with a twinkle in his eye, that there were another few left in his arm, but that he would rather keep 'em for a rainy day. The old timers on the field looked at each other with that knowing look and nodded. After that little exhibition school was out for the day.

Bridges and Stewart, April 23, 1931

St. Louis	000	000	000	0-4-0
Detroit	000	100	000	1-5-0

WP, Bridges; LP, Stewart

Tommy Bridges and his marvelous curveball put a number of entries into the "memorable games" book. One of those was an opening day 1-0 conquest of the St. Louis Browns in 1931. It was an occasion that called for brilliance if for no other reason than that his mound rival, Walter "Lefty" Stewart, was on his game, spacing five hits in a great exhibition of curveball pitchers at Navin Field. Bridges was up to the challenge, converting a fourth-inning run into his first win of the season after having been defeated by the lithe Brownie hurler in Bridges' first outing of the season in St. Louis. The victory came after a seven-game road trip that marked the Tigers' first games in St. Louis and Cleveland. By the time April 23 came around, Tiger fans were more than ready for their favorites' inaugural home contest, and a crowd of more than 30,000 turned out. They were not disappointed. A fourth-inning double by one of their heroes, Charlie Gehringer, followed by a Dale Alexander single, scored the run that proved to be the winning margin in a flawlessly played game, neither team committing an error.

Tommy Bridges split even, four and four, in 1-0 games, and aside from a 0-0 tie in a 14-inning game against Cleveland's Al Milnar, it was his best effort in low-scoring games. He came within an out of a perfect game the next season, against Cleveland once again, defeating them 13-0 in one of his 33 career shutouts, and added to his shutout total with 1-0 games against St. Louis (1932), Washington (1933), and Boston (1936). In a season opener at Cleveland in 1943 he lost a white-knuckler, the winning run having been scored with two out in the bottom of the ninth. Pitcher Jim Bagby's walkoff RBI single drove home the deciding tally. As is often the case in 1-0 games, Bagby's three-hit effort against Detroit was one of his great career games.

Curveball wizard Tommy Bridges. *Brace Photo.*

During the years of the Great Depression there wasn't a better curveball pitcher than Bridges in the bigs, and it's no stretch to put him among the best ever. Such a list might include Bert Blyleven, Sandy Koufax, Mordecai Brown, Herb Pennock, Negro Leagues pitcher Hilton Smith, Camilio Pascual, and, somewhere in the top three of those mentioned, Tommy Bridges.

Feller and Smith, April 16, 1940

Cleveland	000	001	000	1-6-1	
Chicago	000	000	000	0-0-1	

It remained for Bullet Bob Feller to throw the ultimate 1-0 game, a no-hitter that initiated the 1940 season at Comiskey Park. It is—and remains to this writing—the one and only of its kind in baseball's annals. Further, it is one of his more sterling entries, among a number of several significant others, that qualified him for election to the game's Hall of Fame.

The game has been written about in journals, biographies, and numerous other places, hailed as one of the most singular accomplishments in baseball lore. The first of his three no-hitters, it was fashioned on a raw, windy day in Chicago's notoriously unpredictable April weather. Two of the more noteworthy guests at this frigid contest were Feller's mother and baseball's commissioner

Table 1.1. Bob Feller's April 16, 1940, No-Hitter

Cleveland	AB	R	H	PO	Chicago (AL)	AB	R	H	PO
Boudreau, ss	3	0	0	1	Kennedy, 2b	4	0	0	1
Weatherly, cf	4	0	1	2	Kuhel, 1b	3	0	0	11
Chapman, rf	3	0	0	6	Kreevich, cf	3	0	0	3
Trosky, 1b	4	0	0	8	Solters, lf	3	0	0	2
Heath, lf	4	1	1	0	Appling, ss	4	0	0	0
Keltner, 3b	4	0	1	0	Wright, rf	4	0	0	3
Hemsley, c	4	0	2	8	McNair, 2b	3	0	0	2
Mack, 2b	4	0	1	2	Tresh, c	2	0	0	5
Feller, WP	3	0	0	0	Smith, LP	1	0	0	0
					Rosenthal, ph	1	0	0	0
					Brown, rp	0	0	0	0
Totals	**33**	**1**	**6**	**27**	**Totals**	**28**	**0**	**0**	**27**

E: Weatherly and McNair.
2bh: Hemsley.
3bh: Mack.
RBI: Hemsley.
DP: Kuhel unassisted.
SB: Kuhel.
LOB: Cleveland 7, Chicago 6.
SO: Feller 8, Smith 5.
BB: Feller 5, Smith 2.
IP: Feller 9, Smith 8, Brown 1.
Game time: 2 hours, 24 minutes.
Umpires: Geisel, McGowan, Kolls.
Scorer: Ed Burns, *Chicago Tribune.*
Attendance: 14,000.

K-Master Bob Feller.

judge Kenesaw Mountain Landis. Neither was disappointed in the Iowan's performance that day. The great fastballer's counterpart, Eddie Smith, turned in a fair country day's work himself, allowing a single run in the top of the seventh inning, when catcher Rollie Hemsley tripled home Jeff Heath with the game's only run. Feller, still a mere 22 at the time, only needed that single tally to dwindle Sox hopes to nothing.

In the final stanza, the dreaded last of the ninth, the heart of the Chicago order confronted Rapid Robert. Mike Kreevich, a pesky .300 hitter, was an easy leadoff out, followed by the oversized slugger Moose Solters, who also succumbed. That brought up one of the most exasperating hitters in American League history, Hall-of-Famer Luke Appling, who went into his foul ball routine, slicing drives here and there while running the count to 3 and 2. Then Feller, who remarked later that he wasn't about to stand out there and watch Appling foul new baseballs all over the place, intentionally threw the 3-2 pitch just a little outside to walk him. The White Sox were alive with a base runner, but so was Feller's no-hitter. That brought up Taffy Wright, a contact hitter of the first order. Wright offered on Feller's first pitch and smashed a liner into the hole between first and second. For a nanosecond Feller's no-hitter was in serious jeopardy, but second baseman Ray Mack got to it, snared it, and fired to first baseman Hal Trosky, nailing Wright for the final out of the game.

The hero of the game in Feller's eyes? Ray Mack, who fielded Chicago's hardest hit ball all day, and turned it into a game-saver. That ball soon became one of the treasures in the Feller memorabilia collection.

Though it was his most famous, it wasn't the only 1-0 game Bob Feller threw on opening day. In the first post–WWII season of 1946 Bob Feller returned to Chicago to open the White Sox's season once again, this time throwing a three-hitter while fanning ten in a game won on a George Case double and a Hank Edwards' RBI hit that accounted for the winning run. The White Sox this time mustered three hits, but the result was the same as in 1940 when Feller set them down, 1-0. Bob Lemon, who was to carve out a Hall of Fame career as a sinkerball artist, was Cleveland's center fielder in this game, tossing a strike to Lou Boudreau on the back end of a double play that shut down Chicago's only scoring opportunity.

But there was one game in Feller's career, in which he logged a 7-7 record in 1-0 games, that was another of those "only-time-in-history" ball games. On April 23, 1952, in St. Louis, he was paired with Bob "Sugar" Cain. Both pitchers came to the ball park with a full bag of tricks and stuff, and the result was a 1-1 tie in which neither team could come up with more than a single hit. In this extraordinary game St. Louis' only hit came off the bat of Bobby Young, who led off for the Browns with a triple. What followed was a Marty Marion grounder that Flip Rosen, Cleveland third baseman, muffed. Young scored on that play, so there was an unearned run and no RBI credited to the hitter and the Browns took the lead, 1-0. Subsequently, Bullet Man Feller retired 27 Brownies without a hit. Several "no-hitters" like this have been recorded in the major leagues, but none quite like this one.

The only hit that Sugar Cain allowed the Indians was delivered by muscular Luke Easter, who stroked a leadoff single to start the Cleveland fifth. Rosen walked, but a double play doused Indian hopes of scoring, and through the remaining innings both teams forgot how to manufacture a hit. Consequently, the game wound up a 1-1 tie.

One other of Feller's 1-0 log begs mention: the Allie Reynolds no-hitter that defeated Cleveland with Feller on the mound. Despite a fine four-hitter, the Yankees came out a 1-0 winner on the strength of a Gene Woodling seventh-inning homer. In this tilt Bobby Avila reached base in the bottom of the first on a play that was scored as an error by Phil Rizzuto. It might have been scored a hit—but wasn't. Reynolds went on from that point to a no-hitter, walking three, but benefiting from two spectacularly fielded double plays. Feller on that occasion was almost as good, but to no avail. It was the first of two Reynolds no-no's that season. Reynolds, whose career started in Cleveland livery, secured at least a tie for the pennant with his second no-hitter of 1951, and his Yankees went on from that Boston victory to a World Series championship.

And Bob Feller? His Hall of Fame selection assured well ahead of his re-tirement in 1956, the Van Meter, Iowa, farm boy, with that wicked fastball recorded at speeds over 100 mph on the speed guns of his day, had thrown three no-hitters and a dozen one-hit games in a legendary career that put more than one record into the books—not least of which was that 1-0 no-hitter that brought on the 1940 season, a game that Indian fans will not forget, and that is probably remembered in Chicago, as well—but not for the right reasons!

Pierce and Brecheen, April 15, 1953

St. Louis	000	000	000	0-1-1
Chicago	000	000	10x	1-2-1

WP, Pierce; LP, Brecheen

This season opener at Comiskey Park almost atoned for the miseries suffered at the hands of Bob Feller's no-hitter opening the 1940 season. On this occasion Billy Pierce one-hit the St. Louis Browns, the victory posted in the "lucky seventh" on an unearned run. In that frame Jungle Jim Rivera opened with one of southpaw Harry Brecheen's four walks, advanced on a sacrifice, went to third on a throwing error, and came home on catcher Sherm Lollar's sacrifice fly. During Chicago's Go-Go years that was a rather typical exhibition of White Sox offensive "punch," reminiscent of the old Hitless Wonder days at the turn of the 20th century.

The game came within a Minnie Minoso single in the eighth inning of ty-ing the American League standard of two hits in a game set by the Feller-Cain outing on April 23, 1952. Just a year later Billy Pierce and the very able Harry

Brecheen, a former Cardinal ace making his first start for the Brownies, set down the batting order of the White Sox with just three hits. Second baseman Bobby Young, batting eighth, doubled for the Browns in the seventh for their only hit. You will remember him as the same Young who ruined Bob Feller's no-hit bid with a triple.

Vern Stephens' opening stanza single and Minoso's eighth inning safety were Chicago's only hits. Neither figured in the winning tally.

Starting in 1950 with a sixth-place finish, the Go-Go White Sox rose steadily in the American League standings, moving up to fourth and then third in 1952. By 1953 expectations on Chicago's South Side had risen higher than at any time since the days of the Black Sox. And Billy Pierce's 1953 start gave them greater hopes than ever.

Pierce was a driving force in the next several seasons, which culminated in a 1959 pennant. In 1953 Pierce was an All-Star starter for the American League, pitching three scoreless innings. That season he was an 18-game winner, racked up seven shutouts, 51 consecutive scoreless innings, permitted opposing hitters a paltry .218 batting average, which led his league, as did his 218 strikeouts. His 1-0 winner in the 1953 season opener forecast a bright season for the stylish southpaw, and the numbers at season's end underscored those expectations.

There are those games that even the greats would like to forget—but can't. One of those for Billy Pierce occurred on June 27 in 1958 at Washington's Griffith Stadium. With two out in the ninth, and a perfect game on the line, pinch hitter Eddie Fitzgerald punched a screamer just fair down the right field line for Washington's only hit. The next batter, outfielder Albie Pearson, the American League's Rookie of the Year in '58, went down on strikes, which ended the game, a one-hit 3-0 victory, moving his record at that point to seven wins against five losses.

Surrounding that gem were 4-0 and 1-0 conquests on June 17 and 21, respectively, and a follow-up win, 8-1, against Detroit on July 5.

In a career of 13 1-0 games, Pierce won eight of them, and was involved in two 0-0 ties. His last 1-0 victory came against the Kansas City Athletics at Comiskey Park on August 11, 1961. Luis Aparicio's third inning circuit smash won it that day for the Sox. Pierce was matched with Jim Archer, who had the finest outing of his short-lived career, allowing six hits, walking none, and striking out three. Pierce didn't allow a free pass either, in one of those rare games in which no walks were issued.

There was one final 1-0 game in the Pierce log. In this one, played out in the National League, Billy was brought on as a relief pitcher and got credit for a save as the Giants beat Houston at Candlestick Park on July 19, 1964. On that day two old White Sox hands, Pierce and Bob Shaw, helped Bob Hendley tack gain his ninth win of the season. That day Billy Pierce was the last man standing, striking out Houston first baseman Walt Bond to end the game.

Stottlemyre and Brunet, April 10, 1968

California	000	000	000	0-4-0
New York	010	000	00x	1-3-1

WP, Stottlemyre; LP, Brunet

It was the Year of the Pitcher. Of the several seasons crowned as Year of the Pitcher, this one was *it*. To begin with, there were no less than 18 low-hit games (zero or one hit allowed), and six pitchers ran scoreless inning streaks of 30 or more innings, led by Don Drysdale's record-setting 58.1. And there was Bob Gibson, who ran a streak of 15 straight wins featuring a streak within a streak of 95 straight innings during which he allowed but two earned runs, not to mention his 13 shutouts and absurdly tiny ERA, 1.12. Those few numbers cited are just a tip on the proverbial iceberg that were a part of nearly a decade's worth of miniscule ERA's, low-scoring games, and offensive fireworks *in absentia*. And this doesn't take into account the 24-inning marathon staged in Houston, won by the Astros, 1-0, on an unearned run. Add to that a final shot heard 'round the baseball world: the only All-Star game in history won by a 1-0 count, was put together by the senior circuit "bombers" in '68.

It should be said, nonetheless, that there were a few fellows plying the pitching trade beyond the Drysdales, Gibsons, and Tiants. One of those was Mel Stottlemyre, soldiering on in what was fast becoming a Yankee drought of baseball respectability. His 1968 reading included a 21-12 record for a Yankee team that barely nosed over the .500 mark, showcasing six shutouts that included two 1-0 victories, a 2.45 ERA, and a .280 average among the batters he faced in 278.2 innings of work.

The California Angels and a weak opening day crowd of 15,744 fans helped the Yanks open the '68 campaign. Manager Bill Rigney went with George Brunet, who had won in double figures for the Halos in 1967, as Stottlemyre's opponent. It was a good choice. Brunet, though nicked for a second inning tater off the bat of reserve catcher Frank Hernandez, pitched well, allowing only two other hits, both of them by Mickey Mantle, who, in his last season in a fabulous Yankee career, opened the year at first base. Brunet was lifted after seven innings, facing 23 hitters, but two over the seven-inning limit.

But Mel Stottlemyre was better. His log showed a complete game four-hitter, during which he was in control all the way. He matched Brunet's no-walk performance and shut down the Angels' only threat, which came in the game's final frame as California's Jim Fregosi doubled with one out and advanced, ultimately, to third on a groundout that went from Gene Michaels to Mantle. But then Stottlemyre, a sinkerball artist, induced another grounder, this one by Chuck Hinton, that became the game's final out, again from Michaels to Mantle.

It should be noted that this game was delayed in deference to the funeral ceremony of Dr. Martin Luther King, held at Ebenezer Baptist Church in Atlanta. The occasion is remembered here to note the turmoil of the 1960s, which reminded one and all that although Jackie Robinson, whose career by that time was history, was respectfully remembered, all was not yet settled with respect to the racial unrest, neither nationally nor in baseball.

Six seasons later, in 1974, Mel Stottlemyre's record suddenly dropped to 6-7 after nine successive double-figure win seasons. A rotator cuff injury felled him, bringing to an end a career during which he had posted 40 shutouts, six of which were 1-0 victories. Three of those were won on Yankee home runs: the first detailed above; the second by Mantle against California on April 25 in 1965 at Yankee Stadium; and the third by a Bernie Allen homer in an 11-inning struggle that was marked by a stumbling Allen misstep as he rounded first base (you can just imagine the fun his Yankee teammates had with that one in the dugout!). One particularly well-pitched 1-0 win came against Vida Blue and the Oakland A's in 1971, a three-hitter Stottlemyre claimed was one of the better games he ever threw. That would take in a rich backlog of fine pitching.

Matlack, Kern, and Lyle, vs. Guidry, Underwood, and Gossage, April 10, 1980

New York	000	000	000	000	0-4-2
Texas	000	000	000	001	1-4-0

WP, Underwood; LP, Lyle

Some 33,196 die-hard Texans were on hand to watch their Rangers and the Yankees pry the lid off the 1980 season, as two well-seasoned veterans, lefties Jon Matlack and Ron Guidry, wrangled for an upper hand on one of those picturesque Texas spring days when the sun was warming Mother Earth and the state's much-publicized bluebells were in full bloom. Texan bluebells notwithstanding, neither Guidry nor Matlack were around when the single tally of the game was scored. The 12-inning marathon was finally decided on a wild pitch by the big flame thrower Goose Gossage, author of those aspirin-like offerings that were clocked in the 90s on radar guns around the league, which came in a bases-loaded Texas 12th. That enabled the former Yankee and super flake Mickey Rivers to score. Of course, it brought on a wild celebration in the Great Republic of Texas.

What added interest to this game, at least for the players, was the rematch set up by managers Dick Howser of the New Yorkers and the Rangers' Pat Corrales. Just two seasons earlier both Guidry and Matlack were the pitchers of choice to open the 1978 season. In that one Richie Zisk lofted a ninth-inning walkoff bomb out of the Arlington stadium that pinned a 2-1 loss on Gossage, again in relief of Guidry. In two season openers, consequently, against the same team and pitcher, the lean lefty from the Bayous had given up one earned run and had yet to win a ball game. But don't waste your sympathy on Guidry. That very year, 1978, he recovered enough to post 25 wins, devastate AL teams with a 1.74 ERA, and win the Cy Young award plus a World Series ring. It was a Mount Everest year that rated six wins on Bill James' sabermetric rating scale. No Yankee pitcher has ever turned in a better season.

Guidry's opening day opponent in '78, as well as '80, had pitched 18 innings against the Yankees, giving up but a single earned run in total, winning once in the two games. Between the two of them, Matlack and Guidry had pitched some 34 innings of simply great baseball, yielding runs at a bare minimum. In the 1980 tilt Guidry offered up a mere 98 pitches, only 27 balls, and in 1978 Jon Matlack retired the last 18 Yanks he faced and 25 out of the last 26. Goose Gossage's only explanation concerning his wild pitch was that it got away from him. Major league life *does* have its tremendous highs and equally low lows.

1994 Opening Series' Shutouts

At San Francisco: San Francisco 8, Pittsburgh 0 (4/4/94)
At Los Angeles: Florida 1, Los Angeles 0 (4/7/94)
At Montreal: Chicago 4, Montreal 0 (4/8/94)
At San Diego: San Diego 4, Florida 0 (4/8/94)

Four shutouts marked the opening days of the 1994 season. In their first series of the year at Miami, Florida snuffed out the Dodgers in both teams' opening series, the 1-0 victory coming in the third game of the series. Chris Hammond, who started and shut down Los Angeles hitters through eight innings, was the winning pitcher. Bryan Harvey closed out the day in 1-2-3 order.

The next day, April 8, the San Diego Padres opened at home to those same Marlins. This time the tables were turned, and the Pads, on a strong two-hit effort by Chris Hammond plus three Padre homers that accounted for all four San Diego runs, vanquished the Florida Marlins 4-0. Hall of Fame–bound reliever Trevor Hoffman got the save in this one.

An earlier shutout, this one by San Francisco on April 4, resulted in a Pittsburgh defeat by an 8-0 score. The victory went to John Burkett, the defeat pinned on Zane Smith of the Pirates.

A fourth National League shutout (there were no American League shutouts or 1-0 games in 1994's openers) was posted by Chicago's Cubbies, who blanked the Montreal Expos 4-0. In that April 8 encounter the veteran Steve Trachsel went seven-plus innings, giving up only three hits, to get the victory. Cub relievers Jose Bautista and Randy Meyers finished off Montreal at the Olympiad. The Cubs-Expos game brings us to Chicago's own opening game, played four days earlier. The events of that day bear a closer look even though there was no shutout or 1-0 game involved. Read on . . .

The Chicago Cubs' 1994 baseball season opened in the Friendly Confines with the usual, as well as at least one *un*usual opening day ritual. There were, indeed, the traditional lineups along the base lines and other of the accustomed ceremonies. Finally, there was the ceremonial first pitch. This one was not delivered by the president. He was in Cleveland, decked out in an Indians jacket while throwing left-handed. It was mentioned that "Da Prez" played the sax much better than he pitched, but Lefty Clinton got through his opening day assignment passably well.

Some 300 miles to the west of Cleveland, there was a far different opening pitch artist at work. She was, in fact, the president's wife, Hillary, a scatter-armed right-hander who graciously agreed to throw out 1994's first ball at Wrigley Field. If there were to be no other "firsts" or "mosts" that day, at least it could be said that Wrigleyville enjoyed the privilege of hosting the first First Lady's opening pitch!

So unique was that event that it wound up in the erudite pages of the *Atlantic*'s August 1996 issue in an article entitled *Throwing Like a Girl*, written by James Fallows, national *Atlantic* correspondent and sometime speechwriter for former president Jimmy Carter. The following paragraph sums up Hillary Clinton's valiant effort at Wrigley Field on April 4, 1994.

> The next day photos (on April 5) of the Clintons in action appeared in newspapers around the country. Many papers, including the *New York Times* and *Washington Post*, chose the same two photos to run. The one of Bill Clinton showed him wearing an Indians cap and warm-up jacket. The President, throwing lefty, had turned his shoulders sideways to the plate in preparation for delivery. He was bringing the ball forward from behind his head in a clean-looking throwing action as the photo was snapped. Hillary Clinton was pictured wearing a dark

jacket, a scarf, and an over-sized Cubs hat. A right-hander, she had the elbow of her throwing arm pointed out in front of her. Her forearm was tilted back, toward her shoulder. The ball rested on her upturned palm. As the picture was taken, she was in the middle of an action that can only be described as throwing like a girl.

Fallows' whimsical article thoroughly dissected the throwing art in the hands of feminine delicacy, but, from a baseball buff's standpoint, somehow failed to get the real significance of Madame Clinton's efforts at the beginning of a new season—especially one at Wrigley Field! No mayor, president, or foreign dignitary got first-day coverage like that, and after that first wobbly toss, everything was no doubt anti-climactic. As a matter of fact, the Mets of New York, behind Dwight Gooden, followed up with an offensive show that netted a 12-8 win over Mike Morgan and his beleaguered Cubs. No 1-0, no shutout, no win. Just the first day at the office, as it turned out, for a Cub outfit that wound up that season in the basement of their division. At least on opening day, per Hillary Clinton, Wrigleyville enjoyed a happier moment.

Nomo and Glavine, April 8, 1996

Atlanta	000	000	000	0-3-0
Los Angeles	001	000	00x	1-5-0

WP, Nomo; LP, Glavine

As befits this latter day, there is an international flavor to the last game of this opening game review. In a later chapter, 1-0 games in other and foreign venues command our attention, and this one—played in our own international city of Los Angeles—serves well as a glimpse of what lies ahead.

The roster of the Dodgers listed Hideo Nomo as one of its pitchers in two separate hitches, 1995–1998 and 2002–2004. The native Japanese right-hander with the unusual windup was born in Osaka and starred in Japan's Major Leagues before inking a Los Angeles contract enabling him to become the first international to sign as a permanently relocating player. He was a success from his first pitch forward, paving the way for a tsunami of Japanese players on American soil. One of Nomo's five-star accomplishments was to throw a no-hitter in both the National and American Leagues. He is but one of five major league hurlers to accomplish this rare feat.

Hideo Nomo was in fine form on April 8, 1996, when the Dodgers entertained the Atlanta Braves. Though challenged by the powerful 1990s Braves with a pair of stolen bases and five free passes coaxed by Atlanta patience, the Nipponese hero weathered all of that, permitting just two singles and a Jeff Blauser double to abet a modest Dodger attack of a single, third-inning run, thus coming out of the encounter with his and the Dodgers' first win of the season. That sent 53,180 Angelenos home happy. It is well to note that his opposing pitcher on this day was the very able left-hander Tom Glavine, who in that game stifled Dodger bats enough to have won on many another day—three of the five hits he surrendered were bunched in a one-run third.

The opening day game was Nomo's first of two 1996 shutouts. The latter of the two is worth a closer look. Though Nomo had to wait for the last weeks of the season to post another shutout victory, the wait was more than worthwhile. Playing in the elevated surroundings of hitter-friendly Coors Field on September 17, he turned in a breathtaking 9-0 no-hitter. Nomo put the finishing touch to his no-no in the ninth when the top of the Rockies' order, led by Eric Young and Quinton McCracken, both grounded out. That left the hard-hitting Ellis Burks as the last obstacle in the way of his no-hitter, and the able sinkerball artist, who also used a sharp, late-breaking curve as an out pitch, got Burks on strikes to end it in a flourish.

Among the many 1-0 victories registered by major league pitchers, there are a number of choice selections that are spotlighted in the next chapter. We turn now, from opening day victories to some that are beyond sensational.

Notes

1. Henry Thomas, *Walter Johnson: Baseball's Big Train* (Lincoln: University of Nebraska Press, 1995), 354.
2. Thomas, *Walter Johnson,* 155–156.

CHAPTER 2

1-0: The Great Ones during Regular Season Play

Among upward of 500 1-0 regular season ball games to choose from, the more than 20 presented here should give an idea of the games and the heroes that make up the list of some of the best on record. From John "Jocko" Flynn to Randy Johnson, the stories of these games make up a fascinating profile of that *rara avis*, the 1-0 game. (Note, please, that selected no-hitters and perfect games are reviewed in a chapter further on.)

Jocko Flynn, September 13, 1886:
St. Louis Maroons vs. Chicago White Stockings

Chicago	001	000	000	1-3-2
St. Louis	000	000	000	0-4-8
	WP, Flynn; LP, Healy				

By 1886 the National League was well established, having been on the professional baseball scene a decade, and looking to another grand season of play in its eight-team league. By September 11 of that year the Chicago White Stockings had a firm grip on the pennant race, ahead of their closest competitor, the Detroit Wolverines, by four games. Their last game prior to Jocko Flynn's superb effort on September 13 was a thoroughgoing squelching of the Wolverines, 14 to 4, behind John Clarkson, the legendary one who ultimately found his way to the Hall of Fame. The Detroit victory had been his 26th among his 36 victories in 1886. The other big winner on the 1886 Chicago staff was burly Jim Mc-Cormick, a 31-game winner. And then there was John Flynn.

They called him Jocko, and for good reason. He was a *bon vivant* who didn't take his baseball as seriously as he did the spirits available in Chicago's many watering holes. And as far as major league careers go, he was around for only one season. But what a season! He was a 26-game winner, led the NL in winning percentage at .793, fired two shutouts, hit four home runs, completed 29 of his 32 starts, and wound up the season with a 2.24 ERA.

As the 1886 season wore down to its last weeks the Chicago club was scheduled for a long road trip to finish the season. After Clarkson's win at home against Detroit, the White Stockings' home stand came to an end and the team traveled to St. Louis for the first of a three game set. Cap Anson penciled Flynn's name into the starting pitcher's slot for the September 13 game at Robison Field to meet the Maroons of St. Louis. Already at that time the Chicago–St. Louis rivalry was a big one, just as it is today.

What little is known of Jocko Flynn has been put together by the very able baseball historian David Nemec. In his *Great Encyclopedia of 19th-Century Major League Baseball,*[1] he sketches the young gay-blade this way:

> Cocky, insouciant, Jocko Flynn stands beside fellow rookie Jimmy Ryan in the 1886 Chicago White Stockings' team picture. It is [the] lone enduring image of perhaps the greatest one-year wonder in major league history. . . . Flynn won 23 games so quickly that it was said of him: "On the street he looks like one of your lawn-tennis dudes. On the field he is, to quote everybody, a perfect terror."

With four days rest, Flynn was as ready as he would ever be—all things considered. He was matched with a St. Louis favorite, Jack "The Egyptian" Healy, on a day when his winning streak of ten was on the line. *The Chicago Tribune* issue of September 14, 1886, covered the game. The report on the winning run, ignited by Flynn's third-inning single, follows: "Ryan sent a fly out in right field which Cahill caught. While Gore [the next hitter] was preparing to demolish the ball, Flynn made a dash for second, [catcher] Meyers made a wild throw and Flynn kept on to third. Gore then made a base hit and Flynn scored the only run of the game."

The defensive gem of the game was rookie Jimmy Ryan's sensational catch in the eighth inning of a Patsy Cahill drive that was speared inches off the ground after a frantic chase. On great plays like Ryan's catch these 1-0 games so often turn. It usually takes more than super pitching to hold opponents scoreless, and on those very special days it all comes together in a masterful display of drama and artistry on the Elysian fields.

Jocko Flynn went on to retire the Maroons in the ninth, recording his 11th straight in a streak that mounted to 14 before it was over. His meteoric career ended on a losing note on October 5 in New York, bested by Hall of Famer Mickey Welsh, whom he had beaten earlier in the season. But he had had his share of winning, with 26 notches on a star-studded belt.

More than one pitcher's career has foundered on a blown-out arm, and Flynn's was one that suffered that very fate. Others who come to mind are Mark "The Bird" Fidrych, Johnny Beazley, and Smoky Joe Wood. In Flynn's case it wouldn't have been a matter of a healthy pitching limb. Cap Anson, the great White Stockings first baseman-manager, simply wouldn't have put up with Jocko's wayward habits. Further, Anson, who was unable to lead his White Stockings back to their early 1880s prominence, had his hands full with others who enjoyed Chicago's watering holes as much as they did playing ball.

Amos Rusie, May 12, 1890:
13 Innings and One Run at the Polo Grounds

New York	000	000	000	000	1	1-4-2
Boston	000	000	000	000	0	0-3-5

WP, Rusie; LP, Nichols

The *New York Times* reported on this game in gushing superlatives. Played at New York's Polo Grounds and attended by 1,000 or more Giants fans, the Boston Beaneaters were edged by the men of Jim Mutrie in a nerve-wracking 13-inning 1-0 ball game. Considering the quality of play and the hurling of two Hall of Fame pitchers—New York's Amos Rusie and the picture-perfect hurler Kid Nichols, whose fast one suffered little by comparison with the cannon-balling Rusie—one has to grant the *New York Times* its unabashed awe over this marvelously played game. Rusie and Nichols hooked up in one of those classic duels that went from inning to inning without a score, giving every indication that there would be very late suppers for the New York faithful. And, as it turned out, there were.

As so often happens, things changed in the twinkling of an eye. Mike Tiernan stepped into the batter's box in the top of the 13th, looked at a pitch or two, and then fouled one off. A new ball was brought into play and what followed was a heater that Tiernan caught up with and lofted over the center field fence, no mean feat at the Polo Grounds. Suddenly, as if turning on a switch, Tiernan's blast had ruined Nichols' shutout and put the Giants out in front by the barest of margins. Nichols' 2 and 4 record would turn on that one pitch and Tiernan's bomb, moving it to 2 and 5 because the Hoosier Thunderbolt would come on in the bottom half of the 13th to make that run stand up.

But there was more than Tiernan's home run in this one. The *Times*' sports scribe had this to say:[2]

> Never before in the history of the game have the same number of people shown so much enthusiasm on a ball field as there was shown at the New Polo Grounds yesterday when Tiernan knocked the ball over the centre-field fence, winning the game for the New Yorks. Even the people who were at the Brotherhood game [a game between the New York and Boston teams of the rival Players League], and who were watching the [National] League game at the top of the fence, made a great demonstration! And why not? Tiernan had done what few people believed could be accomplished. The ball struck the fence of Brotherhood Park.
>
> Another thing about the game. It was the finest contest ever played by two professional teams, and will go down to record as such, not on account of the number of innings played, but because of the wonderful work done by the pitchers and the brilliant fielding.

Kid Nichols, not quite 21 when this game was played, later in his career referred to this encounter as one that taught him something. Never again would he throw a ball that was just put into play anywhere near the strike zone. Almost exclusively a fastball pitcher, the tall, lean lefty became an outstanding control pitcher and moved on to a 361-208 career record that won Cooperstown honors. But the fifth defeat of his career in 1890 was one that stayed with him a long, long time.

Amos Rusie, a second-year man in 1890, also had much to learn. The 1-0 victory evened his record at 5 and 5 in a 29 and 34 season. There was more to pitching than 95-mile-an-hour screamers. He learned the pitching art, developing a hard, wide-breaking curveball to go along with his fastball, and in the short span of a 10-year career piled up almost 250 wins, the overall record resulting in election to the Hall of Fame.

Grover (Pete) Alexander, September 7, 1911: Phillies vs. Cy Young's Rustlers

Philadelphia	000	000	010	1-6-0
Boston	000	000	000	0-1-0

Even among baseball's immortals the names of Alexander and Young bring an awed deference to conversations about these greats. There is, justly, a pause before launching any discussion about their deeds, or records, or pitching prowess, as one selects with great care from among the more important data. Anything less, or trivial, seems out of place, if not irrelevant. Two of the most victorious pitchers in the game's history (their combined total of 884 career wins is just unbelievable) have etched equally incredible events into baseball

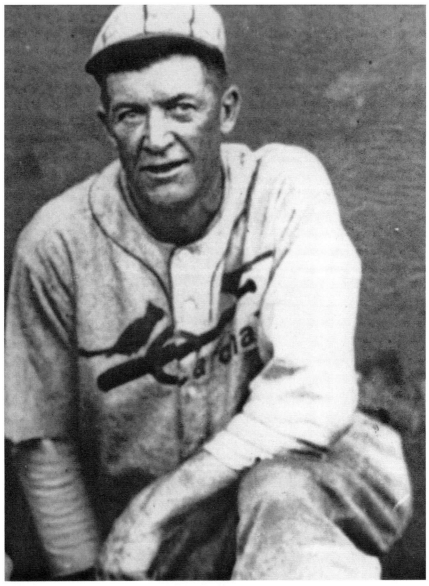

Ol' Low and Away, Pete Alexander.

lore. The annals of the game teem with their many accomplishments. Standing high on the 1-0 ledger—Alexander with 17, and Young with 13—they have any number of games from which to select one or another of particular significance.

The game that brings both together in a 1-0 pairing is perhaps symbolic of the unique place they hold in American baseball. In Alexander's first year and Young's last, they confronted one another at Boston's South End Grounds, home of the Rustlers, later known as the Braves. While this game would result in the 312th loss of Young's career (four days later he lost his 313th of 316 career losses to Christy Mathewson in their only meeting), the victory for rookie Alexander would be his 23rd of 28 in a brilliant freshman season.

A lowly little single off the bat of speedy Hans Lobert scored Dode Paskert in the seventh frame, registering the only run of the game. Cy Young had put the scythe to the Phillies before and after that mini-outburst that cost him a 14th career shutout and 1-0 victory. He had been going very well after one last visit to the fountain of youth in posting 6-0 and 2-1 wins before yielding to the 24-year-old Alexander.

It should be pointed out that the man behind the plate sorting out Alexander's and Young's strikes from the balls thrown in this game was none other than the storied Bill Klem, whose umpiring was so exceptional that he was honored with a Hall of Fame plaque, the first arbiter so recognized. That makes this 1-0 game even more treasured.

Alas for Young, the day belonged to the fellow they soon called "Old Low and Away." As the years rolled on, the pitcher whose entire career was spent flirting with the edges of the outside corner just got better and better despite the ravages of epilepsy, WWI, and just too much of the bubbly. But one would be hard pressed to name a sturdier, sterner competitor in the clutch. He did persevere, finally winding up with 373 wins—the same, incidentally, as Mathewson. You will not fail to notice that the linescore of this game indicates that Boston managed but one safe blow off Alexander, one of the many one-hitters he threw in his career. In those remarkable seasons of 1915-17 he threw 36 shutouts, 12 of them in 1915, and among those 12, four were one-hit beauties which still stand as the best on record.

Cy Young, September 22, 1911: Boston vs. Pittsburgh

Boston	000	000	100	1-4-4
Pittsburgh	000	000	000	0-9-0

This 1-0 masterpiece by Cy Young came a scant two weeks after his 1-0 loss to the Phils. The game took place at Pittsburgh's Forbes Field, an acreage that

Baseball immortal Cy Young, the man with the most "mosts."

was made for hitters, the kind of place where triples and inside-the-park home runs were commonplace. When players like Honus Wagner, Max Carey (a 1910s speed demon), and Tommy Leach were wearing Pirate togs, as they did in this late September tilt, a pitcher needs to be on his game. Young allowed nine hits, each of which proved to be rather harmless, though two of them were two-baggers. The old master bore down just a little harder, especially in the fifth inning when catcher Mike Simon led off with a double, followed by a wild pitch that enabled Simon to move over to third with only one out. On a squeeze attempt by the Corsair's quick leadoff hitter Bobby Byrne, the Rustlers came to the rescue with a fine play at the plate that turned Byrne's bunt into a fielder's choice as they nailed Simon trying to score.

But the inning was not yet over. With Byrne still aboard Carey singled, moving Byrne over to third with another speedster, Vin Campbell, due up. But Young induced a Campbell dribbler in front of the plate and catcher Bill Rariden smothered it, throwing to first baseman Jay Kirke for the third out. The third out prevented Honus Wagner, the next hitter, from doing anything about the Pirate base runners, something, of course, he was more than capable of doing. Young closed out his final 1-0 game in the ninth, fanning Tommy Leach for the win that registered number 511 in his peerless career. (The full box score can be seen in table 2.1.)

Table 2.1.   Boston vs. Pittsburgh, September 22, 1911

Boston	AB	R	H	PO	A	Pittsburgh	AB	R	H	PO	A
Sweeney, 2b	4	0	1	5	5	Byrnne, 3b	4	0	1	0	2
Donlin, cf	4	0	1	0	1	Carey, cf	3	0	2	4	0
Jackson, lf	4	0	1	2	0	Campbell, lf	4	0	1	3	0
Kirke, 1b	4	1	1	11	0	Wagner, 1b	4	0	1	6	0
Miller, rf	3	0	0	2	0	Wilson, rf	4	0	0	2	0
Bridwell, ss	3	0	1	1	5	McKechnie, 2b	4	0	2	3	4
McDonald, 3b	3	0	0	1	1	McCarthy, ss	4	0	0	3	1
Rariden, c	3	0	1	5	3	Simon, c	3	0	1	6	2
Young (WP)	3	0	0	0	1	Clarke*	1	0	1	0	0
						Adams (LP)	3	0	0	0	0
						Leach**	1	0	0	0	0
Totals	**31**	**1**	**6**	**27**	**16**	**Totals**	**35**	**0**	**9**	**27**	**9**

*Batted for Simon in ninth inning.
**Batted for Adams in ninth inning.

Boston	000	000	100	1-4-4
Pittsburgh	000	000	000	0-9-0

Smoky Joe Wood, September 6, 1912: Boston Edges Washington

Washington	000	000	000	0-6-0
Boston	000	001	00x	1-5-0

WP, Wood; LP, Johnson

Smoky Joe Wood. According to Walter Johnson, no one threw harder than Smoky Joe did.

One of the most-quoted lines about Howard Ellsworth Wood, known among baseball's followers as Joe or Smoky Joe, was spoken by Walter Johnson, who, when asked about Wood's speed by a reporter said, "Listen, mister, no man alive can throw harder than Joe Wood!" With that you are introduced to one of baseball's fastest fastball hurlers, whose pitches arrived at home plate so suddenly that it seemed like a trail of smoke was all that could be seen between the mound and home plate.

The story of Wood's matchless 1-0 skirmish with Walter Johnson—who, it just so happens, was also known to throw a little smoke in his day—might need that kind of an introduction because there are so many today who would say, "Who's Joe Wood?" It is quite possible that many today who don't know the ancient Famers' old-time stars will be in need of a few more words about this fellow to set the stage for the epic battle staged during the late summer of 1912 in front of an overflow crowd numbering in excess of 30,000 at the newly christened Fenway Park in Beantown.

Let's start with recalling the Alexander-Young tussle in September of 1911.

During the closing weeks of the season during which Pete Alexander was unveiling his stunning freshman season in the big time, Joe Wood was closing in on his first 20-win season as a member of the fast-improving Boston Red Sox. At 23, just about two years younger than Alexander, there was great promise in store for this youngster. He wound up the 1911 campaign with a sterling 23 and 17 record for the Red Sox, who finished the season tied for fourth place with the White Sox of Chicago.

Both the team and Wood headed into 1912 filled with pennant ambitions and confidence and by season's end found themselves World Series bound, where they shouldered McGraw's Giants aside to emerge from the tussle as world champs. Joe Wood's contribution to that achievement was a monster season consisting of 34 wins, an .872 winning percentage, 10 shutouts, and 35 complete games, all league-leading figures. Among those 10 shutouts were three 1-0 games, two of which came in a succession of blankings against the White Sox, New York, and Washington, in that order. The last of that threesome was the famed Boston-Washington tilt on September 6 staged by the master baseball showman and "Old Fox," Clark Griffith, who was the Senators' manager at the time.

Emile Rothe, a long-time member of the Society of American Baseball Research (SABR) wrote an interesting article about the Wood-Johnson game entitled "The War of 1912"[3] for the *Baseball Research Journal* that was reproduced later on the SABR website. Part of that article appears here:

> As expected the game developed into a *bona fide* pitching battle. Boston put together two singles in the second but Walter [Johnson] escaped that threat as Heinie Wagner raced into the outfield to grab a pop fly in spectacular fashion for the third out. Washington filled the bases in the third, two on walks, but Smoky Joe fanned Danny Moeller for the third out.

The lone tally of this memorable game came in the sixth after Walter had disposed of the first two batters of the inning. Tris Speaker hit into the crowd in left for a ground-rule double. Duffy Lewis, next up, drove a hard liner along the right field foul line which Moeller, the Senator right fielder, almost caught, the ball just ticked his glove as Speaker scored and Lewis reached second.

The Senators had men in scoring position at second in the sixth, eighth, and ninth but Wood was tough when he had to be. In two of those innings he got the final out via the strike out. In all, he fanned nine Senators, and the shutout was one of 10 he registered in 1912.

A word about those shutouts is in order. The 10 were distributed among five different opponents, including New York (victimized three times), Washington, Chicago, and St. Louis (all twice), and Detroit (once). In mid-season three of those came in succession during Wood's 16-game win streak, an achievement that matched Walter Johnson's effort set earlier in the 1912 season. That established the American League mark, but it was several shy of the National League's standard set by Rube Marquard of the Giants, who reeled off 19 in a row from his first win in his first start of the season through July 8, attempting his 20th in a row, only to lose it in Chicago. When did that take place? In 1912, of course!

Rothe concluded his article with these perceptive observations:[4]

Many baseball games are remembered by players and fans for a multitude of reasons; maybe it was the first game a player ever played, or the day he could do no wrong on the field, the first time a boy's father took him to a game, or a game of historical import. Whatever the reason, almost every game will live in someone's memory as long as that someone lives. Some games, though, deserve to be remembered by the entire baseball community for all time. The Walter Johnson-Joe Wood contest, played on September 6, 1912, should be one of those.

Joe Oeschger, April 20, 1920: Boston over the Giants—Prelude to a Marathon

Boston	000	000	100	1-5-0
New York	000	000	000	0-6-1

WP, Oeschger; LP, Toney

Leon Cadore and Joe Oeschger were Chicagoans who were born some 16 months apart. Both grew up to be big leaguers who toiled away in journeyman

Joe Oeschger, who pitched 21 straight innings of scoreless baseball in MLB's longest game, a 1-1 tie on May 1, 1920. *Brace Photo*.

careers that were average in most respects. However, they are part of the record book by virtue of one stupendous entry they made on 1920's May Day. On that famous day in baseball history their work was cast in the Walter Johnson or Pete Alexander mold.

This vignette in our 1-0 history book features a Joe Oeschger ball game that was won on April 20, more than a couple weeks ahead of the marathon of baseball marathons. Coming in the second game of the 1920 season, it was a harbinger of events written in zeroes. The full sequence, stretching from mid-April through the next six weeks, unfolded this way:

April 15: Joe Oeschger pitches a 1-0 shutout, beating the Giants' Fred Toney.
April 20: Leon Cadore defeats Oeschger in 11 innings, 1-0 at Ebbets Field.
April 26: In his next start Oeschger beats Eppa Rixey 10-3 in Boston.
May 1: A 1-1 26-inning game at Boston.
May 13: In his next start Oeschger is defeated 9-3 by Famer Jesse Haines.
May 21: In his first start after May 1, Cadore shuts out Cincinnati, 2-0.
May 25: Cadore adds four more to his scoreless streak, losing to Pittsburgh, 2-0.

A few nuggets regarding that sequence:

- Oeschger, though defeated by Cadore on April 20, became involved in a string of scoreless innings. Save for the fifth inning of that monster marathon and a single run on April 20, an 11-inning game, he hurled 43 innings of shutout baseball out of 45 in the early stages of the 1920 season.
- Leon Cadore put together 45 out of 47 innings of shutout ball between April 20 and May 25.
- Oeschger established a still-standing mark of 16 consecutive scoreless innings in a single game. Further, he joined with Cadore in tossing a total of an estimated 665 pitches to complete the 26 innings. The numbers on each: Oeschger, 320; Cadore, 345.
- Hardly believable is the number of balls used in the May Day, 1920, 26-inning game—*three*. Also worth noting: Oeschger threw a no-hitter the last nine innings of that 1-1 tie, retiring the side on three pitches in the seventh inning.
- And, of course, the 26-inning game is the longest in major league history.

And so, on to the feature 1-0 game of April 25, a 1-0 gem reported by the *New York Times* with an opening that read: "The Giants looked like a pretty slick ball team at the Polo Grounds yesterday, but the Boston Braves were better."

Further into the *Times'* recap of the game there were indications that outstanding defensive play gave substantial support to Big Joe: "Oeschger received commendable support from his teammates. Gorgeous fielding by Maranville and [Walton] Cruise waylaid more than one hit." Cruise stood between the Braves and a tie score when Larry Doyle came up to the plate in the last of the ninth. Doyle got hold of "the ball with the end of his club and poked a screaming drive to right field. . . . The Boston right fielder ran at top speed and skillfully gathered the ball at the tips of his fingers just as it was about to pass him like a stranger." Catcher Steve O'Neill and the wily one, Hall of Famer Walter "Rabbit" Maranville, also contributed run-saving plays. It was a ball game that came together on great pitching, outstanding fielding, and the mildest of offensive efforts, consisting of a Wally Cruise single, a stolen base, and a run-scoring single by the Braves' hard-hitting outfielder, Les Mann. Giant pitcher Fred Toney pitched well, but as the *Times* reporter phrased it: "It didn't matter what the Giants tried, the Braves were always on the job to go them one better."

In 1920, the year Joe Oeschger posted a 15-13 record, he fashioned four 1-0 games, lost two 1-0 tilts (one to Hippo Vaughn and the other to Cadore), and won a 2-0 game against Cincinnati. Four 1-0 victories is more characteristic of an upper division ball club and bespeaks some stellar pitching. During his 12-year career there was one 20-game season, which came in 1921, a year that was highlighted by his last 1-0 outing, coming against Pittsburgh. In Oeschger's career, there were nine 1-0 victories, representing a huge 50 percent of his shutout total. Though his career lasted only 12 seasons (that would be well above the average of a major leaguer's four seasons), his longevity in another respect was way beyond the norm for his day. Joe Oeschger died at 94, the last survivor among the players who played that 26-inning ball game at old Braves Field in 1920.

Jerome (Jay) Hanna Dean, August 16, 1935: St. Louis Cardinals vs. New York Giants

St. Louis	000	000	001	1-5-0
New York	000	000	000	0-3-2

WP, Dean; LP, Schumacher

Dizzy Dean. Madcap. Fractured English Raconteur. The likes of this fellow will not appear again. The mold cast for him was broken and pitched. And speaking of pitching, he was an original in that rare art as well. He not only told you what he was going to do, the odds were that somehow he would do it—no matter how outlandish the claim would be. Only the very few have been able to do that. So it is very likely that he would put together not simply a 1-0 entry in this collection but an exquisite one. Though Dean didn't get around to pitching a no-hitter in a short but very sweet career of dominating pitching, he did come very close, and the three-hit 1-0 gem he hurled in 1935 serves as the very best among his 26 career shutouts.

This victory came in the midst of a taut stretch of games during which the Cardinals and Cubs were whittling away at the Giants' lead. At the close of play on August 15 the Cards and Cubs had pulled to within four of the Terry New Yorkers. They were applying steady heat to the frontrunners and the games on August 16 would be another chance to scrape away at that four-game difference. Over in Brooklyn, the Dodgers and Moose Earnshaw had beaten Chicago's Charlie Root, 2-1, with all the runs accounted for by one-run four-baggers. That meant that a St. Louis victory would put the Cards into second place, inching them to within three of the Giants.

Hall of Fame sports scribe John Drebinger set the stage for the game this way in the August 17 issue of the *New York Times*:

> Dizzy Dean, the elongated ace of the Cardinals, is still tops when the heat is on and the chips are down. The chips were down at the Polo Grounds yesterday and the heat was on, with terrible pressure to boot.
>
> The Cardinals were trailing in the current series with the Giants, two games to one, and they were lagging at four lengths in the National League pennant race. Another defeat would just about have been a crusher for even so indomitable a leader as Frankie Frisch, and a ladies day crowd of 15,000 was on hand fervently hoping that this very thing would come about.
>
> Add to this the fact that Dizzy, in contrast to his amazing triumphs along similar lines last year, had yet to win his first game of the year from the Giants and you have the setting that confronted the tall Oklahoman as he strode to the firing line to oppose Hal Schumacher in the fourth game of the series.
>
> What followed was a pitching classic of the first flight as the incomparable Dean hurled a three-hit shutout to conquer Schumacher, 1-0.

Still scoreless into the ninth frame, with little indication that either team could master the deliveries of two outstanding pitchers on this day, the Cardinals opened the top half of the inning with a Pepper Martin dart to right field, and before the Giants had logged a third out, outfielder Joe Medwick launched a fly ball deep enough to permit Gashouser Martin to put the go-ahead marker on the board.

Enter Diz. The final act of this play called for some pitching and the 19-game winner provided it, retiring the Giants with nary a run to show for their efforts. The victory was Dean's 20th among the 28 he finished with in 1935, and one of eight 1-0 performances in his shortened major league tenure.

Dizzy Dean was not only eccentric and fiercely fast but very athletic and street smart, quite able to pitch with his head and heart as well as his arm. His last 1-0 game, a very able six-hitter accomplished through a careful pitch selection of curveballs and, by his own admission, "nothing balls," would be such a case in point. That game, won on the strength of a Gabby Hartnett tater, was one of those pitched in the days when his arm was all but gone, as he was making do after the All-Star game injury in 1937 that ultimately put an end to his career.

Lon Warneke, September 25, 1935: A Cubs-Cards Classic

Chicago	010	000	000	1-7-0
St. Louis	000	000	000	0-2-0

WP, Warneke; LP, Paul Dean

The *baseball intelligentsia* were pretty much convinced that Bill Terry's New York Giants would wind up in the 1935 World Series either against the Yankees or the defending champions, the Detroit Tigers. By the July 4 milestone their conjectures looked good. The race shaped up this way: The Giants, just having swept a doubleheader at Boston, were out in front by nine games of St. Louis, by 10 in front of Pittsburgh, and 10½ ahead of fourth-place Chicago. Not to worry was the mindset of all three underlings. The race gradually tightened as August wore to a close. Then, the "Least of These," Chicago's Cubbies, went on one of the most famous tears in baseball history, winning 21 games in succession between September 4 and the second game of a twin bill at St. Louis on September 27. At the end of that day, with just two games to play, Chicago was on top with 100 victories and a six-game lead over the second-place Cardinals. The NL race was all over. It would be a Chicago-Detroit World Series. They simply got hot, stayed hot, and bulldozed their way to a championship behind hurlers Big Bill Lee, Larry French, and Lon Warneke with five victories each, and the veteran Charley Root with four during the streak. The "Arkansas Humming Bird," Warneke, put the finishing touches to his 20-13 season with a seven-game winning streak, emerging from a so-so 13-13 log as crunch time approached in the race to the wire. Warneke was in his fifth Cub season, having won 20 in two of the three seasons just past. He was a seasoned veteran, as were Root, Lee, and French.

The Arkansas Hummingbird, Lon Warneke. *Brace Photo*.

What was particularly significant about this Cub pennant was that it was the only championship flag clinched by a 1-0 score, ever. And the hurler of that glitzy clincher was Lon Warneke, whose only 1935 shutout was pitched in that game. He made it a masterpice. Two hits less by the Cardinals and it would have been a no-hitter. Only a single by Lynn King and what was called a fluke double in the *New York Times*, hit by Rip Collins, stood between Warneke and Cooperstown recognition. In support of Warneke's sterling pitching effort there was, well, not much. One run was the sum and substance, and it was provided by a youngster fresh out of Chicago's Lane Tech, the square-jawed Phil Cavarretta, who crushed a Paul Dean pitch that found its way into Sportsmans Park's right-field seats. The rest of the game was one of those classic pitcher duels. But the lanky Warneke made the 19-year-old Cavarretta's homer stand up.

Warneke continued throwing goose eggs on into the 1935 World Series, defeating a tough-out Tiger team in the opener by a 3-0 score, allowing four hits. He came back in game 5 to hold the Detroiters scoreless for six innings of that game, running his scoreless streak to 15 innings. He left that game with a sore shoulder, leaving the mop-up chore to Bill Lee for a 3-1 victory. Sadly for Cub fans, the only W's the Cubs posted were those listed behind Lon Warneke's name, as the Cubs lost the Series in six games.

Lon Warneke got around to serious shutout business on August 30, 1941, when, as a member of the Cards' pitching staff, he no-hit the Cincinnati Reds and Elmer Riddle 2-0. In that game he faced 28 batters, one over the magic 27, as he benefited from two double plays. He walked but one hitter, Lonnie Frey, handcuffing the Reds while picking up his 15th win in a 17 and 9 year, his last big season in a 15-year career.

Wartime Baseball in 1943

America entered yet another international war as of December 8, 1941. During the next year citizens in all walks of life began to feel the effects of that declaration, including the baseball world. By 1943 many of baseball's brightest stars were wearing military uniforms and some of the big changes in the daily life of franchises and their ballplayers included travel arrangements, restrictions on nighttime ball games, spring training arrangements, and equipment. The latter of these was not only in short supply, but in the case of the game's ball, a different substance was introduced to replace cork, which was declared essential to products in the war effort. That substance was balata, declared nonstrategic by the government. It was made from the dried juices of a number of tropical trees and used as a centerpiece for baseballs after spring training began in 1942. The new balls were put into play throughout the training camps, and when opening day came, it was the balata ball that was thrown out for the first pitch.

Major leaguers were willing to put up with a lot because of the wartime situation, but the new ball caused an uproar. It was branded "the fake ball," the "no-ball," the "stone ball," and "Hitler's ball" among the printable names that circulated around the teams trying to hit the deadened sphere. It was about 25 percent less resilient than the 1942 ball. Evidence of its deadened quality surfaced immediately, especially in the opening series of play at Cincinnati which began on April 21.

Just five days later the white flag went up, in the National League at least, when senior-circuit prexy Ford Frick gave NL teams permission to use up what remained of the 1942 balls, and a little later the American League followed suit. The opening series at Crosley Field, home of the Cincinnati Reds, was a major factor in Frick's decision. The Reds and Cardinals managed six runs *combined* in the four-game series. There were three 1-0 games and a 2-1 effort. The Cardinals, whose fine 1942 club led the Nation League offensively, lost the season opener 1-0 in 11 innings, and they lost the next game 1-0, this time in 10 innings. There was a reprieve in game 3, a 2-1 win, and in the final game of that series they prevailed behind Howie Pollet, defeating the Reds by, yet again, a 1-0 score. Of the four games, the second of the series was the most interesting. The line score and recap follow:

Cincinnati 1, St. Louis 0, April 22, 1943

St. Louis	000	000	000	0 0-5-0
Cincinnati	000	000	000	1 1-6-0

WP, Starr; LP, White

A 10th-inning scoring "splurge" gave the host Red Legs a 1-0 victory in the season's second game, attended by only 1,897 fans and played out in just under two hours. Three hits accounted for the extra inning score—all singles, the winner driven home by Bert Haas. Haas, along with Stan Musial, provided the only extra base hits, both triples, but neither figured in a score. The winner was Ray Starr, whose 37th birthday was due just a couple days later. And the losers? St. Louis had suffered through 26 consecutive scoreless innings to start the 1943 season.

A very interesting and whimsical article was written by Noel Hynd for the May 13, 1985, issue of *Sports Illustrated*, dealing with the specifics of the early 1943 season, the balata ball, and its improvements through the '43 season. He noted that after the 1943 season, the government found new ways to manufacture synthetic rubber, thus assuring the major leagues that new baseballs would have more bounce to the ounce. But during the remainder of 1943 there were still some mighty fine 1-0 games—23 of them as a matter of fact.

Over in the American League the Detroit, Chicago, Washington, New York, and Cleveland teams made a race of it until August, when it became apparent that the Yankees were going to take their mission from winning the pennant to the world championships, as they hoped to gain revenge for a World Series loss to St. Louis the previous October. Spud Chandler and Tiny Bonham each pitched 1-0 victories, the White Sox' Orval Grove won another over the Yankees, and on July 9 in Cleveland the Senators won a 1-0 night game in 13 innings before 11,840. All eight AL teams logged shutouts and within the first five games of the season six teams had posted shutouts, four of them resulting in 1-0 games.

AL Games Ending in 1-0 Scores in 1943:

New York: 5
Washington: 4
Cleveland: 5
Chicago: 2
Detroit: 2
St. Louis: 3
Boston: 2
Philadelphia: 0

Total: 23

Don Fisher, September 30, 1945:
New York Giants vs. Boston Braves

New York	000	000	000	000	1	1-6-2
Boston	000	000	000	000	0	0-10-0

WP, Fisher; LP, Hendrickson

You have probably heard of the one-gamer. This player's record is listed as a one-line item. Articles have been written about these players, one of baseball's rare breeds, up for the proverbial cup-o'-coffee and, in many cases, never heard from again as far as major league ballplayers are concerned. There are quite a number of ballplayers whose encyclopedia and franchise entries are taken care of in two-line items, signifying two seasons of baseball, often limited to less than

This fellow was perfect in his MLB career at 1-0. New York Giants pitcher Don Fisher. *Brace Photo*.

20 appearances. And then there are those whose careers are contained in a single season, perhaps making it into the lineup, but not successfully enough to merit another season's play in the bigs. Among all these players many become career minor leaguers, many leave the game to find employment elsewhere, and others continue playing the game they love on the semi-pro level or in amateur baseball. There are human interest stories in every one of those players who continue to play ball, their professional careers over in the batting of an eye.

One of the players from the ranks of those listed above was a husky pitcher whose baseball days prior to a major league appearance or two were played out on the sandlots of Cleveland. His name was Don Fisher, and during WWII many a ballplayer went through the same experiences as did the fireballer from the Forest City. By 1945 major league rosters had been dotted with players ear-marked for the minors once the war was over. They filled out big league lineups, rode the trains to games played around the league, and at the end of one of the wartime seasons, when it came to contract time, theirs were not renewed. Base-ball's grapevine, always active and usually deadly with regard to the disposition of talent, had seen to it that "Benny X," for an example, now with the Reds, or Senators, or Cubs, was earmarked for either the minors, or, worse yet as far as Benny X's future in the bigs was concerned, oblivion. Don Fisher's situation was a similar one, though probably not for the usual reasons.

Don Fisher was signed directly off the Cleveland sandlots to a Giants con-tract in the last months of World War II. Giants manager Mel Ott brought him directly to the Polo Gronds to acquaint him with big league baseball. By mid-season of 1945, which was usually marked by fourth of July doubleheaders, the war on the European front was over, and in the Pacific Theater VJ Day was just a little more than a month away. Major league players were being mustered out of military service. The lineups of quite a few teams, though not up to pre-war standards, were fairly solid.

By August 1, when the Giants were scheduled to play the Boston Braves at the Polo Grounds, the lineups of these two teams boasted stars like playing manager Mel Ott of New York, Ernie Lombardi, Ducky Medwick, Tommy Holmes, Whitey Lockman, pitchers Jim Tobin, Mort Cooper, Bill Lee, Big Bill Voiselle, Van Mungo, and a rookie named Sal Maglie. The teams around the two leagues were gradually getting back into authentic major league fettle. And by the end of that month Ott's latest rookie addition, Don Fisher, was being primed for action. The call came on August 25 when the Giants were at Ebbets Field absorbing a shellacking at the hands of the Dodgers. Led by "The People's Cherce" (as the word was enunciated in Flatbush), Fred "Dixie" Walker drove home six runs, and the Dodgers had mounted a 10-0 lead before the fifth frame got underway. So the call went to the bullpen: "If Fisher's ready, send him." Don Fisher made the long walk, debuting with a relief role that began in the fourth inning. Nine runs, charged to Mungo and Emmerich, who had gone before him, had already been assessed to his predecessors, and the broad-shouldered right-hander was charged with four more, all told, before his five inning mop-up job was completed. Though he hadn't set the world afire, the *New York Times* proclaimed that he had held the Dodgers reasonably well in check. Many, many a rookie had endured a similar experience. Fisher had no reason to hang his head over his outing.

But the weeks hurried by and the call either out of the bullpen or for a start didn't come. Suddenly the Giants were just about out of ball games for the 1945 season, and the last date of the season had come, featuring a season-ending twin bill with the Boston Braves. Mel Ott's choice for game 1 was Don Fisher, paired with James Wallace, a left-hander who had beaten the Giants in his only start of the 1945 campaign just a week prior to this September 30 game. He would have "last-outs" advantage, if it came to that, in this game scheduled for Braves Field. Wallace dueled Fisher through nine innings of scoreless baseball before being lifted for a pinch hitter in the ninth, Bob Nieman. Wallace was replaced by another wartime pitcher, Don Hendrickson, and the teams headed into extra innings. A scoreless, three-inning set went by. Finally, in the top of the 13th, Cuban Nap Reyes caught hold of a Hendrickson offering much to his liking and parked it in the seats beyond the center-field fence to give the Giants a one-run lead. After 12 innings of no-run pitching, Don Fisher was not about to cough up a tying or winning run, nor did he, retiring the Braves in the bottom of the inning to record his first—and last—big league win. Giant pitchers had authored 13 shutouts during the 1945 season, but among them there was only one 1-0 game. That one belonged to Don Fisher.

So Don Fisher and the Giants were through for the 1945 season. In his two appearances he had registered a 2.00 ERA, given up four runs in 18 innings of work, struck out four, walked only two, and allowed 12 base hits. Not too shabby. It would seem that good things would be waiting to happen in 1946.

Fisher, who had signed his first professional contract with the Cleveland organization in 1938 at age 22, and had been out of organized baseball from 1941 to '44, reported to the Giants' Miami training base in the spring of 1946.

Because he had not reached the mark of 50 innings pitched, he was still considered a rookie, and with all the other "rooks" wondered whether he would be going north to open the season. He did go north, but not to New York. Instead, he was assigned to the Jersey City Giants, where he was in the lineup for nine games as a pitcher and 10 as a hitter (he hit .474 in his limited number of at-bats). The call to the majors never came. By March 18, 1947, at the Cardinals' training base, he was released once again, never to appear in major league—or minor league—togs again. The end had come as abruptly as his emergence from Cleveland's sandlots, pitching for the semipro Bartunek Clothiers in 1945.

There seems to be something wrong with this picture. Yet, as was the case with thousands who unsuccessfully tried to make big league lineups directly after WWII, Don Fisher was left behind. His satisfaction for all the trouble had to be the game that turned out to be the only one of its kind in the 1945 land of the Giants.

Leroy "Satchel" Paige, August 20, 1948: Indians Beat the White Sox behind Ol' Satch

Chicago	000	000	000	0-3-0
Cleveland	000	100	000	1-8-0

WP, Paige; LP, Wight

The record book had him down for 42. Nobody believed it. And they were no doubt right because Satchel Paige had been around for a baseball eternity. Nonetheless, at a ballplayer's advanced age Ol' Satch made his debut, following Jackie Robinson and Larry Doby into the bigs on July 9, 1948, in a two-inning relief stint against the St. Louis Browns. Later in the season manager Lou Boudreau named him the starting pitcher for a game against Chicago's White Sox at Cleveland's cavernous Municipal Stadium. The response? Cleveland won that Friday night game, for one thing. For another, 78,382 turned out to see this ancient mariner of the baseball wars. Paige's 1-0 shutout win rewarded the Tribe's fans beyond all expectations. It was the lithe right-hander's fifth in a 6-1 season that helped the Indians win the '48 blue ribbon. Further, he tossed a few pitches in game 5 of the Indians' winning World Series sequence. That, too, was a part of a scoreless inning.

A lot of ink has been splashed on behalf of Mr. Paige, and that will be reviewed in a later chapter where leagues beyond the majors, in different venues, will be examined. There, the Japanese and Negro Leagues receive just due as some of the more famous 1-0 games in those circuits are examined. Satchel Paige's start was made during the 1926 season with the Chattanooga Black Lookouts in the Negro Southern League, and his last professional appearance was made with the Peninsula Grays of organized baseball's Carolina League in 1966, topping out a 40-year career in baseball.

But more of that later. The spotlight in connection with major league 1-0 games, for this moment, falls on the evening of August 20, 1948, and here are some of that date's more significant highlights:

- The 1-0 blanking of the White Sox was Paige's second shutout in a row.
- The attendance mark of 78,382 exceeded the previous record of 74,747 set at Yankee Stadium in May of 1947.

40-something Satchel Paige, baseball's oldest 1-0 winner.

- Paige retired the side in order in six of the nine innings and no Chicago base runner got as far as third base.
- With his victory the Cleveland pitching staff completed 39 straight innings of shutout ball, just two shy of the 1903 Cleveland staff's record. In the next game they played, Bob Lemon extended that record to 47, as he held the White Sox scoreless until the ninth frame, when a three-run uprising not only broke the string of scoreless innings but proved sufficient to break an eight-game Cleveland winning streak.
- In the three games Paige started, including the August 20 victory, the Indians drew 201,829 in attendance, an average of 67,276 per game.
- Larry Doby, a black center fielder in his first major league season, drove home the winning tally with a fourth-inning single.

Table 2.2.   Cleveland vs. Chicago (AL), August 20, 1948

Chicago	AB	R	H	A	Cleveland	AB	R	H	A
Hodgin, rf	4	0	0	0	Mitchell, lf	4	0	2	0
Lupien, 1b	3	0	1	0	Clark, rf	3	0	1	0
Appling, 3b	4	0	1	0	R. Kennedy*	0	0	0	0
Seerey, lf	3	0	1	0	Boudreau, ss	4	1	2	1
A. Robinson, c	3	0	0	0	E. Robinson, 1b	4	0	0	0
Philley, cf	3	0	0	0	Keltner, 3b	4	0	2	0
Kolloway, 2b	3	0	0	4	Doby, cf	4	0	1	1
Michaels, ss	3	0	0	6	Berardino, 2b	3	0	0	4
Wight (LP)	3	0	0	0	Hegan, c	3	0	0	0
					Paige (WP)	3	0	0	2
Totals	**29**	**0**	**3**	**10**	**Totals**	**32**	**1**	**8**	**8**

*Bob Kennedy was a pinch runner for Clark and replaced him in center field.

LOB: Chicago 3, Cleveland, 8.
Game time: 1 hour, 50 minutes.
Umpires: McKinley, McGowan, Boyer.

Chicago	000	000	000	0-3-0
Cleveland	000	100	000	1-8-0

Satchel Paige closed out the game with a 1-2-3 finishing touch that saw the White Sox' Ralph Hodgin fly out to Larry Doby, Tony Lupien go down the same way, this time to left fielder Dale Mitchell, and Hall-of-Famer Luke Appling ground out, Johnny Berardino to Eddie Robinson. And pandemonium reigned, as the Indians moved a step closer to their 1948 pennant and world championship laurels. The full boxscore of that momentous game appears in table 2.2.

Karl Spooner, September 26, 1954: Brooklyn vs. Pittsburgh

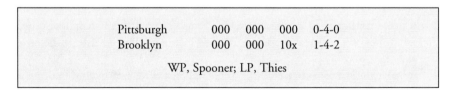

In the June 14, 2010, issue of the Mighty Casey Baseball website, an article entitled "Stephen Strasburg Was No Karl Spooner" put two names together, possessors of career openers that shocked the baseball world. In this segment of

Karl Spooner, whose two consecutive shutouts as career openers set a major league record. *Brace Photo*.

the 1-0 chapter about games played during the regular season, we're about to take a longer look at one of them, a game played at Ebbets Field back in 1954. The article cited above started out its comparison this way:

> Perhaps you caught his first major league start—the one where Stephen Strasburg launched his career with a masterful fourteen strikeout performance against the Pittsburgh Pirates.[5] Strasburg fanned the last six batters he faced and eight of the last nine—an amazing performance.
>
> Perhaps you caught his second start on Sunday—where Strasburg seemed a bit flustered by his lack of comfort on the Cleveland Indians mound but still only allowed a run and two hits over five-plus innings. If you did, you may know that Strasburg now has 22 strikeouts in his first two major league starts.
>
> It's the second best start, in terms of strikeouts, in the history of major league baseball. However, unless you are a long-time fan, someone who remembers games played in old Ebbets Field in Brooklyn, you've probably never heard of the guy who set the record by striking out 27 batters in his first two major league starts. Both complete games. Both shutouts.
>
> His name is Karl Spooner, and like Strasburg he was an easy throwing fireballer with a very professional demeanor and a hard fastball that captivated baseball fans immediately upon arrival.

Before Strasburg's career is over there will no doubt be some 1-0 entries. Our concern at this point, however, is Karl Spooner, whose major league debut was quite unlike any other major league hurler's. The pitcher's line for his first game, in which he defeated the New York Giants on September 22, 1954, looked like this:

IP	H	R	ER	BB	SO	BF	Record
9	3	0	0	3	15	34	1-0

He followed up that sparkler with a 1-0 season closer on September 26:

IP	H	R	ER	BB	SO	BF	Record
9	4	0	0	3	12	34	2-0

Spooner had struck out 27 in his first two games for a major league record that still stands—going on upwards of 60 years. Quite an accomplishment. Those two rookie starts put some new numbers into the record book, to whit:

(a) Spooner was the first (and still is) rookie to fan 27 in his first two starts; (b) he bettered the mark of Dazzy Vance (1926 and 1928) striking out 27 in two regular season games; and (c) he joined four other pitchers in pitching shutouts in his first two major league games.

His 27 strikeouts in those two games tell only a part of his domination of the Giants and then the Pirates in the Dodgers' last game of the season. The big lefty with a 95-mph hummer that moved ominously as it approached the plate didn't get much of an offensive cushion as he faced equally tough Jake Thies of the Pirates. The Dodgers got but four safeties, as many as the Pirates managed off the slants of Spooner. But one they did get was Gil Hodges' 42nd homer into the left-field stands, and it proved to be enough to carry the day for the Dodgers.

The Dodgers of the 1950's were kingpins in the National League, so Karl Spooner, who threw another shutout in 1955, picked up two championship rings in the two seasons he toiled in Dodger togs. Indeed, only two seasons was the sum and substance of Spooner's major league career. Unfortunately, Spooner's career actually ended, for all practical purposes, in 1955's spring training exercises, as he came into one of those early games unprepared to really let loose, which he did in a relief appearance. That was enough to bring about a series of disappointments and finally disability, as he spent the next several seasons in and out of minor leagues, with a transfer to the Cardinal system, and finally out of the game. What had started with such promise ended all too soon, and the Spooner memories of those two bright and shining starts in late 1954 were about all that he had to take with him.

Ballplayers are forever wary and looking over their shoulders. All of them wonder if the injury monster will strike on some sunny day, depriving them not only of the rewards they strive for but their very careers. For Karl Spooner the end came quickly; for others it takes longer; and for still others there is even a recovery (Tommy John comes to mind as the foremost example among those who stayed the advances and ravages of Father Time and the injury demon). But for a higher percentage than one would dare think, there is no reprieve or return. Such was Karl Spooner's fate.

Warren Spahn, September 6, 1961: Milwaukee vs. Philadelphia

Philadelphia	000	000	000	0-3-0	
Milwaukee	100	000	00x	1-5-1	

WP, Spahn; LP, Buzhardt

Hall-of-Famer Warren Spahn, baseball's winningest southpaw.

Warren Spahn won more games than any left-hander in baseball's history, with 363 victories. That number broke Eddie Plank's record by 27. That wasn't Spahn's only foray into the record books. His superiority and durability, even at an advanced age for a pitcher, was evidenced by notching 20 or more victories per season for a record-tying 13 consecutive seasons. At 42 he logged a 23-7 season and he pitched a no-hitter at age 40. One would expect that over the course of 21 major league seasons he was also active in 1-0 games. Table 2.5 contains his 1-0 ledger.

His 1-0 record is 10 and 8, including the 15-inning game in 1951. Spahn confronted four Hall of Fame pitchers, winning against Robin Roberts and Don Drysdale and losing to Juan Marichal and Jim Bunning.

The 1-0 game of interest was Spahn's 18th win of the season and came at the expense of the Phillies and John Buzhardt, who, in a night game at County Stadium in Milwaukee on September 6, 1961, threw a very creditable, five-hit game that was just not quite good enough to bring the Phillies home a winner. For all practical purposes the game was over in the first inning. The tilt's only run came about as a result of a Hank Aaron sacrifice fly that sent home Roy McMillan, who had walked and was singled to third by Eddie Mathews. After that tiny "outburst" it was a 0-0 game, Spahn permitting but three safeties and Buzhardt four.

Table 2.5. Warren Spahn's 1-0 Games

Date	Score	Opponent	Opposing Pitcher
August 14, 1947	0-1	Brooklyn	Lombardi
September 14, 1947	1-0	Chicago (NL)	Erickson
May 15, 1948	1-0	Brooklyn	Barney
June 21, 1948	0-1	St. Louis	Brazle
September 10, 1949	1-0	Philadelphia	Roberts
May 19, 1950	0-1	Pittsburgh	Chambers
August 7, 1951*	0-1	Philadelphia	Heintzelman
September 9, 1952	1-0	Cincinnati	Nuxhall
September 20, 1952	0-1; 10 innings	Brooklyn	Erskine
May 23, 1953	0-1	Pittsburgh	B. Hall
May 28, 1957	1-0	Cincinnati	Gross
April 30, 1959	1-0	St. Louis	Kellner
April 28, 1961	1-0, no-hitter	San Francisco	Jones
September 6, 1961	1-0	Philadelphia	Buzhardt
June 28, 1963	1-0	Los Angeles	Drysdale
July 2, 1963	0-1; 16 innings	San Francisco	Marichal
September 4, 1963	1-0	Pittsburgh	Friend
May 5, 1965**	0-1	Philadelphia	Bunning
August 31, 1965***	2-0	Milwaukee	Burdette

*This was a 15-inning game. Spahn relieved for 3.2 innings and was charged with the loss. Heintzelman pitched the last 5 innings and was credited with the win.
**Jim Bunning won this game with a 6th-inning home run.
***This was Spahn's last shutout—against his former Milwaukee teammate.

This victory marked a milestone in the great lefty's logbook. It was Spahn's 306th victory, the record-breaking win that made him the winningest left-hander in the annals of the game. Further, his game-ending strikeout of Charlie Smith raised his K total to 100, making it the 15th straight season in which he had erased at least 100 batters via the strikeout route.

In the Phillies' fifth, Spahn picked off Tony Gonzalez with that very deceptive, quick move of his to first base. It was a rally killer, one of many he had squelched over the years with that same lightning-like move to first base, à la Whitey Ford.

One other 1-0 game—one of baseball's most famous—begs attention, the 16-inning marathon staged by the then 42-year-old Spahn and Juan Marichal. The review of that scintillating ball game awaits our attention in a later chapter. And there is another rather impressive game that merits attention in a later chapter on 1-0 no-nos: the no-hitter Spahn threw as a frisky 40-year-old against San Francisco's Sam Jones. That April victory was Spahn's 290th and was completed in conjunction with an assist once again from Hank Aaron, who singled home the game's lone marker in the first inning. The run came about as the result of a Frank Bolling single followed by a passed ball on the part of Giants' catcher Ed Bailey and then Aaron's line shot to right field. From that point on, as in his 1-0 win against the Phils in 1963, the offense went south as the pitchers took absolute command of the ball game. No doubt San Jones wondered about that first-inning pitch to Aaron for a long time.

Dean Chance, September 25, 1964: Another Victory in an Angels Year to Remember

From 1964 to 1966 Dean Chance was among the top three pitchers in baseball, if not baseball's best. His 1964 season was one of those once-in-a-lifetime seasons, and that is the season during which so much happened that it's hard to track it all down. But some of the more incredible achievements of that Cy Young Award-winning season, presented then to only one pitcher, include these:

- Among his 15 complete games were 11 shutouts.
- He allowed only seven home runs in 278.1 innings pitched.
- In 50 innings of work against the Yanks he allowed *one* run.
- He won nine straight at one point during the season, six of them shutouts, and among the six shutouts were four 1-0 games.
- Among his nine losses were four by the score of 1-0.

- On September 25 he won his 20th game and his sixth 1-0 win of the season, tying him with Walter Johnson, Bullet Joe Bush, and Carl Hubbell for all-time leadership in that category.

Table 2.6 lists Chance's pitching log for the 1964 season, and one can see how overpowering it was. Note, if you will, that Dean Chance went un-

Table 2.6.   Dean Chance's 1964 Season

Date	Opponent	Opposing Pitcher	Score	Record
April 17	Detroit	Lary	8-3	1-0
April 28	Save vs. Washington	Save		
April 29	Save vs. Washington	Save		
May 3	Chi	Buzhardt	6-2	2-0
May 5	Save vs. Kansas City	Save		
May 15	Baltimore	Bunker	1-6	2-1
May 17	Save vs. Baltimore	Save		
May 24	New York	Bouton	3-0	3-1
May 29	Baltimore	Roberts	2-3	3-2
June 2	Boston	Lamabe	1-0	4-2
June 15	Washington	Rudolph	2-3	4-3
June 23	Washington	Daniels	2-0	5-3
June 27	Kansas City	O'Donoghue	1-2	5-4
July 1	Baltimore	McNally	2-4	5-5
July 11	Chicago	Talbot	1-0	6-5
July 15	Detroit	Regan	1-0	7-5
July 19	Minnesota	Grant	4-0	8-5
July 26*	Kansas City	Wyatt	4-3	9-5
July 28**	New York	Williams	3-1	10-5
August 1	Boston	Wilson	2-1	11-5
August 5	Baltimore	Bunker	1-0	12-5
August 14	Washington	Koch	7-0	13-5
August 18	Detroit	Aguirre	1-0	14-5
August 22	Cleveland	Siebert	0-3	14-6
August 25	Kansas City	Meyer	5-3	15-6
August 29	Detroit	Gladding	3-2	16-6
September 2	New York	Bouton	4-0	17-6
September 7	Boston	Morehead	4-1	18-6
September 11	Boston	Monbouquette	0-3	18-7
September 15	New York	Downing	7-0	19-7
September 23	Chicago	Wilhelm	1-2	19-8
September 25	Minnesota	Kaat	1-0	20-8
September 29	Chicago	Howard	1-2	20-9

*Won in relief in a 10-inning game (2 IP).
**NY's run was on Mantle's homer.

defeated between July 11 and August 25, during which time he won nine straight, allowing but one run per outing (his victory in relief was a two-inning stint on July 26). There were four saves during the early stages of the season. After May 12 Chance was used in starting roles, except for his relief win on July 26. In 1964 the Angels won 10 of their 82 victories by 1-0 scores and Chance represented 60 percent of that total. If one were to take even half of Chance's 1-0 victories away, the Angels would have been a sub-.500 ball club. And one last note: after July 11, and to the end of the season (19 games), he allowed a mere 17 runs.

In case you might be wondering about the gap between June 2 and 15, Mr. Chance had one other shutout date with the Yankees. On June 6 at Dodger Stadium, where the Angels played their home games in 1964, he made his way through extra innings in a 0-0 game in which he went 14 stanzas of the 16 played. The Yanks won that one, scoring twice in the top of the 16th. Willie Smith was the Angels' loser. Chance gave up a miserly three hits, only two free passes and struck out 12 with a no decision for his labors. Before the season was over it would be said of his work against the Yankees that it wasn't CBS who owned the Yanks, but Chance—lock, stock, and barrel. It was the Yanks' Mickey Mantle who scored the only run off Chance all season long, and he insisted then, and long afterward, that Dean Chance was the toughest pitcher he ever faced.

Going into his September 25 engagement with the Minnesota Twins, Chance stood at 19 and 8, facing Jim Kaat, a very capable lefty who came into the night game at 17 and 8. That match-up drew only 8,000 fans, partially because neither the Angels nor the Twins were anywhere near pennant contention. Those who chose not to take in this one missed a beauty. Chance and Kaat retired the side in order three times each, but the young lad they called Groove got the three that counted most, retiring the heart of the Twins' order, Harmon Killebrew, Jimmie Hall, and Don Mincher, to put the lid on his 20th conquest of the year, a sixth 1-0 effort. It added still more credentials on what would soon be proclaimed a Cy Young Award year. Those 20 wins marked the first time in the Angels' history that they could boast a 20-game winner. The very supportive Angels' owner, Gene Autry, was elated and, as usual, showed up in the clubhouse when it was all over.

The Halos waited until the bottom of the eighth to give Chance his narrow victory margin. Chance himself (a self-proclaimed atrocious hitter) started out the inning with a weak tap to Kaat that quickly became the first out. That ultimately brought up Bob Perry, who had not exactly burned up the baseball world with his hitting. In fact, the final game of his two-year major league career was just a week away, But on this night, and on this at bat, he lashed a "tweener" that was good for three bases, putting the go-ahead run on third. Manager Bill Rigney then sent swift Willie Smith in to run for Perry. Up came Jim Piersall, and a Kaat delivery got away from the Twins' ace, enabling Smith to score. That was all that Dean Chance needed, and three outs later the Twins were toast.

By 1968 Dean Chance, then with Minnesota, was into what should have been the middle years of his career. He posted a 16-16 record for a very weak-hitting Minnesota lineup, logging a 2.53 ERA with six more shutouts and a pair of 1-0 games. But before the 1969 season was underway there was a lengthy salary squabble with the parsimonious Twins owner, Calvin Griffith Jr., and after its settlement one of the results was that Chance reported late to spring training. Hurrying to get himself in shape, and doubtless appearing before he was really ready for the stress his delivery demanded, he suffered a back injury that brought his career to a premature end, as he sputtered through the 1969 season and on to a bitter end two seasons later. Chance was among the many whose outstanding careers had gone down before him when debilitating injury struck. Nonetheless, before his last major league pitch there had been a generously sized hatful of franchise and major league records that spoke so well of his 11-year career.

Bob Gibson, September 20, 1968: St. Louis vs. Chicago

Chicago	000	000	000	0-5-0
St. Louis	001	000	00x	1-4-0

WP, Gibson; LP, Jenkins

Baseball's 1968 was a delight for pitchers; for hitters it was a nightmare. There was something wrong, and that something wrong was a loss of the delicate balance between pitching and hitting. The strike zone had been enlarged to extend from the shoulders of the hitter to the bottom of his knee five seasons earlier and the pitchers took full advantage of that little gift. Gradually, between 1963 and 1967, pitching began to dominate, and by 1968 that domination was crushing. Baseball authorities, players, and writers branded 1968 as the Year of the Pitcher. There were seasons, nevertheless, that matched 1968's domination. The numbers in table 2.7 (1969's are for comparison with 1968)

Table 2.7. Periods of Pitching Domination

Teams / Year	SHO	CG	% SHO / Team	MLBA
16/1907	271	1728	15.	.245
20/1968	339	897	16.9	.237
20/1969	300	982	15.0	.248
30/2010	329	165	10.9	.257

Cardinal great Bob Gibson.

are from three especially depressed hitting years, 1907, 1968, and 2010, low in comparison with the 1995–2009 era.

Escaping the clutches of deadball-era scoring, the ravages of the 1960s, and lately of the 2010 season, these figures, to say the very least, raised eyebrows. In each instance baseball's masterminds came out—at least in the 1920's and late 1960's—with new decrees that helped the hitter. The 1920 season began with notices about doctoring the ball and putting clean baseballs in play as warranted, which led to a serious hitting boom. Major league teams in 1921 averaged .290 as compared with 1907's .245. 1969 pitchers went to work with a 10" mound, down five significant inches from the 1968 hill. It was a tonic for 1969's hitters, who raised the ML standard 11 percentage points from 1968.

Although no important changes were made in the game's basic measurements, there is a noticeable difference in the seasonal numbers between 1968 and 1969. Nor were any basic changes made in the production of baseballs, or in the specifications for bats used by major league hitters. Nevertheless, major league ball games were closely watched. Balance between hitting and pitching is *always* under surveillance. Table 2.8 shows team numbers on the season's 1968, 1-0 games.

There was something wrong with MLB during the 1960s, and the culprit was the imbalance between pitching and hitting. But there was nothing wrong with Bob Gibson's 1968 season. No matter what the circumstances might have been, Gibson would have been magnificent. It is some kind of wonder that he lost as many as nine games in 1968, a fact partially explained by one nine-game stretch during the season when he was backed by an offense that produced only nine runs and hit .147. That surely doesn't make things easier, but he survived and as time went on tightened his grip on the jugular vein of senior circuit hitters to go into the World Series with an other-planetary ERA of 1.12.

Gibby was involved in three 1-0 losses during the seasonal wars. Any one of those, or more, might as easily have been won as lost. He lost games three times by the score of 3-2, one each to Larry Dierker, Don Sutton, and Bobby

Table 2.8. 1-0 Games in 1968

National League		American League	
St. Louis	8	Detroit	1
San Francisco	6	Baltimore	6
Chicago	5	Cleveland	6
Cincinnati	0	Boston	2
Atlanta	3	New York	5
Pittsburgh	1	Oakland	2
Los Angeles	5	Minnesota	4
Philadelphia	5	California	2
New York	7	Chicago	7
Houston	7	Washington	5
Totals	**47**	**Totals**	**40**
ML Totals	**88**		

Bolin, and Don Drysdale beat him 2-0 in Los Angeles early in the season. But there were also victories, 20 of them, and here is one that took place at Busch Stadium on June 20. The pitchers were the side-arming Gibson with his sweeping delivery and rising fastball, and Fergie Jenkins, whose career had Hall of Fame written on it. And the two of them put on a Hall of Fame display of pitching.

In this game, attended by more than 25,000 Cards' enthusiasts, Gibson and Jenkins retired the side in order nine times (Gibson with five), and Gibby wound up the affair in the ninth by fanning dangerous Billy Williams and then causing Al Spangler and Ron Santo to fly out. It was the final out of a five-hit, six-strikeout effort. Except for one pitch that resulted in a triple off the bat of Lou Brock, who scored on a Curt Flood single one batter later, Jenkins was even better. He held the Cardinals to four hits, two of them in the third that posted the game's winning margin and K'd 11, three of which tied Cardinal cleanup hitter Orlando Cepeda in knots. Gibson snuffed the only Cub scoring threat in the fourth stanza when, with Ron Santo on third, he nailed Lou Johnson on a two-out grounder that ended the inning. The win raised his season mark to 7 and 5, as he was emerging from his early season disappointments to move on to a 13 and 4 record for the remainder of his Cy Young season.

What to do for an encore? How about a 17-strikeout game in the 1968 World Series opener against Detroit? That was part of a 4-0 shutout that got the NL champs off to a roaring start. The record set in that game still stands.

Luis Tiant, July 3, 1968: Cleveland vs. Minnesota

Minnesota	000	000	000	0	0-6-1
Cleveland	000	000	000	1	1-4-0

WP, Tiant; LP, Merritt

The Baseball Digest issue of July 2002 carried an article by Bob Dolgan that showcased the 1968 season of the man known as El Tiante. It was *some* season. Dolgan had this to say:

> Luis Tiant wasn't just another good pitcher. He was one of the most entertaining hurlers in baseball history.
>
> His choreographed windup had a wide range of motions. He would bob his head, turn his back on the batter, look skyward or

into the field boxes, then deliver the ball from a bewildering array of angles, overhand, sidearm, or even underhand. . . .

Tiant was at his best in the spring of 1968, when he threw four straight shutouts. . . . It was an unforgettable season for the Cuban right-hander. A few weeks after the four straight zeroes, he struck out 19 while winning a 10-inning game, 1-0. . . .

Tiant began his spectacular shutout streak on April 28, 1968, throwing a two-hitter over the Senators in Washington for a 2-0 victory. Senator slugger Frank Howard struck out on Tiant's hesitation pitch. "I give him shoulder, back, foot, and the ball last," he told the Cleveland Press.

"He threw everything at me but the ball," Howard said.

Tiante went on to conquer the Twins, 4-0, the Yankees, 8-0, and Baltimore's O's, 2-0, by which time his ERA had almost fallen out of sight, at a skimpy 1.03. 1968 was a pretty good year for that kind of stuff, but even then, that 1.03 during his remarkable streak is something to write home about.

Tiant's 21-9 season was a Cy Young Award season—just about any year but 1968, when Denny McLain's 31-6 was pegged for that prestigious award. That season, "the Fred Astaire of baseball," as he was dubbed by Reggie Jackson, logged league-leading marks in ERA, with 1.60 and in opposing hitters' batting average at .168. His 4.4 wins, by sabermetric measure, tied McLain's at 4.4, best in the AL, and second best to Gibson's 7.6 NL mark. By the numbers:

- Tiant won 9 by shutout scores.
- He won one 1-0 game (10 innings and 19 K's).
- He lost 2 1-0 games.
- He lost 5 shutout games.
- He defeated New York four times without a loss.
- He defeated Jim Merritt (Minnesota) three times.
- Tiant was undefeated between May 26 and July 24 (12 straight).

El Tiante's game of note during the 1968 season took place on July 3 at Municipal Stadium with 21,136 fans on hand. The game was finally won in Cleveland's 10th, when with none out Tiant's Cuban battery mate, Joe Azcue, singled home Lou Johnson. Tiant's incredible control was evidenced by his 19 K's and no free passes. The only error in the game, by Cesar Tovar, set up the winning run by permitting Lou Johnson to advance to scoring position as a consequence of his (Tovar's) error in a routine ground ball play.

National League 1, American League 0, July 9, 1968:
The Only 1-0 Score in All-Star Game History

American League	000	000	000	0-3-1
National League	100	000	00x	1-5-0

WP, Drysdale (LA); LP, Tiant (Clv)

The first All-Star game was played in Chicago at the home of the White Sox, Comiskey Park. It was a part of the 1933 World's Fair and included among the Windy City's many celebrations during its Century of Progress Exposition that year. Stars selected by the fans gathered to initiate a baseball gala that has been played every season since as a sort of midway point in the major league regular season games. The 39th renewal of the All-Star Game was played indoors for the first time at Houston's Astrodome. It was, from the perspective of its score, representative in every respect of the status of the game in 1968. One to nothing was its score and the game was won in the first inning on an unearned run, a combination of a Willie Mays leadoff single, an error, a wild pitch, and Willie McCovey's gounder, which resulted in a double play that enabled the game's MVP, Mays, to score while Rod Carew, Jim Fregosi, and Harmon Killebrew were busy completing the DP. It was fatal for the American League's starting hurler, Luis Tiant, who was tagged with the defeat. His teammates that day garnered only three hits off National League pitchers, among whom was the game's winner, Don Drysdale. After Mays' first-inning single, the senior circuit hitters could come up with but four more, each harmless as both offenses sputtered to a close in regulation time. It was the only 1-0 score in All-Star play and has remained so to this very day. Significantly the scores of the two games preceding 1968's were 2-1, both won by the NL. It took another score of years to register a tight, low-score game, this one won by the AL, 2-1 again, in 1988.

Among the 81 1-0 games, there were stellar performances by a number of fine hurlers in both leagues. We'll put a wrap on 1968 by taking a look at some of those pitchers and their superlative efforts. Tables 2.9 and 2.10 detail pitchers

Table 2.9.   1968 Low-Hit or No-Hit Performances

Name	Team	Date	Hits	Opponent	Spoiler
Gaylord Perry	San Francisco	September 17	No-hitter	St. Louis	
Rick Wise	Philadelphia	August 8	1	Los Angeles	Bart Shirley

Note: There were 52 two-hit games and 13 one-hit games in 1968.

Table 2.10.   1968 Scoreless-Inning Streaks

Pitcher/Team	No. Innings	Dates	1-0 Games in Streak
Don Drysdale, Los Angeles	58.1	May 14 to June 8	5/14 vs. Chicago (NL) 5/18 vs. Houston
Bob Gibson, St. Louis	48.2	June 2 to July 1	6/2 vs. Chicago (NL)
Ray Culp, Boston	40	September 7 to September 29	9/25 vs. Washington
Joel Horlen, Chicago (AL)	37	May 11 to May 29	5/11 vs. Oakland
Ken Holtzman, Chicago (NL)	29	July 20 to August 7	7/28 vs. San Francisco
Jim Maloney, Cincinnati	27	September 21 to September 29	9/22 vs. Pittsburgh

who contributed no-hit, perfect, and one-hit games to the record books in 1-0 games, as well as those who chalked up streaks of scoreless innings during the season. Recognition, in a preliminary way, goes to the following:

- Catfish Hunter, who pitched the first perfect game in 46 years
- Joel Horlen, who won four and lost two 1-0 games in the AL (Chicago)
- Bob Gibson, who won four and lost one 1-0 game

Mickey Lolich, August 20, 1974: Detroit Tigers vs. California Angels

Detroit	000	000	000	01	1-4-0
California	000	000	000	00	0-10-0

WP, Lolich; LP, Ryan

The California Angels performed flawlessly through an 11-inning scoreless game. Nolan Ryan was throwing lasers at the Tigers, clocked in at 100.9 on the speed gun. They were playing at home and a decent-sized crowd was there to cheer them on. It was a perfect evening for baseball in Anaheim, California, and everything was about letter perfect except for one thing: the Angels forgot to score. The visiting Tigers, behind the stout Mickey Lolich, messed up the proceedings by slamming the door on each scoring threat mounted by the Angels, and though touching the Bengal southpaw for 10 singles (there were no extra base hits in this game) the Halos bowed to Detroit by a 1-0 score. For Angel fans it was an ugh-night; for Tiger fans back home in Detroit is was oh-so-sweet.

Prior to this game Mickey Lolich had been involved in 28 Tiger decisions, breaking even at 14 and 14, barely adequate by major league standards. His 16-year career won-loss mark, as a matter of fact, wound up on the better side of .500 baseball, but not by much: 217-191 is better than half only by some 26 decisions. And in 1974, Lolich, a sinkerball pitcher with an excellent changeup, stood right at 14 and 14 on the eve of his match up with Nolan Ryan. Nearing the end of his 12th tour of duty with the Tigers, he had previously thrown six 1-0 games, and he would add a seventh on this occasion. An innings-eater throughout his career, his total would be 308 in 1974, the fourth consecutive time he had reached the 300 level. He was one of the more durable pitchers in the Detroit franchise's history, and though he took his whippings, he was there when it counted, particularly during the 1968 season and especially when he subdued the Cardinals in game 7 of the World Series in the Year of the Pitcher.

During the 1974 campaign Lolich had been victimized by shutouts five times previously, and on August 20 it began to look like Nolan Ryan was going to pin number six on him. Ryan had surrendered but two harmless singles through 10 innings. Then came the top of the 11th. Ron LeFlore became Ryan's 19th strikeout victim to start the inning, and then Gary Sutherland, the Tigers' elongated second baseman, popped up for the second out. Two out and another zero in the making. But Ben Oglivie stepped in and lined the Tiger's third hit into center field, promptly stole second, and Bill Freehan followed with another single to score Oglivie. That run did the trick and Lolich found himself on the W side of the ledger after one last threat by the Angels to tie it up. Here is what happened in California's last-gasp chance. Second baseman Bobby Heise opened the frame with a single to put the tying run on base. Rudy Meoli then sacrificed Heise to second. But with one out the veteran Bobby Valentine grounded out, third to first. Now two were out and Mickey Lolich was one out away from a well-pitched victory. Standing in the way of that victory was a very dangerous warrior, Frank Robinson, whose exploits as a hitter were so gold-plated that he was a sure Hall-of-Famer. Detroit manager Ralph Houk was not about to play Russian roulette with this fellow, so he ordered him passed, putting runners on first and second, but also setting up a ground ball out at any base. The strategic move on Williams' part, though the right one, proved unnecessary as first baseman Bob Oliver lofted a fly ball to Jim Nettles, ending the game. It was the Tigers' 58th victory of the season, at least somewhat easing the pain of their last-place miseries in the AL East.

The last shutout Mickey Lolich threw was a 2-0 conquest of the Atlanta Braves during his one season with the New York Mets. On July 18 in the Bicentennial Year, by then a grizzled veteran, he gave up two hits, retiring 14 Braves in a row before an error put Rod Gilbreath on base with two out in the ninth. He then took matters into his own hands, fanning Jim Wynn to end the game.

It was his 41st career shutout. Lolich left the game behind in 1979 after a two-year stint with the San Diego Padres. There were no regrets for the fun-loving, easy-going Oregonian. He had made the scene, won a World Series ring, and recorded victories more than 200 times.

Jim Palmer, April 12, 1977:
Baltimore Wins in Sudsville, 1-0

Baltimore	000	000	001	1-5-0
Milwaukee	000	000	000	0-2-2

Smooth-as-silk Jim Palmer lost his first game of the 1977 season to Texas in a nerve-wracking, 10-inning season opener in Baltimore. The Texans got to him in the top of the tenth to score the winning run of the day. Bert Blyleven was the winner, 2 to 1. Four days later, the 6'3" Baltimore ace, who had won 20 or more in six of the previous seven seasons, found himself embroiled in another ball game that featured strings of goose eggs on the scoreboard, this time before a record-breaking crowd of 55,120 at Milwaukee's County Stadium. Palmer was opposed by 23-year-old Bill Travers, a 15-game winner in 1976, and the two of them were locked in a nail-biter in the Brewers' home opener. This time, however, Jim Palmer was in complete control while crafting a one-hitter through the first eight innings. During that time he had retired the side in order five times, running up 18 consecutive outs before the Milwaukee left fielder, Jim Wohlford, opened the bottom of the ninth with a single. It was the second and last hit Jim Palmer gave up. Assisted by a fine play on a bunt that catcher Rick Dempsey turned into a double play, Palmer then induced a pop fly in short right to finish off the Brewers. It was the first of his 20 victories in 1977. His 1-1 record as of April 12 came after 19 innings of play during which the run-starved Orioles had managed but two tallies, rather thin gruel for a team with pennant aspirations.

Jim Palmer's 20 wins and 319 innings pitched, a career high, were league-leading figures in 1977. He had won the Cy Young Award three times in the space of four previous seasons (1973, 1975, and 1976) and he didn't miss by much in 1977. This one was bound for Cooperstown. During his career he posted 53 shutouts, which put him at number 53—tied with Gaylord Perry—on the all-time list. His last two shutouts came in a reprise, 15-5 season in 1982. One of them was a towering two-hitter thrown at Yankee Stadium on the first day of June. A fifth-inning unearned run was all he needed to subject the Bronx Bombers to a 1-0 humiliation.

A final Palmer note of interest: If his opponents harbored any intentions of poking one of his pitches into the seats with the bases jammed, they might

Table 2.11.   Baltimore vs. Milwaukee, April 12, 1977

Baltimore	AB	R	H	A	Milwaukee	AB	R	H	A
Bumbry, cf, lf	4	0	0	0	Joshua, cf	4	0	0	0
Dauer, 2b	4	0	0	3	Yount, ss	2	0	0	9
Singleton, rf	3	0	2	0	Cooper, 1b	3	0	0	1
DeCinces, 3b	3	0	1	4	Bando, 3b	3	0	0	4
Murray, dh	4	1	1	0	Lezcano, rf	3	0	1	0
L. May, 1b	2	0	0	2	Money, 2b	3	0	0	4
Dempsey, c	3	0	1	2	Quirk, dh	2	0	0	0
Kelly, lf	3	0	0	0	Wohlford, lf	3	0	1	0
Robinson, ph	1	0	0	0	Moore, c	3	0	0	2
Harlow, cf	0	0	0	0	Travers (LP)	0	0	0	3
Belanger, ss	3	0	0	2					
Palmer (WP)	0	0	0	0					
Totals	**30**	**1**	**5**	**13**	**Totals**	**26**	**0**	**2**	**23**

Game time: 2 hours, 8 minutes.
Umpires: Garcia, Chylak, Palermo, Brinkman.
Attendance: 55,120.

Baltimore	000	000	001	1-5-0
Milwaukee	000	000	000	0-2-2

just as well have forgotten about it. *Not once* in his career did Jim Palmer permit that to happen. Among the 254 batters he faced with the bases fully occupied in his career, he gave up a relatively scant 36 hits (that averages out to .195), meaning that four out of every five hitters came up empty handed. That is a rare accomplishment, indeed.

The full box score of the April 12, 1977, game at County Stadium, Milwaukee, appears in table 2.11.

Frank Tanana, October 4, 1987: And on to the Playoffs!

Toronto	000	000	000	0-6-0
Detroit	010	000	00x	1-3-0

WP, Tanana; LP, Key

Nearing mid-May in 1987 the Tigers seemed destined for a miserable season, having won but 11 of their first 30 games. No one seemed to be hitting and their pitching seemed to be in disarray. But, as so often happens, they suddenly went on a tear starting with a 15-2 slaughter of California and won 8 of their next 10 games. It put them back into the AL East race. The race settled down into a struggle for supremacy between New York, Toronto, and a Tigers team that was gradually showing its teeth to the rest of the league. By mid-July, on the 17th, in fact, they shut out the Mariners behind the magic of a three-hitter pitched by Frank Tanana. The Tiger southpaw, by this time into the crafty-and-slower stage of his career, was in top form, spotting pitches artfully and mixing speeds, arm angles, and pitches that set Seattle back on its ears.

However, Toronto, with a talented lineup that replaced the Yankees in the division's race for first place, managed to stay ahead of the pack, and going into the last six games of the season was out in front of the Detroit Tigers by two and a half games. Despite the onrushing Tigers, they were expected to take the AL East, having won seven in a row, two of which came at Detroit's expense in Toronto. With seven games yet to play, they had become prohibitive favorites to represent the AL East in the divisional championships. Then "stuff" began happening. They lost the last game of the three-game set with Detroit in 13, and at home. Milwaukee moved into Toronto for the second-to-last three-game set of the season and took three in a row. Now their lead was down to a game and a half, and their final series of the season loomed as something murkier than the nights ahead of them.

Detroit had come a long way since those early season frustrations and had turned what well might have been "just another series" into something that could turn the Motor City upside down. And sure enough, the Tigers won a throbber behind Doyle Alexander, who had been acquired in exchange for John Smoltz on August 12, and proceeded to win nine straight down the stretch. The win cut the lead to one and a half games. Detroit fans were agog. The next night Detroit won again, this time in 12 innings, with reliever Mike Henneman picking up the victory.

The race had come down to the last game of the season, winner take all. At this point, enter sports scribe Roy Johnson of the *New York Times* in a size-up of the final game of regular season play.

> Dateline: October 4, 1987
>> Miracle Finish?
>> Incredible Flop?
>> Tigers Win It
> It will either be remembered as one of baseball's most inspired comebacks or one of its most embarrassing collapses. The Detroit Tigers, a team that some predicted would be among the worst in its

division, captured the American League East title this afternoon with a dramatic 1-0 victory over the Toronto Blue Jays for a stunning three-game sweep of the season-ending series in the tightest pennant race of the year. . . .

The game's only run was provided by Larry Herndon, the Tigers' right fielder. Herndon spoiled an otherwise outstanding three-hit pitching performance by Toronto's Jimmy Key (17-8) with a second-inning home run over the left-field fence. The fly ball was aided by the blustery conditions that marked the entire series. . . .

In notching his fifth complete game and his third shutout of the season, the 31st of his career, Tanana (15-10) defused the already frustrated Blue Jay hitters. He allowed just six hits, striking out nine batters, tying his highest total of the season.

Interviewed by no less than Jim Palmer after the game, Frank Tanana revealed that he had to make some mechanical changes in his delivery, which recently had been sending his curveball to home plate "flat," making the pitch easier to pick up and, consequently, easier to hit. His adjustments restored the effectiveness of his curveball, making his fading fast one more effective. The 13 infield assists in this pressure-cooker game attest to the effectiveness of his curve and changeup pitches and accounted for almost half of the Blue Jays' outs.

Almost lost in the midst of a championship on the line in the season's last game is the 1-0 gem Tanana threw. This one brought with it a championship, one of the few in the game's history that was a last-ditch, season closing coup. The game showcased two of 1987's premier hurlers. Jimmy Key, who led his league with a 2.76 ERA, matched the crafty Tanana pitch for pitch and, though touched for Herndon's wind-blown four-bagger, was as effective with his sharp breaking hooks, striking out eight while facing only 27 hitters. Lou Whitaker's two safeties, both singles, were erased in double plays, and Key subjected the Detroiters to four out-in-order innings.

But the hero of the day was Tanana. His 1-0 masterpiece was the only one of its kind during the 1987 Tiger season and it gave Motown's faithful something to cheer about. The book on Tanana's 1-0 games showed more than a rare entry or two. For example, during his flame-throwing days with the Angels, he both lost and won 1-0 games in the same season, 1975, to the same hurler, Jim Palmer, who was his interviewer after his championship victory. His first 1-0 game was hurled as a Halo in his second major league season, defeating the Tigers on August 19, 1974, in a night game in Anaheim. That night he walked one and struck out nine. He had to wait until the bottom of ninth for the tally that sealed his victory. It came, finally, on a passed ball and a sacrifice fly with one away, moving his record to 9 and 14 in a 14 and 19 season.

Roy Halladay, September 6, 2003:
Doc Tames the Tigers

Detroit	000	000	000	0	0-3-0
Toronto	000	000	000	1	1-6-1

WP, Halladay; LP, Rodney

Roy Halladay closed out the 2002 season, a breakout year for him, with a 1-0 two-hitter over the Tigers that moved his record to an impressive 19 and 7. It was his third career shutout and first 1-0 conquest. Earlier, in 1998 as a rookie, he served notice that great things were ahead with a one-hit performance as he defeated those same Tigers 2-1, the Tigers garnering their only run on that one hit, a home run by Bobby Higginson delivered with two out in the ninth. When it came time to open the 2003 season, this very accomplished right-hander was ready. A master of the strike zone and several pitches, he put on a pitching mechanics clinic every time he pitched. He is on a direct-line course to Cooperstown, having emerged from relative obscurity despite his numbers in the earlier stages of his career.

In 2003 it took him a couple games to get thoroughly warmed up to the task at hand, but when he did it was Nellie bar the door. Between May Day of 2003, when he edged Texas 7-6, and August 1, exactly three months later, he went undefeated, winning 15 in a row. It was the foundation piece for the Cy Young he was awarded for his 2003 efforts. Among his 22 victories were 13 in which he allowed two runs or less. He hurled completions nine times and shut out opponents twice, and one of those shutouts was a stellar 1-0 game late in the season, our feature game in this 1-0 review.

Running his record to 18 and 6, he defeated the Yanks on September 1, 8-1. His next assignment was at Toronto's Skydome against Nathan Cornejo, Detroit's 6'5" right-hander. Young Cornejo pitched extremely well, furnishing Halladay all the competition he could ask for, allowing only five hits in a full nine innings of work. Scoreless at the end of nine, the game went into extra innings and Detroit went down in order for the seventh time in the game. For the bottom of the 10th, manager Alan Trammel brought on reliever Fernando Rodney. A Dominican, he hadn't yet tasted victory during 2003, and apparently this was the wrong day for that to happen because the Blue Jays pushed across the winning run on a Bobby Kielty single, putting the ball game on ice and hoisting Halladay's record to 19 and 6. Three victories later that record was 22 and 7 as he wound up beating Cleveland in his final appearance of the season.

Through the 2005 season he had posted a complete game record of 14, accompanied by eight shutouts. Although there were no additions to the 1-0 ledger, neither were there any defeats. Only 28 at that time, there were, barring injury, many years ahead for the dominant pitcher of his day. He was the best pitcher in baseball between 2000 and 2005 and gave every indication that it would remain just that way.

Randy Johnson, September 2005: Incredible Speed and Incredible Achievements

At 6'10" it seemed that Randy Johnson's pitching arm almost reached to home plate. Factoring in the blinding speed of his deliveries, it's small wonder that hitters didn't look forward to an afternoon or evening of Johnson heaters. On one of his more incredible outings, August 25, 2002, at the "mere" age of 39, he was clocked at 102 mph as he K'd the Cubs' first baseman to end the seventh inning of a 7-0 shutout. That afternoon he subdued the Cubs, fanning 16 with at least one Cub victim in every inning. The only hurler to throw heat as long and as hard as Nolan Ryan, he joins Walter Johnson, Lefty Grove, Ryan, and Bob Feller as the top fastball pitchers in the game's history. And when his last days had come, logging the last of his 303 victories as a San Francisco Giant, he was still throwing in the 90-mph range.

Just about everything about this fellow was unique, including the very professional way he went about his hobby, photography. The Johnson record on 1-0 games is a bit skimpy. Not so with his 2-0 conquests. There are 15 of them, and when combined with his 1-0 log (in table 2.12), it's impressive.

The year 1999 was a bit of a speed bump for Johnson. On June 25, 1999, he lost the first four straight, as follows:

- June 25: to St. Louis, 0-1
- June 30: to Cincinnati, 0-2
- July 5: to St. Louis, 0-1
- July 10: to Oakland, 0-2

Two weeks later, on July 25, he lost to Los Angeles, 2-1.
His 1-0 and 2-0 totals follow:

- 1-0 games: won 8, lost 3
- 2-0 games: won 14, lost 3

Table 2.12. Randy Johnson's 1-0 and 2-0 Games

Date	Score	Opposing Team (LP)	Noteworthy
June 2, 1990	2-0	Detroit (Robinson)	No-hitter
August 15, 1990	2-0	Baltimore (Harnisch)	4-hitter
May 17, 1991	**1-0**	New York (AL) (Leary)	7 IP, 10 K, first 1-0 victory
April 11, 1992	**1-0**	Kansas City (Appier)	11 K, 4-hitter
April 20, 1992	2-0	Minnesota (Tapani)	4-hitter
May 25, 1994	**1-0**	Oakland (Darling)	9 K, 4-hitter
June 4, 1994	2-0	Toronto (Stottlemyre)	6-hitter
June 5, 1995	2-0	Baltimore (McDonald)	2-run HR by Buhner, 3-hitter
June 8, 1997	2-0	Detroit (Moehler)	2-hitter
August 20, 1997	**1-0**	Cleveland (Nagy)	6 IP, 2 hits, Slocumb SV
August 28, 1998	2-0	Pittsburgh (Cordova)	7 hits
September 7, 1998	**1-0**	Cincinnati (Parris)	14 K, won on Derek Bell HR
June 14, 1999	2-0	Florida (Dempster)	4-hitter
April 9, 2000	**1-0**	Pittsburgh (Schmidt)	13 K, 5 hits
September 2, 2001	0-1	Arizona (Kim)	Johnson started and pitched the first 7 innings (no decision); the game was lost when Klesko hit a walk-off home run in the 13th
April 1, 2002	2-0	San Diego (Jarvis)	Season opener, Mark Grace 2-run HR won it
August 5, 2002	2-0	New York (NL) (Estes)	2-hitter
May 18, 2004	2-0	Atlanta (Hampton)	17th perfect game in MLB history; fastest pitch in this game at 98 mph
August 15, 2004	2-0	New York (NL) (Trachsel)	8.1 IP, Aquino SV
August 31, 2005	2-0	Seattle (Hernandez)	4-hitter, Rivera SV
September 11, 2005	**1-0**	Boston (Wakefield)	3-hitter, Giambi HR, Rivera SV
April 19, 2009	2-0	Arizona (Scherzer)	7 IP, 1 hit, Wilson SV

To conclude this chapter on significant, 1-0 regular season games, we're going to take a closer look at the last of Randy Johnson's 1-0 victories. It came on the afternoon of September 11, 2005, at the ripe old baseball age of 41. On this particular day he was wearing a New York Yankee uniform, facing another seasoned veteran, the knuckleballer Tim Wakefield.

Because New York is New York, with all that means for its baseball teams, things hadn't gone too well for the most recent of Yankee star acquisitions. Brought to New York for the 2005 season by George Steinbrenner, Johnson was a bit less than overwhelming in Yankee pinstripes. Still, he had managed a 14-7 season prior to his September 11 date with the Bosox. More than likely, the New York front office and press rather expected that by that late date the electrifying southpaw would have been around the 20 mark in wins. After all, he *was* Randy Johnson and he *was* in New York. Well, it just didn't work out that way, and "The Big Unit" looked a tad less than a Big Unit.

Prior to his September 11 date with Boston, New York's archenemy, Johnson had put together a run of 23 innings during which he gave up but a single run in 5-1 and 2-0 victories. The 23 frames included the last five of a 6-2 loss in Chicago. That didn't seem to impress many New Yorkers. In the *Times'* feature "Sports of the Times" article of September 12, after a dominant, stellar whitewash job, William C. Rhoden wrote:

> After "New York, New York," the city's theme song could be, "What Have You Done For Me Lately?" . . .
> With 20 games left, the questions are just beginning. Where has this Unit been hiding? Is he coming back? Was his performance yesterday a mirage?

Without commenting on those typical New York press corps remarks, it is sufficient to point to the record of Johnson's 2005 performance in a Yankee uniform. As Casey Stengel once said: "You could look it up."

Here we have Johnson coming off his 23-inning stint of excellence and capping that with a magnificent 1-0, three-hitter that brought the New Yorkers of Joe Torre to within three of the front-running Bosox. It was a pressure-laden afternoon for New York, which desperately needed a W to stay within reach of Boston. This game was pivotal, and Torre, as well as the entire ball club, knew it.

In the Yankee's first, Jason Giambi took advantage of a rare Wakefield curveball to stroke the circuit smash that won the game. After that the Bronx Bombers, hardly bombing their way on this occasion, spent the afternoon chasing Wakefield knucklers that sent them back to the dugout 12 times, victims of strikeouts.

Meanwhile, Randy Johnson set to work protecting his slim one-run margin. In near-perfect fashion he disposed of one Boston hitter after another, retiring the side in six of the seven innings he pitched. The only hit he gave up, a single to Kevin Youkilis, proved harmless in his seven-inning tenure. The last hitter he faced, Kevin Millar, was a strikeout victim on a 90+ mph swiftie. Reliever Tom Gordon was brought on in the eighth and the incomparable Mariano Rivera in the ninth to wrap things up.

The Unit had spoken and there was really little left to be said about the big win. However, it didn't silence New York sports scribes, who went on and on as is their wont. Nonetheless, the 1-0 victory sparked the Yanks to a 13 out of 15 surge that ultimately reduced the Boston lead to a point where the last series of the 2005 season at Fenway might just bring home a championship. Johnson won 2-1 and 11-3 games against Baltimore in the interim and in that final series faced off against Tim Wakefield once more. In the most crucial series of all with respect to the AL East, old Randy beat Wakefield yet another time, running his season record to 17 and 8, as well as assuring New York at least a tie for divisional honors. Sorting everything out after that could be left to playoff wars. Randy Johnson had at least brought them this far.

Further on, you will encounter Randy Johnson once again, this time listed among the game's hurlers who pitched no-hit and perfect games among their 1-0 victories. We turn next to the blue ribbon games that were played in championship playoff and World Series settings.

Notes

1. David Nemec, *The Great Encyclopedia of 19th Century Major League Baseball* (New York: Donald Fine Books, 1997), 290.

2. *New York Times*, May 12, 1890.

3. *Baseball Research Journal*, volumes 1–3 (Cleveland: SABR, 1974), 132–133.

4. *Baseball Research Journal*, 132–133.

5. Strasburg debuted with a 5-2 victory over Pittsburgh and followed that with a 9-4 win at Cleveland on June 13, 2010, in an interleague game.

The Grand Old Warriors. In 1947 the New York Yankees brought together these Grand Old Warriors for their Reunion and Old Timers celebration. Pictured here left to right, with career 1-0 game records, are: Cy Young, HOF (W13, L7); Lefty Grove, HOF (W8, L6); Jack Coombs (W5, L2); George Earnshaw (W1, L0); Ed Walsh, HOF (W13, L8); Stan Coveleski, HOF (W12, L5); Red Faber, HOF (W7, L2); Albert "Chief" Bender, HOF (W5, L3).

CHAPTER 3

1-0 Games at the Summit

Between the American League's 1901 entry into the major league mix and the 2005 World Series' conclusion with its 1-0 thriller, there have been 23 of these exceptional 1-0 games. The only 19th-century tilt of this kind that came close to making this distinguished list involved winners of both halves of the NL's 1892 season. It was an 11-inning tie between Cleveland and Boston on October 17. This one was a brilliantly pitched, scoreless game featuring Jack Stivetts, who that season logged more than 400 innings pitching for the Boston Bean-eaters. He threw a no-hitter against Brooklyn and won 35 games while completing 45 of his 54 starts in a heroic effort that matched teammate Kid Nichols' 35 victories.

Another youngster—in his third big-time season—enjoyed a huge year in 1892. His name was Cy Young. During the 1892 season he led the league in wins (36), ERA (1.93), and shutouts (9), which included a 0-0 tie, a 2-0 victory and one outing of the 1-0 variety.

Classifying a championship series as a World Series came into vogue during the 1880s when playoffs between the National League and the American Association pitted their champions against one another for professional baseball's top honors. Thus, Boston and Cleveland (better known as the Spiders at that time) met for laurels in the 1892 World's Series. The first of what became known as the *modern* World Series games were played in 1903, and again we find the name of Cy Young, this time with the AL's Boston Americans (later, the better-known Red Sox) making headlines with two wins against the NL's Wagner-led Pittsburgh team. Table 3.1 lists all 23 World Series games with a 1-0 score. From this listing eight World Series have been chosen that will provide nine heart-stoppers (two successive games from the 1966 Fall Classic are listed as one entry).

It might just be well to remind ourselves, before plunging into some of baseball's best 1-0 World Series games, that these championships are among

73

Table 3.1. World Series Games with a 1-0 Score

Date	Winner	Winning Pitcher	Loser	Losing Pitcher
October 17, 1892	0-0 tie, Boston (NL)	Stivetts	0-0 tie, Cleveland (NL)	Young
October 13, 1905	New York (NL)	McGinnity	Philadelphia (AL)	Plank
October 12, 1906	Chicago (NL)	Brown	Chicago (AL)	Altrock
September 5, 1918	Boston (AL)	Ruth	Chicago (NL)	Vaughn
October 11, 1920	Cleveland (AL)	Mails	Brooklyn (NL)	Smith
October 13, 1921	New York (NL)	Nehf	New York (AL)	Hoyt
October 12, 1923	New York (NL)	Nehf	New York (AL)	Jones
October 6, 1948	Boston (NL)	Sain	Cleveland (AL)	Feller
October 5, 1949	New York (AL)	Reynolds	Brooklyn (NL)	Newcombe
October 6, 1949	Brooklyn (NL)	Roe	New York (AL)	Raschi
October 4, 1950	New York (AL)	Raschi	Philadelphia (NL)	Konstanty
October 9, 1956	Brooklyn (NL)	Labine	New York (AL)	Turley
October 7, 1957	Milwaukee (NL)	Burdette	New York (AL)	Ford
October 6, 1959	Chicago (AL)	Shaw; Donovan, save	Los Angeles (NL)	Koufax
October 16, 1962	New York (AL)	Terry	San Francisco (NL)	Sanford
October 5, 1963	Los Angeles (NL)	Drysdale	New York (AL)	Bouton
October 8, 1966	Baltimore (AL)	Bunker	Los Angeles (NL)	Osteen
October 9, 1966	Baltimore (AL)	McNally	Los Angeles (NL)	Drysdale
October 18, 1972	Cincinnati (NL)	Billingham	Oakland (AL)	Carroll
October 18, 1986	Boston (AL)	Hurst; Schiraldi, save	New York (NL)	Darling
October 27, 1991	Minnesota (AL)	Morris (10 innings)	Atlanta (NL)	Pena
October 28, 1995	Atlanta (NL)	Glavine	Cleveland (AL)	Poole
October 24, 1996	New York (AL)	Pettitte; Wetteland, save	Atlanta (NL)	Smoltz
October 26, 2005	Chicago (AL)	Garcia; Jenks, save	Houston (NL)	Lidge

the sporting world's most tension-laden events. One pitch, one out, or one hit might have "all the marbles" written on it. Tom Boswell, who analyzed and wrote about baseball, once said, "Baseball is really two sports—the Summer Game and the Autumn Game. One is the leisurely pastime of our national mythology. The other is not so gentle."[1] That "not so gentle" phrase is a delicious understatement pulling together the way things are done and the players who go about their championship business. Great plays, even embarrassing miscues, are part of almost every game, often occasioned by the pressures of the moment. The tensions created by the big bucks riding on nearly every play in these games are often crushing and usually directly related to the prestige and notoriety that accompanies winning. With that in mind, let's turn to the 1905 World Series for a look at the first 1-0 game in modern World Series play.

1905 was a year of titanic proportions. Albert Einstein published papers that introduced the theory of relativity to the world, a Russian revolution nearly deposed Tsar Nicholas II, and the western movement continued in both Canada and the United States. America's American and National League champions had been decided, the two set to meet for baseball's ultimate honors after a year's absence in 1904.

In 1905, the Giants' front office and their fiery *major domo*, John McGraw, finally consented to a renewal of the classic initiated in 1903. There was a lot at stake, especially for the McGraw-men. Their skipper publicly proclaimed his opponents White Elephants, turning up his nose at Connie Mack's Athletics as inferior—just like the rest of the league he represented—to his Giants. And in this series, he was right—barely. The rosters of the two pitching staffs included five future Hall of Fame hurlers, including Rube Waddell (sidelined by an injury), Albert "Chief" Bender, Eddie Plank, Christy Mathewson, and Iron Man Joe McGinnity. These were two very accomplished ball clubs.

This Fall Classic was the first—and only—in which one pitcher won three games via the shutout route. That moundsman was Christy Mathewson, a national sports idol, who entered the series on the heels of an awesome 32-8 record and a 1.27 ERA, making McGraw's task much less complicated, no matter how much his managing skills were touted.

The other of the M-Boys, McGinnity, had won 35 in 1904, his best season in a Hall of Fame career. His work in '05 showed over 300 innings pitched, a league-leading 46 starts, and a pair of shutouts. That, too, made things a little easier for the Giants.

It was McGinnity who pitched the fourth game of the '05 Classic, shutting down the Mackmen yet again on six scattered hits. There wasn't an extra base hit to be reckoned with. The Athletics reached base only seven times, including one error and one free pass. None of that bothered the Iron Man, who breezed through his assignment in utter control of the proceedings.

This is the way the *New York Times*, with a nod toward Eddie Plank's equally fine performance, characterized the pitching in this almost scoreless tilt.

> McGraw manifested clever generalship when he decided to have McGinnity pitch, for the Iron Man, with an even break, would have captured his game on Tuesday.[2] Yesterday he twirled to perfection, and at no time did the raiders give evidence of seriously hammering his deliveries. Plank, be it inscribed to his credit, hurled them over with almost equal skill, and had not a fatal error by Monte Cross been made in the fourth, when the single tally of the game was recorded, baseball history might tell a different tale today. McGinnity had everything on the list that was desirable, and with perfect fielding support carried the day. His delivery was mainly of the speedy type, an occasional floater[3] going over, and he struck out the Athletics every time when strikeouts were needed most."[4]

The only real threat to McGinnity's supremacy occurred in the eighth stanza when the tiny A's speedster Topsy Hartsel, who walked to start off the inning, finally wound up on third with hard-hitting "Socks" Seybold due up. Seybold, however, became a McGinnity strikeout victim to the roar of approval registered by a capacity Polo Grounds crowd. The Iron Man set down the Athletics in 1-2-3 order in the ninth, a strikeout closing the day. And then the roar was deafening. Mathewson's third shutout the next day was almost anticlimatic, despite the majestic singularity of his effort. It wound up a truly magnificent "pitchers' series," one that would be hard, if not impossible, to match.

WORLD SERIES GAMES

The 1918 World Series, Game 1: The Babe Takes On Hippo Vaughn, September 5, 1918

Boston Red Sox (AL)	000	100	000	1-5-0	
Chicago Cubs (NL)	000	000	000	0-6-0	

WP, Ruth; LP, Vaughn

There seemed to be no way that a baseball game was going to be ordinary if Babe Ruth was in the middle of it. Major league games have had their moments of sensational, or bizarre, or once-in-a-lifetime events. But put the Bambino into the mix and it was almost always a whole different thing!

He could pitch, too. "The Babe" established the World Series consecutive scoreless innings mark.

The first game of the 1918 World Series was just such an example. In fact, it had more than its share of extraordinary goings-on. For one thing, the First World War was heading toward its final, climactic months of warfare in the beleaguered European countryside. Major League baseball played its part, cutting short the season by more than 20 games, thus enabling the leagues to stage their

World Series, its prestigious event barely salvaged, a month earlier than usually scheduled. Another of the outcomes of that tragic conflagration was the necessity of lodging the military-in-training in camps throughout the land. One of those was the naval base at Great Lakes, just north of Chicago. Out of that base proceeded a special flight bound for Chicago, its assignment a flyover of 60 Army Air Force planes, targeting Comiskey Park as a part of opening ceremonies to the 1918 World Series. The flyover was the first of its kind in baseball history (or in sports history for that matter). Parades, decorations, marching troops, service bands, and anything associated with the patriotic themes on display were all a part of the ceremonies on this very special occasion. The drone of 60 aircraft in flight over Comiskey Park while all the other program events took place, along with the unfurling of a special flag for the occasion, must have been stirring.

In order to accommodate more fans, the Cubs' front office negotiated with Charles Comiskey to use his ballpark for the Cubs' Series games. So the series opened up at Comiskey Park, where, by special arrangement to abet wartime travel restrictions, the first three games were slated for Chicago, and however many more might be needed beyond that were to be played at Fenway Park.

We have yet to address a rather incongruous situation that arose when players from the two championship teams threatened to sit down before the fifth game at Fenway Park. It was the only one of its kind inasmuch as it was to be staged *during* a World Series, another of those incredible things that attached itself to this championship series. As usual, the potential stumbling block to play was money. The split in shares for winners and losers was at stake in this one, and negotiations, if they may be called that, failed to produce a satisfactory solution. The dust settled when the players realized that they were about to look small, indeed, in the face of a war effort, palpably present in the form of thousands of Red Sox guests who were injured and handicapped veterans. The backlash came in game 6, attended by only 15,238 fans. The threatened strike only added to the extraordinary nature of this series' events.

But there were, beyond all else, ball games, one of which in this Fall Classic was extraordinary. That would, of course, involve the one and only Mr. Ruth, the strapping 23-year-old lefty who had made it through the season shuttling from mound to various positions afield, hitting an even .300 and winning 13. Chosen to pitch the crucial first game of the series against Cub ace Hippo Vaughn, he was faced with a stern challenge. He took matters in his own hands, as he had before and would continue to do through the remaining years of his Hall of Fame career. In the 1916 series Ruth had pitched a game 2, 14-inning victory, giving up a first-inning run and following that with 13 shutout innings against the Brooklyn Robins. In his second World Series pitching appearance, the first game of the '18 series, he continued his whitewashing artistry as though there were no interruption, save for the 1917 season, when it was the White Sox who were playing at Comiskey Park, not the Carmine. After another nine innings in the '18 series' initial game, he had amassed 22 consecutive frames without a run to stain his work. Fast forward to game 4 of the same series, and here we find the big lefty tacking on another 7.2 scoreless frames to set the record in that category at 29.2. That record stands on a par with many of his awesome hitting marks; we might compare it to his original record of 29 home runs that marked his last Red Sox season the very next year, 1919, or, in Yankee togs, the 54 he hit to break his own record in 1920.

It was in the fourth inning of the Series opener that the Red Sox got to Hippo Vaughn for the contest's only marker. It came about this way: Leadoff hitter Dave Shean worked Vaughn for a free pass, followed by Amos Strunk's failed sacrifice attempt that the Cubs' lefty snared. With Shean still on first base, outfielder George Whiteman lashed a clothesliner to center. The ball was so sharply hit that Shean had no alternative but to hang tight to second base. The play brought up World Series–wise Stuffy McInnis, brought to Boston in January of 1918 in a multiplayer deal. The former Athletics' captain found one of Vaughn's offerings much to his liking and rifled it down the left-field line, sending Shean on his way home. This is the way the *New York Times* (April 7, 1918, issue) described Shean's homeward dash:

> Leslie Mann, Chicago's left fielder, raced over and checked the truant ball [hit by McInnis]. Shean did not even stop to look, but tore around third base toward home as Mann picked up the ball and hurled it to Killifer . . . as he [Shean] galloped home, taking the last few yards with a long, desperate slide, and beat the ball in by inches."

The side was retired without any further damage and the rest of the game was played out in pitching splendor, Ruth's curves keeping the Cubs at bay, and Vaughn, who settled down, silencing Red Sox batters while waiting on his teammates to score at least a run that would tie things up. It never came. Ruth—and a particularly sensational play on a line drive that was converted into a 6-3 putout by Ev Scott—prevailed in the taut pitcher's duel. That kind of "Ruthian" outing (these kinds of super-performances were to be hailed later and regularly as "Ruthian") was already a part of the Legendary One's bag of tricks.

The 1948 World Series, Game 1: Bob Feller's Pickoff Magic, October 8, 1948

Cleveland (AL)	000	000	000	0-4-0
Boston (NL)	000	000	01x	1-2-2

WP, Sain; LP, Feller

Boston again . . . only this time the Braves were Boston's champions and, in 1948, were hosts to the World Series' first game, a game in which one of the Fall Classic's most controversial plays took place.

In the '48 series Boston won the battle but Cleveland won the war—and the opening battle was a stunning beauty, with Johnny Sain, a wily breaking ball right-hander, throwing a magnificent four-hitter at the Cleveland Indians. Bob Feller, the equal of Sain in this one, limited the Braves' howitzers to two hits in a tense 1-0 thriller that had everyone on the edge of their seats right down to the last out. Feller's misfortune was a highly controversial call on a pickoff play at second base in the eighth inning. Hall of Fame sports columnist of the *New York Times* Arthur Daley wrote about the base on balls that brought it all about in his "Sports of the Times" column for October 7.

> It was a walk which brought about Feller's downfall, a pass to Bill Salkeld to open the eighth. Ah, those bases on balls! The ghost of George Stallings, the manager of the 1914 Braves, must have shuddered when that walk came. It was he, you know, who supposedly lay in state in his coffin when a mourner remarked, "What a fine looking man! What was it that killed him?" Thereupon Stallings bolted upright and exclaimed, "Bases on balls!"
>
> Yes, it was a walk which killed Feller today. Phil Masi replaced Salkeld as a baserunner, went to second on a sacrifice, almost was picked off and then went tearing like crazy around the paths, his hat clutched firmly in his hand and his hair waving in the breeze, when Holmes drilled his slice to left.

And what about that pickoff play? It was "the play of the day," one of those plays that historians will never let you forget. Feller opened the bottom of the eighth with a walk issued to Braves catcher Bill Salkeld. Manager Billy Southworth replaced Salkeld with a faster base runner, Phil Masi, and then ordered Mike McCormick to sacrifice Masi to second base. The next hitter, Eddie Stanky, was intentionally passed, putting runners on first and second. Lou Boudreau, the Indians' playing manager, then signaled Feller for a pickoff play, successfully negotiated on a count that triggered the throw from Feller to Boudreau. At least Lou Boudreau thought so. But not Bill Stewart, the second base umpire. Boudreau put up a furious argument, but to no avail. The call stood, and after a Johnny Sain fly ball brought on the second out, Tommy Holmes shot a screamer through the Cleveland infield to score Masi, putting the Braves ahead 1-0 going into the Cleveland ninth. Sain, with his bag of slow-breaking stuff in command, saw to it that the score stayed that way, and the Braves went home with a one-game lead in the series. Papers across the nation hailed the pickoff play as the pivotal play of the game, showing one photo that made Boudreau's argument look very good. The photo showed Boudreau, with the ball in his mitt, between Masi and second base. In 1990, when Phil Masi's will was opened, there was a statement indicating his admission that he was out.

Years later, in the *Montreal Gazette* issued on October 17, 1975, sports scribe Dick Carroll wrote an article about the play. It seems that Stewart, who was also a hockey referee, was well known in Canada and often appeared there with his Canuck and Canadien's friends. Many of these hockey cohorts came together for the opening of the 1978 season, and before the lidlifter between archrivals Toronto and Montreal, over a friendly libation or two, the conversation got around to Stewart's call in the '48 series, 30 years earlier. Toe Blake, a veteran Canadian "hockeymeister," joined the back-and-forth with this observation: "It was strictly a judgement call, and no umpire is perfect," he pointed out. "That may have been the only mistake Stewart made all season, but a lousy photographer got a picture of it and the whole world sees it. That was just Stewart's tough luck."

The furor over this play went on for years, and it almost completely overshadowed the Series itself. The Gene Beardon–led Tribe won out in six games, while the pitchers of note, Sain and Feller, were deprived of any victories thereafter. Indians fans observed, sadly, that Bob Feller's two-hitter was wasted. Braves fans, on the other hand, felt that Sain's work was every bit as good as Bullet Bob's and, further, even pointed to the likelihood of another miracle, similar to the one in 1914. But the baseball gods had declared otherwise.

The 1956 World Series, Game 6:
Clem Labine's Great Day, October 9, 1956

New York (AL)	000	000	000	0	0-7-0
Brooklyn (NL)	000	000	000	1	1-4-0

WP, Labine; LP, Turley

In the 1956 World Series the boys from Flatbush mustered but one run in the Classic's last three games, shut out by Don Larsen's perfect game in the fifth tilt, finally scoring a run in the tenth that prolonged the Series, and shut out again in the deciding seventh game. One run in 28 innings. The Yankees weren't much better in games 5 and 6, coming up with a pair of runs to support the Don Larsen miracle, and none at all in a superb pitching masterpiece by Clem Labine in game 6, which was, considering the devastation of the Larsen perfecto, a major miracle in and of itself. But the Dodgers hung on until they finally edged home a winner in the 10th frame of game 6, which if nothing else kept them alive to fight on another day.

As 1-0 games go, especially those played out in the pressure-cooker intensity of world championship play, this one stands right up there in the rarified atmosphere of top performances. Credit Clement Walter Labine, better known as Clem, ace reliever among Dodger pitchers, who, during the 1956 season, had chalked up a league-leading 19 saves. In a Series that exhausted both pitching staffs, skipper Walt Alston turned to the sinkerball artist from Rhode Island, hoping for several good innings from him while his Dodgers scored a few runs to get far enough ahead should he falter later in the game. Clem Labine responded with a masterful exhibition, getting stronger instead of weaker as the game progressed. Inning followed inning, first three, then another three and then, incredibly, another three without a score. That meant extra innings—and there would be but one.

Labine retired the Yankees on a strikeout and a pair of grounders in the top half of the 10th frame. He was first up in the Dodger 10th, and Walt Alston let him hit, the decision no doubt having been made that Labine would start another inning if necessary. Labine opened the inning with a pop out to Billy Martin behind second base. Jim Gilliam, Brooklyn's leadoff hitter, then worked Bob Turley for a walk and moved on to second courtesy of a perfectly executed sacrifice bunt by Pee Wee Reese. Casey Stengel then ordered an intentional pass for the dangerous Duke Snider. That put runners on first and second, with Jackie Robinson coming up.

Even though Robinson was in the last year of his Hall of Fame career, putting him on wasn't much of an option. That would only choke the bases, and with Gil Hodges due up behind Robinson, Turley would be forced to pitch to Hodges with the bases loaded. So the contest between hitter and pitcher boiled down to Turley—who had eked a pop up out of Robinson his previous time up—and Robinson, who rarely in his career followed one embarrassment with another. It was not to happen this time around, either, and a ringing single brought home the walkoff RBI run that put the Dodgers in a position to win a second straight world championship at the expense of the Bronx Bombers. That wasn't to be, but it wasn't of any great consideration on October 9, 1956. On that day the Dodgers ruled supreme, toasting Clem Labine as The Great One.

The performance of these two pitchers, not among the better-known names of the game, merits further attention. Number one, major leaguers are in the bigs because they have super talent. Whether there for what the veterans of the game call a "cup-o'-coffee" or to endure through Hall of Fame–bound careers, those who pull on major league uniforms can make the plays, hit the ball, pitch, and field better than the millions of "wannabes" who just don't seem to have that extra within themselves or the natural talent to play ball with the big boys. Some, indeed, have just enough to get that cup of coffee and are gone in the twinkling of an eye. Others hang on for several seasons, and others have long

Baseball's first southpaw 300-game winner, Eddie Plank.

careers as journeymen, rarely heard of. Both Labine and Turley fall into this class, famous for a meteoric moment, Labine with his 1-0 World Series win and Turley with his 1958 Cy Young Award. Very good, but not consistently good enough or sensational enough to become headliners in the fiercely competitive environment of major league baseball. It is a game in which even the least of the

Hall of Famers is a marvelously gifted athlete who is far better than the ordinary, everyday players next door.

Then, too, another look at Clem Labine's effort in the 1956 World Series merits attention. The game marked only the second time since 1913 that Fall Classic contenders had played through nine innings without scoring. That earmarks it as a truly momentous event. That 1913 struggle between Christy Mathewson and Eddie Plank was waged between two Hall of Fame pitchers, lending still more prestige to that kind of performance. It would take another 40 years to produce another 1-0 game that was won in extra innings.

We are looking at one of baseball's rarities here. To say that both pitchers were on their game on that Ebbets Field date in 1956 would be something of an understatement. For both Labine and Turley (especially Labine) it must have ranked among the finest one or two games of their major league careers.

The 1966 World Series, Games 3 and 4: Baltimore's Goose Egg Boys, Bunker and McNally, October 8 and 9, 1966

October 8

Los Angeles (NL)	000	000	000	0-6-0
Baltimore (AL)	000	010	000	1-3-0

WP, Bunker; LP, Osteen

October 9

Los Angeles (NL)	000	000	000	0-4-0
Baltimore (AL)	000	100	000	1-4-0

WP, McNally; LP, Drysdale

For a score of years starting in the 1960s and extending into the 1980s, Baltimore pitching was more often than not the scourge of the American League. The franchise scheme for providing outstanding pitching was ably spearheaded in 1966 by the Orioles' commandant, Hank Bauer, who moved his pitchers in and out of games with a deft alchemistic touch. The Baltimore staff was never better or more lethal in its effectiveness than in the 1966 World Series, during which they permitted Los Angeles hitting to score a mere pair of runs in a four-game sweep.

Two of those runs came singly, one in the second and one in the third inning of game 1; 33 scoreless innings followed. When they calculated the staff ERA it was booked at 0.50, surpassed only by the 1905 effort of the New York Giants, figured at 0.00 since, unbelievably, the Athletics failed to score an earned run in that five-game series. Two of the 1966 games, numbers 3 and 4, have been selected as exemplars of supreme 1-0 artistry in Fall Classic play worthy of inclusion on this distinctive listing.

After Jim Palmer's four-hitter that moved the O's to a two-game bulge in the Series' second encounter, the teams left the West Coast and headed for the next three-game set on the other side of the nation in Baltimore's spacious Memorial Stadium. Palmer won his game with a stylish four-hit smothering of the Dodger sticks. At not quite 21, he was half of the Youngster Set the Orioles sent after the Dodgers, which also set a record for youngsters in World Series play.

After that one, Bauer would be all smiles, knowing that another pair of aces would be working in the Orioles' backyard. And even though what should be is not always what will be in baseball, this time it was. Wally Bunker made sure of that in the third contest and Dave McNally in the fourth, Series-winning game. Each threw 1-0 games, one as sparkling as the next; and though Dodger pitching was but a shade less brilliant than Baltimore's, the Orioles' singletons in each game were enough not only to win the huge trophy emblematic of World Series supremacy but to set a record that will be seriously difficult to surpass: 33 consecutive scoreless innings by a team pitching staff. Thirty-three—that's the better part of four games. Straight! Along the way, Baltimore pitching resulted in a wrong-way hitting record, set by the Los Angeles nine, for hitting a measly .142, managing but 17 hits in the four games.

The two games cited from this World Series showcased Baltimore's Wally Bunker, only 20 years old, and the veteran Dave McNally, who opened the series but gave way to an outstanding piece of relief work by Moe Drabowsky, the game's winner. In that appearance Los Angeles' only runs scored in the series were charged to the unflappable southpaw. But he came back in game 4 to write *fini* to that game—and the series—with his four-hit gem. Between the two of them they allowed only 10 hits, no runs, and not a semblance of an offensive threat in the last of the series' 33 record-setting innings of scoreless baseball.

In the midst of all this Baltimore pitching brilliance a word or two about the pitching of the Alston-men is in order. The Drysdale and Koufax 1-2 punch was as formidable as any in professional baseball's history going all the way back to Larry Corcoran and John Clarkson of the 1880's Chicago White Stockings, the McGinnity-Mathewson twosome, the Lefty Gomez and Red Ruffing duo of McCarthy's Yankees, and more recently the "Terrific Three," Maddux, Glavine, and Smoltz of the 1990s Atlanta championship era. These and many superlative pitching staff combinations, however good they might have been, were never any better than either the Baltimore or Los Angeles units that belabored hitters in the 1966 World Series.

The greatest Dodger left-hander, Koufax, and Drysdale, among the top three Dodger right-handers of all time, formed a fearsome dual threat to opposing 1966 hitters. Sandy Koufax earned his 1966 Cy Young Award in the final year of his career with league-leading marks like these: a career high 27 victories, 323 innings of work, 317 K's, a stingy 1.73 ERA, and 41 starts for Alston's Dodgers. In the only game he started against the Orioles, he worked through six innings at a 1.50 ERA clip, victimized by shoddy Dodger fielding that the O's capitalized on for a three-run fifth inning. That was more than enough for Jim Palmer, who slashed through Dodger hitting with a four-hitter. In game 4 Don Drysdale hurled a four-hitter. Unfortunately, one of those hits was a Frank Robinson bomb that put Baltimore ahead in the fourth inning of the final game. Neither of the Koufax and Drysdale outings was all that "under par" as to cause one to think that, if only they had been up to their usual standards, they might have won. They pitched well enough to win, but McNally, Bunker & Company were, on those days, even better.

A month after the '66 Series ended Sandy Koufax announced his retirement, his Hall of Fame career relegated to the history books. The November retirement came during the banquet season when players and teams were being honored at those festive occasions where hump-backed loopers became line drives and the fastballs of pitching heroes were reported as "high in the 90s." Wally Bunker, Jim Palmer, Dave McNally, and Moe Drabowsky, the only pitchers the Orioles needed to win the 1966 Fall Classic, were in on the banquet circuit that season.

The 1991 World Series, Game 7:
The Morris Spectacular, October 27, 1991

| Atlanta (NL) | 000 | 000 | 000 | 0 | 0-7-0 |
| Minnesota (AL) | 000 | 000 | 000 | 1 | 1-10-0 |

Between the 1966 and 1991 World Series, there were only two 1-0 games, one in the third game of the 1972 championship clash between Cincinnati and Oakland, and the other in 1986, which pitted New York's Mets against the Boston Red Sox. Well into the era of relief specialists, neither of those contests featured complete game victors.

The 1991 World Series between the Minnesota Twins and the Atlanta Braves put the 1-0 complete game back into the mix of almost scoreless games. And the air in this one was heavy with breathless moments. Game 7 can do that to a World Series.

Always a tough competitor, Jack Morris won that 1-0 nail-biter to wrap up a World Series crown for the Minnesota Twins in 1991.

In the 1991 feature Jack Morris was the headline maker with as gritty and determined a performance as any 10th-inning 0-0 ball game could be. Asked prior to the final stanza whether he could make it through another, the 36-year-old warhorse, the very guts of the Minnesota roster, didn't even reply. He simply headed toward the mound. A gamer, just the kind of hard-nosed competitor you would want on the mound in a game 7 classic, Morris would have asked for the ball 10 innings later, were he still able to grunt. And the last couple innings weren't easy for him even though he made it look so.

Two ground outs and a strikeout disposed of the Braves in the ninth. By the time the 10th frame began, the top of a very workman-like Braves order was due to test Morris's tiring right arm once again. But again, in 1-2-3- order, Morris saw to it that Blauser, Smith, and Pendleton wouldn't get too far with whatever mischief they might have been thinking about.

Five Twins hitters later, in the Minnesota 10th, it was all over. There would be no more worries or speculation under the Heartburn Dome, home of the 1991 champs, the Minnesota Twins. That was seen to by an inning-opening two-bagger by Gladden, a sacrifice bunt by Knoblauch that sent Gladden to third, intentional walks to Kirby Puckett and Hrbek, clogging up the sacks, and a climactic pinch hit by Gene Larkin that soared over the heads of the drawn-in Braves' outfielders. The Twins had done it. They had provided the Series' MVP, Mr. Morris himself, with just enough to emerge from the fray a World Series winner. Jack Morris wasn't the first 30-something pitcher to preside over a 1-0 World Series game, nor will his effort go down as the last. Just the same, there aren't any to date who have turned that special trick beyond Jack Morris' age. Joe McGinnity (1905, at age 34) comes closest.

The 1991 Minnesota pitching staff was headed by Morris with a league-leading 35 starts. His two shutouts were 7-0 and 5-0 victories, nowhere near the 1-0 effort he summoned in the game of games both for the Twins, and for himself. The pitching staff included three pitchers embroiled in 1-0 conflicts: Scott Erickson and David West, who won their games, and Kevin Tapani, who lost his to Toronto on an unearned run. That was it . . . three 1-0 games all year, until 1991's finale in the World Series came along.

The 2005 World Series, Game 4: The Freddy Garcia Special, October 24, 2005

Chicago (AL)	000	000	010	1-8-0
Houston (NL)	000	000	000	0-5-0

WP, Garcia; LP, Backe

Freddy Garcia was called on to finish up the 2005 baseball season. His assignment: get past the Houston Astros to wrap up Chicago's first World Series championship since 1917, some 88 years earlier. For White Sox fans, long-suffering and clamoring for just one more victory, the game was more than monumental. It was an evening when they dared to hope—something foreign to their psyche these many, many years.

Sox manager Ozzie Guillen had wiggled and wobbled through the three previous white-knucklers, using every last trick in the book to get to game number 4 ahead in games, 3-0. This 3-0 standing might seem improbable when considering the World Series thus far, game-by-game:

Game 1: The Sox win at Comiskey Park, now known as "The Cell," behind Jose Contreras, a well-traveled Cuban with an indomitable will. Opposing Roger Clemens, the Sox pulled off miracle number one: disposing of Clemens, who usually toyed playfully with Sox hitters, but with lethal intent. Clemens was gone this time after a mere six outs, though it must be admitted that a dangerously sore hamstring, as much as Chicago's hitters, put him back in the dugout. Meanwhile, old Jose plodded on, squeezing every ball he rubbed up into soft sawdust. Finally, after Guillen was not about to risk any more of Contreras' aging arm, he called on reliever Cotts, and later Jenks, the hefty closer, to round out the first game with a tight, 5-3 victory.

Game 2: Miracle number two happened in the bottom of the ninth when singles-hitter Scott Podsednik crushed one to give the Sox a nail-biting 7-6 win over a disbelieving Houston crew.

Game 3: Miracle number three. In 14 innings at Houston, site of the first World Series game ever to be played in Texas, the two teams used just about everyone listed as a pitcher in the elaborate World Series program. Guillen started Jon Garland and followed up with these eight: Politte, Cotts, Hermanson, Hernandez, Vizcaino, Jenks, Damaso Marte, and stalwart starter Mark Buehrle, who got the save. Houston countered with its corps of Oswalt, their starter, followed by seven other twirlers who threw anywhere from one third to three innings of relief. Miracle number four: Stan Blum, in his only World Series at bat, blasted one into the seats in the top of the 14th to win it for Chicago.

Game 4: The White Sox win their fourth straight in this series, by that minimalist victory margin of 1-0. And, miracle number five, a ball hit by Jermaine Dye, commonly known among baseball cognoscenti as a ball with seeing-eyes, made its way over the mound with just enough oomph to get to center field, scoring Willie Harris, who had delivered a pinch hit single to open the inning.

Freddy Garcia had throttled Astro hitters, fanning seven while giving up five harmless singles and keeping Houston far enough from home plate to register seven scoreless innings. Finishing his seventh season in the style all pitchers hope for, the Venezuelan threw a mixture of pitches at varied speeds, getting hitters to hit ground balls that very often resulted in infield outs. He was in top form this World Series evening. One of the Houston grounders off the bat of Adam Everett was converted into a double play, Crede to Iguchi to Konerko, sabotaging a potential fifth-inning rally by the Astros. Garcia, a rangy right-hander who worked another two frames before giving way to Cotts and Politte once again, was followed by Bobby Jenks, who picked up his second Series save.

For Chicago's South Siders, the long wait was somewhat of a carbon copy of Boston's frustrating and nigh interminable wait. The red-stockinged Boston club had won it all just a year earlier, an 82-year wait that began after the 1918 championship. The year before that one, 1917, was the last Chicago triumph, long before most of Chicago's 2005 fans were born. And the year after Boston's victory in 2004, it was Chicago's turn.

After the 24th 1-0 game in World Series history, there were none to follow. However, both before and afterward, a number of significant championship play-off games, in the elimination tournament that finally names a pennant winner, have thrilled the autumnal crowd. We turn to a sampling of these thrillers next.

PLAYOFF GAMES

ALCS, Game 2:
Dave McNally in 11, October 5, 1969, at Baltimore

Minnesota	000	000	000	00	0-3-1
Baltimore	000	000	000	01	1-8-0

WP, McNally; LP, Boswell

It didn't take long for 1-0 games to surface in the majors' new playoffs setup to determine league pennant winners. Barely into the first season's postseason games, the Baltimore Orioles—behind the same lefty Dave McNally who had tested the 1-0 waters before in the 1966 World Series—came up with an 11-inning winner at Memorial Stadium before 41,704 Baltimoreans.

Between a fourth-inning Tony Oliva single and a walk issued to Rod Carew in the eighth frame, the curveballing southpaw retired 14 Twins in a row and in the top of the 10th struck out the side among his 11 K's for the day. You would have to say he was pretty much in command, despite facing four dangerous hitters in Rod Carew, Tony Oliva, Harmon Killebrew, and Bob Allison. On this day McNally was the man in charge.

Dave McNally, one of the many fine Orioles hurlers in the 1960s and 70s. *Brace Photo*.

Dave Boswell, a long-armed right-hander who used a sharply breaking curveball for his out-pitch, gave up seven Oriole hits and as many walks, but mostly kept Baltimore hitters at bay. Except for a pair of Frank Robinson two-baggers in the third and eighth innings, Oriole hits were confined to singles, and a pair of double plays aided the Minnesota cause considerably. But in the 11th Boswell faltered. He walked leadoff hitter Boog Powell, who was promptly advanced on a Brooks Robinson sacrifice. A Belanger pop-up was the second out of the inning. Davey Johnson, the Orioles' second sacker, was then intentionally passed, putting runners on first and second. At that point skipper Sam Mele brought on lefty Ron Perranoski, a veteran reliever, to replace the fast-tiring Boswell. Elrod Hendricks was due to face the left-handed Perranoski, so Oriole manager Earl Weaver replaced him with the right-handed-hitting Curt Motton.

Motton hopped on a Perranoski offering that simply didn't get to its intended spot and hammered it into right field to bring home Powell with the winning run on his walkoff RBI single.

Dave McNally was a fine pitcher for many years, rating not that far below Hall of Fame status. Bill James[5] rates McNally near the far end of the top 100 pitchers, all time. During his career he pitched 33 shutouts. Among those 33 were nine of the 1-0 variety, and among those two have been cited here in championship play. His final shutout, a 7-0 victory over the Yankees, was a complete game effort in his last Baltimore season, 1974. McNally's two finest career outings, however, came in the stressful setting of playoff and World Series competition and get five-star ratings.

NLCS, Game 1:
October 8, 1986, at Houston

New York	000	000	000	0-5-0	
Houston	010	000	00x	1-7-1	

WP, Scott; LP, Gooden

Roger Craig, the master and mentor of all things falling into the category of split-fingered pitching, took Mike Scott aside and showed him a pitch, the split-fingered fastball, that stormed the baseball world during the last score of years in the 20th century. Between his 1979 debut and the 1985 season, Scott was a middling hurler. But a breakout season, rated at better than four wins[6] in 1986, went into the record books as a 300-plus-strikeout season, accompanied by 18 wins and league-leading numbers in ERA (2.22), innings pitched (275.1), and shutouts (5). Actually, his big season followed a 1985 season that already gave indication that he had been an apt pupil of Professor Craig. In 1985 he was an 18-game winner, moving up from the 150 strikeout range into the 200s. The big Californian now had a reliable arsenal to call on, mixing speeds clocked as high as the mid-90s and locations with his hopping heater. And he carried that stuff right into the National League Championships against the New York Mets and their young sensations, Darryl Strawberry and "Doctor K" Dwight Gooden.

In the series' first game Mike Scott prevailed with a sparkling 1-0 effort that exceeded Gooden's. But not by much. Aside from Glenn Davis' second-inning home run, the Astro bats were rather silent, Gooden having found a way to shut down any scoring at all. The difference this day came by way of the 14 Scott strikeout tally; 14 is over half of the 27 putouts needed to eat up nine innings. It's usually—though not always—indicative of a dominating pitching perfor-mance, as was this one.

Three games later Scott faced off against Sid Fernandez and came up big once again, logging a 3-1 winner. In this one it took the Mets another eight in-nings before they were able to post a marker, making it 16-plus straight innings of scoreless frustration endured at Scott's hands.

Unfortunately, no one beside Mike Scott could beat the Mets in this se-ries, and the Mets prevailed despite him. But in Scott they had found a mighty dominator who had pitched one of the very best 1-0 games in championship playoff history.

ALDS, Game 3:
The Moose Shuts Down Oakland,
October 13, 2001, at Oakland

New York	000	000	010	1-2-0	
Oakland	000	000	000	0-6-1	

WP, Mussina; LP, Zito

It only took one swing. The Bad Boys from New York's Bronx ruined a wondrous Barry Zito pitching performance in the pivotal third game of the 2001 American League Divisional championships when catcher Jorge Posada's fifth-inning moon shot provided the winning margin in this 1-0 game. The only other hit the Yan-kees came up with was a double by Shane Spencer that followed Posada's homer. Trying to get himself together after the four-base blast probably had something to do with Spencer's two-bagger off Zito, who succeeded in pulling things together so well that the Yanks were put right back to sleep the rest of the game.

The other pitcher in this tilt was a chap named "Moose" Mike Mussina. A combination of one of baseball's premier starters during the Joe Torre era of New York supremacy, along with baseball's peerless reliever Mariano Rivera, whose two-inning stint sealed Mussina's victory, went about business just a little better than did Zito and the Oakland reliever, Mark Guthrie. That little extra was the difference on this Oakland evening.

Before a troublesome fourth inning, Mussina had sailed through the first 10 A's consecutively. Then two Oakland singles put the A's in a position to get something on the board, but the fellow with four or five varieties of fastballs finally put a stop to that by inducing a Jeremy Giambi ground-out ending the threat—and the inning. In the seventh stanza the Yankees' Derek Jeter came to the rescue, chasing down an errant relay throw and flipping the ball backhand to catcher Jorge Posada for a miraculous put-out. Manager Torre then brought on Rivera for the eighth- and ninth-inning wrap-up.

A team rarely gets to the World Series in a preliminary format that puts an elimination tournament between the end of the regular season and the Fall Classic unless it has the kind of pitching that wins these kinds of nerve-wracking ball games. For every 1-0 game there are others of the 2-1, 3-2, and 2-0 variety. In each of those scenarios a Mike Mussina, Dwight Gooden, Roy Halladay, or Randy Johnson puts in an effort that rides on craftsmanship, intensity, and great athletic ability. Pitchers like Barry Zito, Roger Clemens, Steve Carlton, and Vida Blue, to mention but a few, even though they might lose a big game in playoffs or the World Series from time to time, all have the wherewithal to match the Mussinas and Glavines. Two of these master craftsmen, plus a pair of able relievers, produced a gem of a game at Oakland's Network Associates Stadium in 2001. Give Mussina, Rivera, Zito, and Guthrie the credit they're all due.

NLDS, Game 1:
Curt Schilling Wins a Chiller,
October 9, 2001, at Arizona

St. Louis	000	000	000	0-3-1
Arizona	000	010	00x	1-8-1

WP, Schilling; LP, M. Morris

Mark McGwire was in the on-deck circle when Jim Edmonds grounded to second baseman Craig Counsell, who threw to Mark Grace for the last out of the division opener at Bank One Field, Phoenix, Arizona. McGwire, the muscular Cardinal home-run champion, put it all in perspective when he later mentioned that it was the best game he had ever seen, indicating further that although it wasn't much of a game for a hitter, it was an unbelievable game as far as the pitching was concerned.

Indeed, it was a gem. Two 22-game winners in regular season play, Arizona's Curt Schilling and St. Louis' ace Matt Morris, battled pitch for pitch through nine stifling innings of championship baseball. As is so often said about games like this, it's too bad someone had to lose. In this one Schilling gave up a pair of hits to Cardinal shortstop Edgar Renteria and a single to Jim Edmonds—and that was it over the nine-inning affair. Morris, back from a full year layoff in 1999 caused by reconstructive surgery, was nicked for six hits during his seven-inning stint, working out of several jams and overall holding the Dbacks in check well enough to keep the Cards in the thick of the tussle. Already in the first inning, the game barely underway, Morris, whose two- and four-seam fastballs were the scourge of the National League in 2001, found himself in a fix with Arizona runners at the corners and none out. But he maintained his poise and focus, working his way through Luis Gonzalez (57 homers in '01), Reggie Sanders, and Mark Grace, in order, without a ball getting out of the infield. On seeing that kind of exquisite pitching, Schilling knew then and there that it would take everything he had or his Diamondbacks would be on the short end of the score.

Schilling, beyond doubt, gave it everything he had, hurling a little more than 100 pitches—most of them in the mid-90s—at Cardinals hitters. Further, to beat a sturdy Cardinals crew of hitters like Albert Pujols, Edmonds, J. D. Drew, and McGwire, Schilling's offerings needed to be at or just off the corners. And he did the little things, which often turn out to be big things. Damian Miller was hit by an errant Morris pitch to open the fifth inning. That brought up Schilling, who got the bunt signal which would hopefully advance Miller to scoring position. The big fella fouled off his first and second bunt attempts, and still boss man Brenly kept the bunt sign on. On his third attempt the whole thing clicked, and when it was over Miller was at second waiting to score. Steve Finley, in his 13th season, followed with a rope to right-center field that scored Miller with the run that will burn brightly in his memory bank long after his playing days are over. It was the only run Curt Schilling needed, and his successful bunt was a part of it.

Curt Schilling may or may not some day make it to Cooperstown, but his work in postseason play during the 2001 season, which included the following A+ record in playoff and World Series play, was incredible.

- Game 1, NLDS, 1-0 win over Cardinals
- Game 5, NLDS, 2-1 win over Cardinals
- Game 3, NLCS, 5-1 win over Atlanta
- Game 1, World Series, 9-1 win over New York
- Game 4, World Series, game tied 1-1 when he left after 7.1 innings
- Game 7, World Series, starting pitcher, 7.1 innings pitched (allowed two runs) in the game won by Randy Johnson to win the World Series

The totals add up to seven runs in over 50 innings of championship play.

For Curt Schilling the dramatic conclusion to the 2001 season must have been even more thrilling than his conquest with the 2004 Red Sox, in which he was paired once again against Matt Morris and the Cardinals. He won that one, too.

In a career that covered 20 major league seasons, 2001 was his most distinguished effort. His 22 wins, 35 games started, and 256.2 innings pitched were all league toppers, all supported by a 2.98 ERA—and a magnificent postseason log without blemish.

Notes

1. Tom Boswell, *How Life Imitates the World Series* (Garden City, NY: Doubleday, 1982).

2. McGinnity started the series' second game against Albert "Chief" Bender, who snuffed out the Giants' offense with a four-hitter, a shutout that made the fifth blanking in this series, unmatched ever after in World Series play.

3. Joe McGinnity often delivered his pitches underhand and at different speeds. The floater referred to in this account was no doubt a change-of-pace curveball.

4. *New York Times*, October 14, 1905.

5. Bill James, *The New Bill James Historical Abstract* (New York: Free Press, 2001), 916–918.

6. Wins: A sabermetric term designating how many victories a pitcher added to his team's total in a given year, beyond victories achieved by a league-average pitcher rated at 0.00. Wins beyond three indicate outstanding seasons.

CHAPTER 4

No-Hit Wonders

For those who like their baseball in huge doses of pitching summitry it doesn't get much better than a 1-0 no-hitter. And if perfection is the best of all possible baseball worlds, the perfect game 1-0 victory has to be the ultimate baseball achievement. There haven't been many who have personally witnessed either of these baseball gems. Since 1871, as a matter of fact, there have been only eight perfect games resulting in a 1-0 score, and only seven with a single pitcher. The list of those astonishing feats appears in table 4.1.

As you might expect, the no-hit game list with either bases on balls, hit batsmen, or errors is considerably longer. Beginning with a Pud Galvin masterpiece on June 12, 1880, and continuing through the Kevin Millwood no-no pitched on April 27, 2003, there have been 31 1-0 no-hit games. (That list is presented in Appendix A.)

The complete list of nine-inning perfectos and no-nos, thus, rises to 37, and from those 37 another listing awaits your perusal, containing the five best no-hitters in the game's history. I admit to its subjectivity, but the five choices I've made (including a tie for third place) follow.

The Most Impressive No-Hit, 1-0 Game: Hendley and Koufax, September 9, 1965

Chicago (NL)	000	000	000	0-0-1
Los Angeles	000	010	000	0-1-0

WP, Koufax; LP, Hendley

Table 4.1. 1-0 Perfect Games

Date	WP/Team/League	LP/Losing Team
June 12, 1880	Lee Richmond, Worcester (NL)	Jim McCormick, Cleveland
October 2, 1908	Addie Joss, Cleveland (AL)	Ed Walsh, Chicago
September 9, 1965	Sandy Koufax, Los Angeles (NL)	Bob Hendley, Chicago
September 30, 1984	Mike Witt, California (AL)	Charlie Hough, Texas
September 16, 1988	Tom Browning, Cincinnati (NL)	Tim Belcher, Los Angeles
April 11, 1990*	Mark Langston, California (AL)	Gary Eave, Seattle
May 29, 2010	Roy Halladay, Philadelphia (NL)	Josh Johnson, Florida
August 15, 2012	Félix Hernández, Seattle (AL)	Jeremy Hellickson, Tampa Bay

*The April 11, 1990, game is the only one of the eight above with multiple pitchers. Mark Langston (WP), and Mike Witt (SV) were the California pitchers and Erik Hanson (SP, ND), Gary Eave (RP, LP), and Keith Comstock (RP, ND) were the Seattle pitchers.

There are 51 or 54 outs in most nine-inning games. In this one 15 of the 18 at bats resulted in a 1-2-3 order half-inning. The only run of the game was unearned and the winning pitcher hurled a perfect game. The only hit in this amazing display of baseball perfection was a Texas League double that fell just out of reach along the left-field foul line. It was one of those proverbial hump-backed liners. There was only one free pass issued, the one that wound up eventually at home plate with the winning and sole marker of the game.

The pitchers, Sandy Koufax of the Dodgers and Bob Hendley of the Chicago Cubs, had combined for 53 outs of no-hit ball, and except for a fifth-inning lapse by both Hendley and several of his teammates, the spectators witnessed almost total perfection. The 29,139 in attendance plus all the others connected with the game who were there saw an exhibition of baseball that they could have realistically expected no one else would ever see, such was the magnitude of this game's artistry—*and* its rarity. It would be possible to top such an exhibition, of course, but it would take a near miracle, and it would be against all odds that it would happen again soon. Indeed, not since September 9, 1965, has something like this one happened.

The run that actually won this game, though necessary for the Dodgers to win, soon took on a bit role in this drama. The whole show stood out there in the middle of the diamond 60'6" from home plate. Sandy Koufax, standing at the top of his career, was astonished himself at how his stuff was working. What he sent to the plate must have been barely, if at all, visible.

Sandy Koufax, whose 1-0 perfecto against the Cubs was one of the greatest 1-0 games in baseball history.

Prior to this game some had been worried about the great left-hander. For nearly a month before this game Koufax had not been doing well. After defeating the Pirates on August 14 he lost three and had a no decision in a 13-inning game the Dodgers won, 6-3, over the Phils. It was a four-game stretch rather forgotten about, but it *did* accomplish one thing: it set up his September 9 assignment against the Cubs, making the achievements of that sparkling evening look just that much more wondrous.

There is somehow more than a little poetic justice, as far as both pitchers were concerned, with regard to the run that won this game. It came about without benefit of a hit and went into the books as an unearned run. Dodger left-fielder Lou Johnson walked to begin the bottom of the fifth inning. He was sacrificed to second and on his successful steal of third, rookie catcher Chris Krug threw wildly past third baseman Ron Santo. Johnson kept right on going and scored what turned out to be the only run. In the seventh, as though to make up for having to steal his way around the sacks, Johnson was the one who poked the only hit of the game into just the right place, winding up on second with a double. But Ron Fairly, who followed Johnson in the batting order, grounded to Don Kessinger, who threw to Ernie Banks for the third out. That was the end of any offensive threat by either team.

This much-heralded game is thoroughly and meticulously covered in a number of accounts both circular and between the covers of several books.[1] The perfect game Sandy Koufax threw against the Cubs brought about a rematch of the two hurlers a few days later in Chicago. The baseball gods seemed to have ordained some satisfaction for Bob Hendley on that occasion. On September 14 in Wrigleyville Hendley turned the tables and this time bested Koufax 2-1. The two had broken even through 18 innings, four runs, 10 hits, 27 strikeouts, and five bases on balls. The two games were superlative pitching duels.

1965 was the second of Koufax's three Cy Young years. His 1965 record showcased league-leading numbers in victories (26), winning percentage (.765), innings pitched (335.2), ERA (2.04), and strikeouts (382), among still others. His 1965 record was further garnished by the following eight shutouts. The three 1-0 games are bold.

3-0 vs. Houston on May 13
5-0 vs. New York on June 12
3-0 vs. Chicago on July 16
1-0 vs. Pittsburgh on August 14
1-0 vs. Chicago on September 9
1-0 vs. St. Louis on September 18
2-0 vs. St. Louis on September 25
5-0 vs. Cincinnati on September 29

Though his career ended prematurely, the Koufax touch was on his next and final year, 1966, which, save for 1965's perfecto against Chicago, was even better. The Hall of Fame electors wasted no time in enshrining him in 1972. He was the youngest honoree ever to be elected to baseball's ultimate award.

An October Game Extraordinaire: Walsh and Joss, October 2, 1908

Chicago (AL)	000	000	000	0-0-1
Cleveland	001	000	000	1-4-0

WP, Joss; LP, Walsh

There haven't been many seasons that compare with 1908. Pennant races, players with exceptional seasons even by Hall of Fame standards, individual games and events during a tumultuous season, and the race to the end of the season, capped by a Tiger-Cub World Series, made just about every day throughout the season something of an adventure. The story of that remarkable season is ably told by one of baseball's best historians, David Anderson, in his *More Than Merkle: A History of the Best and Most Exciting Baseball Season in Human History.*[2]

One of the pivotal events in the 1908 American League pennant chase gets its just due in Anderson's chapter entitled "October: Down to the Wire." That event would be an all-time classic between Cleveland and Chicago, staged on October 2 at Cleveland's League Park. There is a more often told story about another event in that riveting 1908 season, however. That would be the famed Merkle incident that to all intents and purposes cost the New York Giants a pennant. That will be left for others to tell, mentioned here only because it tends to overshadow, however unfortunately, one of the finest games played in all of baseball history. It was the tilt that matched friendly rivals: Addie Joss, the angular right-hander whose 1908 season was bettered only by Christy Mathewson, and Ed Walsh, whose 40 wins that season have never been matched since. Those three Hall-of-Famers were joined by the likes of Mordecai Brown, Cy Young, and Ed Reulbach in a campaign during which they won 195 games combined, an average of nearly 30 per pitcher.

Only two weeks prior to the Joss-Walsh match-up, Addie had beaten the grizzled warrior Cy Young in one of those heart-throbbers by a narrow 1-0 margin. The winning run in that one didn't come until a single marker was registered in the ninth inning.

But on October 2 there was nothing to compare with what was transpiring in Cleveland on a crisp, sunny fall day. On that day Addie Joss took down Chicago's White Sox 1-0, not permitting one Chicagoan to become a base runner. When the last batter, hard-hitting John Anderson, had been retired it marked Joss' 27th in a row. It was Addie's 24th conquest of the season and

by far his most brilliant among them all. That total included three 1-0 games
and six other shutouts.

May 12, New York (Doyle)	2-0
June 17, Washington (Cates)	2-0
June 24, Chicago (Owen)	6-0
August 3, New York (Hogg)	2-0
September 1, Detroit (Winter)	**1-0**
September 7, Chicago (Walsh)	6-0
September 17, Boston (Young)	**1-0**
September 22, New York (Hogg)	7-0
October 2, Chicago (Walsh)	**1-0**

Big Ed Walsh won 40 games in 1908, a stupendous feat. His famed spitter
bedeviled every American League hitter at one time or another and, coupled with
his lightning-like pickoff move and his fielding (Walsh was arguably the best fielding pitcher in the game's annals), simply outdid opponent after opponent through
an incredible 464 innings of work. And on this October afternoon he pitched
superbly, striking out 15, allowing but four hits and walking only one hitter. It
was the only free pass in the game. The chink in his armor this day was the one
that got away and it cost him the ball game. This is the third-inning sequence
that doomed the White Sox: Dode Birmingham, Nap Lajoie's agile center fielder,
led things off with a single. Birmingham's lead at first base revealed larceny in his
eyes, and Walsh was not minded to put up with it. He whipped a pickoff throw
to first baseman Frank Isbell and Birmingham was trapped, leaning the wrong
way. There was only one thing for Birmingham to do, and that was to hightail it
for second base, hoping to beat the throw or to slide around a tag that might yet
land him safely at second. The ball never got to second base in a rundown that
went awry. Isbell's throw hit the fleeing Birmingham and the ball wound up in
right field where outfielder Ed Hahn retrieved it. But Birmingham kept right on
running, winding up just 90 feet away from home plate. At that, Big Ed got the
next two hitters and was ahead in the count on leadoff hitter Lefty Good, having
slipped two strikes past him. Everyone thought they knew what was coming, but
they guessed wrong. This time Walsh chose his fast one over the spitter, fired it at
the outside corner, but threw it too far outside for catcher Ozzie Schreckengost to
get a glove on it and Birmingham dashed on home with the only run of the game.
It turned out to be the winning run. Bill Bradley, Cleveland's fine third baseman
who was batting while the crucial play was unfolding, fielded the last out of the
game. Later, Franklin Lewis reported Bradley's account of the game's last play:[3]

> There have been stories about that play, but there was nothing un-
> usual about it until I threw the ball. I knew something about John

Table 4.2.   1908 No-Hitters

Date	Pitcher	Team / Opponent	Score
June 30	Cy Young	Bos / NY (AL)	8-0
July 4	**Hooks Wiltse**	**NY (NL) / Phl**	**1-0 (10 innings)**
September 5	Nap Rucker	Brk / Bos (NL)	6-0
September 18	Dusty Rhoads	Clv / Bos	2-1
September 20	**Frank Smith**	**Chi (AL) / Phl**	**1-0**

Anderson. He was a powerful man who played in the outfield and at first base. Once before, when I had been playing shortstop in place of Terry Turner, who was hurt, I almost got a triple play when Anderson sent a terrific liner to me. He was a pull hitter, and so when he came up in Addie's big game, I moved closer to the base. John hit his grounder rather sharply over the bag. I was playing deep and . . . threw to [George] Stovall, but I threw low. George made a fine pickup of the ball out of the dirt.

Five other no-hitters were thrown during that unusual season of 1908, listed in table 4.2.

There is always a huge outpouring of emotion following a rare and outstanding athletic event. In Cleveland on that special October 2, 1908, an overflow crowd poured out of the stands and roped-off barriers to engulf their heroes. The party went on and on. Clevelanders reveled into the night, sure at that point that not only the world's best pitcher, at least in their eyes, but the world's best team, also in their eyes, were on their way to the World Series. That had to be inevitable after this fantastic victory. There might be disappointments ahead, but not for Addie Joss and his Forest City following the evening of October 2, 1908.

One added note: the choice between this game and the Koufax-Hendley game for the number one spot in no-hit, 1-0 games was a difficult one to make. The paper-thin difference between the two came down to a one hit total in the Koufax victory, and the passed ball, four-hit loss suffered by the White Sox in the final climactic and stressful weeks of the 1908 pennant race.

2 Games, 3 No-Nos and 1 Heartbreaker

Two games, each from a different era, share the limelight in third place in this exclusive list of no-hitters. These games include the Toney-Vaughn extra-inning game that featured two nine-inning no-hitters, and the Harvey Haddix loss to

Milwaukee in 1959 despite his 12 perfect innings. These extra inning affairs are factors that unite them uniquely in our listing's third position. Another would be the 1-0 score that further binds them. A century later, nonetheless, Fred Toney and Jim "Hippo" Vaughn, the better known of the two, are figures from a dark and distant past, not well known except to those who really know their baseball history, despite having pulled off the only feat of its kind in the game's history. Harvey "The Kitten" Haddix, who crafted that magnificent perfect game through 12 innings, is a better-known baseball figure whose singular performance on the long night of May 26, 1959, etched his name into baseball's historical record. The two games follow.

Goose Eggs All Around:
Toney and Vaughn, May 2, 1917

Cincinnati (NL)	000	000	000	1	1-2-0
Chicago	000	000	000	0	0-0-2

WP, Toney; LP, Vaughn

The second of May was a cold spring day in Chicago featuring a raw mist, its chill cutting to the marrow of the bone. Not more than 3,500 Cub rooters turned out to see their favorites take on the Cincinnati Reds. Mound opponents at Weeghman Park, the still-new home of the Cubs, would be Hippo Vaughn, the powerfully built Cubs ace, 3 and 1 on the season thus far, and Fred Toney, ace of the Reds' pitching staff, who at 4 and 1 was on his way to a 24 and 16 season that would be highlighted by seven shutout victories and a 2.20 ERA. Vaughn's 1917 record was on an even keel with 23 victories in almost 300 innings of work, two fewer shutouts than Toney's, and an even stronger ERA at 2.01. Though the day was not at all favorable for an epoch-making event, the two veterans would set to the task to see what they could do.

What they would do was to deny opposing batsmen a single hit in the first nine innings of play, something never before done, and, as the years rolled on even to this very day, not done since. There were base runners—Cy Williams for one—who worked Toney for a pair of free passes, and the little Cincinnati leadoff hitter, Heinie Groh, also got free transportation to first base. But double plays erased them. Both defenses came up with answers to any problems in the making. And so the two worked through inning after inning until both teams were out of innings, at least as far as regulation nine-inning games were concerned. That meant, chill and discomfort aside, that there would be extra innings. But not many. In the

Unheralded Fred Toney, the big (6'6", 245 lbs) Cincinnati right-hander, was "the other" pitcher in the famed double-no-hitter in 1918, hurling 10 innings of 1-0, no-hit ball. *Brace Photo*.

top of the tenth the Reds sent third baseman Gus Getz to the plate to lead things off. Vaughn promptly fanned him. He was followed by shortstop Larry Kopf who shot a darter past the outstretched glove of Cub first baseman Fred Merkle. And that was the shot heard 'round Chicagoland. Big Hippo's no-no was history, but at least it was brought down by a clean shot.

This time a single was not a harmless hit. Before the inning was over, it had paved the way—by dint of misplays in the outfield and at home plate—for a run the Cubs could not match in the bottom of the 10th. The sting of defeat, coming as it did after such majestic effort, was even more devastating, to players and fans alike, than was the loss of Vaughn's no-hitter. Catcher Artie Wilson broke down in tears after the game and there was certainly no joy in Wrigleyville that day.

Though much has been written about this game, most of it from the vantage point of Hippo Vaughn and the Cubs' loss, one should not lose sight of Fred Toney's greatest moment. After opening the bottom of the 10th with a strikeout, Toney suffered through a seriously anxious moment on a Fred Merkle fly ball that had the lift to carry to the park's left-field fence. But with his back to the infield, Manuel Cueto caught it. There remained only one out separating the big fastballer from a no-hitter *and* victory in the person of the very capable Cy Williams, now into the fifth season of a productive 19-year career. It was a good at-bat, the two measuring each other in a count that went the limit of 3 and 2. Instead of throwing his heater, Toney chose to bend one in an attempt to hit the outside corner. The sharply breaking curveball found its mark. Cy Williams didn't, whiffing to end the game. Toney had thrown 10 innings of no-hit ball and had extended his record to 5 and 1. It was his best day in the bigs.

With regard to the afterlife of this game, the eminent sabermetrician Bill James said: "When I was a kid the double no-hitter was one of the most famous games in baseball history. But you rarely hear about it anymore because baseball history has become the purview of the television people, who aren't interested in anything for which there is no tape."[4] Sad, but true.

Heartbreak City, U.S.A.:
Haddix and Burdette, May 26, 1959

| Pittsburgh (NL) | 000 | 000 | 000 | 000 | 0 | 0-12-1 |
| Milwaukee | 000 | 000 | 000 | 000 | 1 | 1-1-0 |

WP, Burdette; LP, Haddix

The other party to tie for third place in this no-hit 1-0 review is the little Pirate southpaw Harvey Haddix. You have to accomplish something out of the ordinary in order to be the central figure in a baseball loss, and Haddix certainly did. His was the misfortune of going through 12 perfect innings only to lose a ball game *and* perfection. And, much like the game previously covered, the winning run was scored amid a blur of confusion. In Heartbreak City, on this occasion known as Milwaukee, Wisconsin, the hometown nine won the game, devastated both Pittsburgh and its doughty veteran, and succeeded in winning the game on a ball hit over the fence at County Stadium that was ruled a double. Here is how that all happened.

After an error that opened the bottom half of the 13th inning, Felix Mantilla was at first and Eddie Mathews was due up. Although Haddix's perfect game was now gone, his no-hitter was still intact. Needing but one run to win, the wise thing to do was ordered, and Eddie Mathews, though one of baseball's heavy hitters at the time, sacrificed Mantilla to second with a perfectly placed bunt. That brought up the ever-dangerous Hank Aaron. Once again, baseball wisdom prevailed and Aaron was put on with an intentional pass, thus putting a twin-killing in play. Successfully executed, it would end the threat and the inning. In this lethal succession of Milwaukee hitters in the middle of the batting order Joe Adcock was up next. He caught hold of a Haddix slider, lofting it to deep right-center field. It escaped Bill Virdon's leap and sailed over the 375-foot marker, ostensibly a home run. But what followed sliced the four-bagger in half and the run-scoring bomb turned into a double. At that point the dejected Haddix turned and left the mound, thinking the game, his perfect sequence, and the no-hitter, had all vanished in a moment's notice. But that was only partially true.

On the base paths there was confusion. Hank Aaron, between first and second, thought it was possible that the ball had hit the bottom of the outfield fence and, consequently, hesitated, finally heading for the dugout, thinking that Mantilla's score had already won the game. Meanwhile, Joe Adcock, who had seen the umpire's hand signal for a circuit smash, was into his home run trot and passed Aaron on the basepaths. Aaron was subsequently ruled out on the play, and after a period of time it was thought that even though Aaron had been ruled out, both Mantilla and Adcock had scored to make the final count 2-0. In any case, the winning run had scored, ruining the evening for Haddix and the Pirates.

National League president Warren Giles cleared things up the next day by ruling that since the hitter could not be treated as having hit a home run, and since the play was recorded as a two-base hit, it was not logical to treat the base runners as if the hitter had hit a home run.

So it had all come to naught as far as Harvey Haddix was concerned. But look at what he left in the wake of that ball game:

- He had pitched 12 innings of perfect baseball.
- He had thrown 115 pitches, averaging between 9 and 10 per inning, a remarkable few.
- 33 of his pitches were called balls, 19 called strikes, and there were 12 foul balls.

- There were 13 fly balls for outs and 8 strikeouts
- And, lest it be forgotten, there were no hits through 12.1 innings.

To this day the game, the pitcher, the achievements, and the records left behind on that one evening of play in Milwaukee are indeed among the game's most distinguished.

Bob Feller's Opening Day—and Some Other Days

We've paid our respects before to the Bob Feller masterpiece on opening day at Comiskey Park in 1940, and many more of his achievements are equally breathtaking. His no-hit achievement ranks as number 5 in our listing of the top five no-hit games. To round out the Feller coverage, here are a few more things about his career.

The opening day no-no in 1940 started off Bob Feller's best all-around single-season effort. During that same year he came close to pitching another no-hit ball game, beating Philadelphia 1-0 while allowing only one hit, an eighth-inning single by the A's' first baseman, Dick Siebert. When the firing was over in the '40 campaign, Feller had won a career high 27 games with over 300 innings pitched and 261 strikeouts, just about one for every inning he pitched. At 22, his career was just in its beginning phases. He leveled off at his career high point and maintained it for many seasons after. As late as 1951, during the 13th of his 18 major league seasons, he won 22 games, the sixth of his 20-win campaigns.

During a 1946 stretch of five games extending from July 24 to August 13, he allowed just two runs in 45 innings. On July 20 Feller whipped Washington 10-2, the two runs coming in the fifth inning. From that point forward he gave up just two runs over a 48-inning span. The next five games, beginning with Bob Feller's 18th victory on July 24, are detailed in table 4.3.

Table 4.3.   Bob Feller's 1946 Streak

Date	Score	Opposing Team / LP	K / Hits	Noteworthy
July 24	1-0	Philadelphia / Bob Savage	9/3	Hank Edwards HR won it
July 28	2-0	Washington / Bobo Newsom	10/4	Feller at 19 and 6
July 31	4-1	Boston / Mickey Harris	9/1	One hitter (Bobby Doerr)
August 8	5-0	Chicago / Orval Grove	5/1	*1-hitter (Frankie Hayes)
August 13	0-1	Detroit / Dizzy Trout	7/4	8 IP, Feller at 21 and 7

*Bob Feller pitched 12 one-hit games in his career.

The last of Feller's shutouts, which were 44 in number, was thrown on May 1, 1955, in game 1 of a Red Sox–Indians doubleheader at Cleveland's Municipal Stadium, and he made it a good one, drawing back on his halcyon days with a one-hit, 2-0 blanking, beating Frank Sullivan. On that day his longstanding battery mate, Jim Hegan, drove home both runs, one in the second frame and another in the sixth, scoring Ralph Kiner on a booming triple that iced the game. In a route-going performance he walked only one batter and struck out two. After all the innings he had thrown, he still had enough in the tank to shut down the opposition.

Bob Feller was better remembered as one of the fastest fastball pitchers the game has known. There is a select list of those hurlers which includes hallowed names like Cy Young, Amos Rusie, Lefty Grove, and Walter Johnson, all of whom were active before reliable measuring devices came along. Bob Feller stands astride both eras. He was clocked at over 100 mph long before the more sophisticated speed guns in use today were available. In these latter days, however, equipment has it "down to a science," and an accurate one at that. Recently a new list appeared, numbering, in order, the 15 fastest mph readings. The top 10 appear in table 4.4.

Bob Feller threw lasers, but acknowledged just how important to successful pitching control and location are. Shortly before turning 30, Feller injured his shoulder, and that, plus having lost prime years to military service, combined to sap his once blazing speed. He had to learn, just as Lefty Grove did, "how to pitch." Note the quotation marks, indicating the time-worn code for the art of pitching. Implicit in the phrase is the knowledge and capability that require more than lightning speed. That very demanding requirement of throwing to batters' weaknesses, changing speeds, spotting the ball in the strike zone, and having the control to put any given pitch exactly where it should be makes the difference between winning and losing ball games. The great ones had it down. The greatest of them, like Bob Feller, wind up in Cooperstown.

Table 4.4.   Fastest Pitches on Record

FFE	Pitcher	Throws	K's per 162-Game Season
108.1 (Doppler radar)	Nolan Ryan (1974)	RHP	246
107.6 (FFE artillery)	**Bob Feller (1946)**	**RHP**	**167**
105.1 (3 videos)	Aroldis Chapman (2010)	LHP (relief)	not listed
104.8 (3 videos)	Joel Zumaya (2006)	RHP (relief)	85 in 2009
103 (radar)	Mark Wohlers (1995)	RHP (closer)	71
102.6 (3 videos)	Jonathan Braxton (2009)	RHP (closer)	not listed
102.5 (FFE artillery)	Steve Dalkowski (1958)	LHP	not listed
102.2 (3 videos)	Brian Wilson (2009)	RHP (closer)	not listed
102 (radar)	Bobby Jenks (2005)	RHP	not listed
102 (radar)	Randy Johnson (2004)	LHP	271

FFE: Speed at 50-foot equivalent.

And with Respect . . .

To conclude this look at pitchers who crafted no-hit 1-0 games, we present three games and their pitchers spread over more than a century of baseball. These games are listed chronologically and deserve honorable mention status. They include professional baseball's first perfect game, pitched by John Lee Richmond, and one of the more unlikely complete game pitchers; Hoyt Wilhelm, who entered the Hall of Fame as the game's first relief pitcher to be so honored; and Mr. No-Hit himself, Nolan Ryan, whose seven no-hitters are a major league record. The very special nature of these pitchers and games merits more than a passing note. Consequently, the honorable mention games follow.

The Class President and His No-Hit Wonder:
June 12, 1880

Cleveland (NL)	000	000	000	0-0-2
Worcester	000	010	00x	1-3-0

WP, Richmond; LP, J. McCormick

John Lee Richmond was a man of exceptional gifts. In his lifetime he was a practitioner of the medical arts, a teacher, principal, professor at Toledo University, orchestra conductor, golfer, and southpaw curveball artist. It is the latter distinction—curveball artist—that claims attention in this collection of noteworthy no-hit games. It was John Lee Richmond, president of Brown University's graduating class, who threw the first perfect game in baseball history. That, by itself, is a singular claim to fame. The honor was achieved under the most unlikely of circumstances but stands, nonetheless, as a remarkable achievement, given the circumstances and the date of its accomplishment, June 12, 1880.

Richmond's perfecto was the first of but 23 between 1880 and the 2012 season. The second perfect game, rather astonishingly, came just five days later. It was John Ward's 5-0 conquest of Providence. And then there was a quarter century gap until Cy Young defeated Philadelphia of the fledgling American League, 3-0. Irregularly spotted throughout the next century of baseball's history came 14 of these rare gems. But it was Mr. Richmond's perfect game that came first, a forerunner and grandfather of them all.

Under the prevailing circumstances, the most unusual was the ruling that allowed batters to signal the pitcher where they wanted the pitch to cross the plate, whether higher or lower in an enlarged strike zone. The other was the ruling that mandated the pitcher to make his pitches underhanded no more than 45 feet from the pitcher's plate. The game was played under decidedly more genteel circumstances, encouraging hitting and scoring above fastball and pitching artistry. And yet the pitching masters of the day often prevailed with low-scoring games that helped promote pitching and defensive skill.

On June 12, amid graduation ceremonies and celebrations, the Worcester Ruby Legs engaged the Cleveland Blues, and Richmond's curveballs—a puzzling novelty to National League hitters—had Blues' hitters swinging at the cool June air in Massachusetts. But in the fifth inning Cleveland's Bill Phillips tagged one of Richmond's curveballs, sending it on a line through the gap between first and second on its way to right field. However, the ball was hit so sharply that the Ruby Legs' right fielder, Captain Lon Knight, converted it into a 9 to 3 ground-out. It was one of several outstanding defensive plays, as reported by newspaper accounts, which saved the day for Richmond's perfect game.

Although hitters caught up with Richmond's breaking ball offerings in his brief major league career during baseball's formative years, the young college grad certainly had his moment in the sun, prevailing on that momentous occasion to pitch baseball's first perfect game.

75 Years Apart but No-Hitters Just the Same

Refinements in the way the game is played, in the ballparks, in the equipment, and in the skills displayed in the modern era have been profound, but there has always remained a conscious effort to maintain a continuity and connection with the early game. As a result, despite the years between John Richmond and Hoyt Wilhelm—who put together our next no-hitter of distinction—there are a number of significant connecting points. One is the delivery of the ball itself. In Hoyt Wilhelm's case, the prime choice of delivery was the knuckleball, something seldom seen in major league ball games. Another was in the two pitchers themselves, both self-effacing and patient individuals who were respected and well-liked professionals. Wilhelm might have been nicked for a base runner or two, but his opposition, the Bronx Bombers from New York, could not find a way to come up with a base hit. That has happened to the New Yorkers only seven times in their history, and there followed a 45-year gap until their next no-hitter on June 11, 2003, when the Astros used a combined staff of six pitchers to embarrass the Yanks at Yankee Stadium by an 8-0 score.

At Memorial Stadium in Baltimore in one of 1958's late September games, the Yanks lineup had another of its murderer's rows in place; it surely didn't lack for hitting, featuring these seasoned hitters: Richardson, Mantle, Skowron, Berra, Slaughter, Bauer, and Elston Howard—not a patsy in the bunch. But Wilhelm's dancing knucklers had them popping up, grounding out, and whiffing the thick air of Baltimore's early autumn.

There were a few of baseball's many trivia at play on this date in baseball history. Here are four of the more significant:

- Wilhelm's opposing starter was the pitcher of record in the only perfect World Series game, Don Larsen, and through six innings of this game he was almost perfect again, allowing only a bunt single. Casey Stengel removed him, however, bringing on Bobby Shantz for the seventh stanza.
- Gus Triandos, who provided the only scoring of the game with a moon shot of more than 400 feet, tied opposing catcher Yogi Berra's single-season home run record with the smash, his 30th of the season. He was, incidentally, a former Yankee, picked up in a 1954 trade.[5] Amiable Gus, a favorite in Baltimore, was nobody's speed merchant, but he didn't need to be. All he needed was his home run trot.
- Hoyt Wilhelm was originally signed to a free agent contract with the New York Yankee franchise in 1948.
- Since the latest no-hitter against the Yankees was a combined effort of six pitchers, Wilhelm's no-no is the last one by a single pitcher, dating back a half century from 2008.

Paul Richards, Baltimore's manager, made one defensive move that paid dividends in the ninth inning, helping Hoyt Wilhelm on the way to baseball history. He had moved outfielder Willie Tasby from center field to right field and brought in defensive wizard Jim Busby to play center field. Enos Slaughter tested that move with a line shot that the swift Tasby just did catch.

A year earlier, almost to the very day, on September 21, 1957, Snacks, as he was referred to by teammates and friends, had been claimed on waivers from the Cleveland organization, for whom he had gone 2 and 7 prior to coming over to the Baltimore Orioles. He added only one victory, but it was a monster, his third in a 3-10 season, the no-hitter that baffled not only the Yankees, but baseball's cognoscenti, who hardly believed it possible that a knuckleballer could throw a no-hitter.

Hoyt Wilhelm, wounded in 1945's Battle of the Bulge, was awarded the Purple Heart. The reward for his pioneering efforts on another field, the baseball diamond, was his selection for Hall of Fame honors in 1985.

A Litter of Seven

Nolan Ryan knew he was blessed with rare and overwhelming speed, but he also knew that his control problems might well be the end of his major league

He threw smoke—and 7 no-hitters. Nolan Ryan, who at one time was clocked at 101 mph.

career. Being an intense and conscientious fellow, he set about maximizing the one and ridding himself of the other. One would have to say that he managed both and was successful, overall, in a number of ways. His long hours of work, conditioning, and mental preparation paved the way to Cooperstown, where he arrived with other members of the class of 1999, one of 26 elected in his first year of eligibility. Another consequence should be noted: his 5,714 career strikeouts and seven career no-hitters are indelibly noted in the record book. Concerning those no-hitters, one is of utmost importance in a book devoted almost exclusively to 1-0 ball games. The game of concern occurred on the first of June 1975, a 1-0 marvel in which the Baltimore O's looked helpless, going without a semblance of a hit through nine innings. Orioles starter Ross Grimsley pitched well enough in the early part of the game to limit the Angels to a single run driven in by Dave Chalk in the third inning. But Wayne Garland, who relieved Grimsley, was much better, allowing only one hit the rest of the way in over four innings of work. Neither could match the Ryan Express, however, as he notched his fourth no-hitter in the span of two years. Of the victory Ryan said that he would prefer to have an outstanding year, with a 27-5 record or something like it, and that people would then know that he was great all year instead of on just one day.

While it is true that the Ryan Express was derailed more than a time or two (Ryan lost almost as many as he won), there were any number of seasons when the number 18 or more appeared under his W column, and his ERA dipped below the 3.00 mark (eight times) during an era of robust hitting. He endured, the Methuselah of his time, still throwing blistering heaters at age 45. Ryan's success on June 1, 1975, is ably detailed in the box score in tables 4.5 and 4.6.

Table 4.5. Baltimore vs. California, June 1, 1975

Baltimore	AB	R	H	RBI	California	AB	R	H	RBI
Singleton, rd	4	0	0	0	Remy, 2b	3	0	1	0
Shopay, cf	3	0	0	0	Rivers, cf	4	1	1	0
Bumbry, lf	4	0	0	0	Harper, dh	4	0	1	0
Baylor, dh	2	0	0	0	Chalk, 3b	3	0	2	1
Davis, dh	2	0	0	0	Llenas, lf	3	0	1	0
Grich, 2b	2	0	0	0	M. Nettles, lf	0	0	0	0
May, 1b	3	0	0	0	Stanton, rf	2	0	1	0
B. Robinson, 3b	3	0	0	0	Bochte, 1b	3	0	1	0
Hendricks, c	3	0	0	0	E. Rodriguez, c	3	0	0	0
Belanger, ss	2	0	0	0	B. Smith, ss	2	0	1	0

Table 4.6. Baltimore vs. California, June 1, 1975: Pitching Stats

Baltimore	IP	H	R	ER	BB	K
Grimsley (L, 1-7)	3.1	8	1	1	0	1
Garland	4.2	1	0	0	1	1

California	IP	H	R	ER	BB	K
Ryan (W, 9-3)	9	0	0	0	4	9

Notes

1. Michael Coffey, *27 Men Out* (New York: Atria Books, 2004), and Ronald Mayer, *Perfect* (Jefferson, NC: McFarland, 1991).

2. David Anderson, *More Than Merkle: A History of the Best and Most Exciting Baseball Season in Human History* (Lincoln: University of Nebraska Press, 2000).

3. Franklin Lewis, *The Cleveland Indians* (New York: Putnam's, 1949), 46.

4. Bill James, *The New Bill James Historical Abstract* (New York: Free Press, 2001), 913.

5. The Triandos trade was one of the most complicated and massive ever. The particulars: New York traded Gene Woodling, Harry Byrd, Jim McDonald, Hal Smith, Willie Miranda, and four more players named later. In exchange with Baltimore they (the Yanks) received Don Larsen, Bob Turley, Billy Hunter, and four players named later, November 17, 1954. Baltimore received Bill Miller, Don Leppert, Ted Del Guercio, and Kal Segrist on December 1, 1954. New York, on the same day, received Darrell Johnson, Jack Hamilton, Mike Blyzka, and Jim Fridley.

CHAPTER 5

The Titans

The Big Train: Walter Johnson

When passenger trains included Washington, Chicago, and New York on their itineraries in the 1910s and 1920s, they were commonly known as the Big Trains. Extra cars were added and the operation was entirely spit and polish as these Big Trains sped on their way to the big cities. Above all, these trains were incredibly fast. The many lines in operation vied with one another to get their Big Trains to their big-city destinations faster than their competitors. The Big Train seemed to be an appropriate way to characterize Walter Johnson's fastball, and it wasn't long before he was referred to as The Big Train. Now, there were others in the bigs during Johnson's era who could throw rockets. Lefty Grove, who came on during Johnson's waning years, and Cy Young, who finished up his legendary career during Johnson's first years, come immediately to mind. Apparently, however, Sir Walter's heater made such an impression on ballplayers, media, and fans that they had no trouble labeling the Johnson express the best they had ever seen.

Walter Johnson's numbers must have been made on another planet. Many of them in the record book are a good distance removed from other greats in one category or another. But when it comes to limiting opponents to no runs, he is really not in the same world as others. The number 36 stands beside his name when it comes to 1-0 ball games. That's roughly *twice* as many as Pete Alexander, the second-place hurler on this list of titans, has posted. With respect to 1-0 games, Johnson is immortal.

A look at this broad-shouldered, long-armed right-hander's dossier is an eye-opener, particularly with regard to low-scoring games. To give you an indication, here is an example or two. There weren't only 62 games in his 1-0 log; there were also a total of 65 games in which his Washington teammates failed to

A younger Walter Johnson, whose 36 1-0 victories top the list. *Brace Photo.*

score a run while he was on he mound. He hurled 110 shutouts, an overwhelming number, including 11 in 1913 alone, when his ERA disappeared in the nether regions of 1.09. And one more: he led the American League in strikeouts 12 times, as well as holding opposing teams scoreless, at one point, through 55.2 consecutive innings.

The speed of a ball approaching home plate is something baseball players and fans talk about from generation to generation. And the more speed the better. Fans couldn't get enough of it. Hitters actually feared it. There is one engaging story about Walter Johnson's speed that simply must be included before getting on to his 1-0 exploits. Steve O'Neill, one of the game's great receivers, tells this story:[1]

> Clyde Milan once told me of an exhibition game the Senators played against the Braves. Johnny Evers, a cocky little cuss, doubled off Walter in his first time at bat. When the inning ended and Milan trotted past second base, Evers refused to keep his big trap shut. "So that's the great Walter Johnson," he said to Milan. "Listen, we got a half dozen pitchers in our league who are faster than he is." Milan sat alongside Johnson. "Walter," he said, "Evers just told me that there were a dozen pitchers in his league faster than you are." But Johnson never said a word. A few innings later Evers came to bat again. Walter threw him three pitches and Johnny hasn't seen any of them yet. Evers was still pale and shaking when he met Milan at the inning's end. "You big blabbermouth," he screamed. "You told Johnson what I said, didn't you?!"

The 1-0 record below includes pairings with eight Hall of Fame pitchers, including Ed Walsh (3), Babe Ruth (2) Addie Joss (2), Red Faber, Waite Hoyt, Eddie Plank, George Sisler, and Albert "Chief" Bender. Johnson posted a 6-6 record in extra inning games, the most famous his encounter with Eddie Rommel on opening day 1926, a 15-inning affair. The contest was quite probably the most artistic opener on the part of two accomplished pitchers in the game's history. Johnson walked three, struck out nine, and gave up only six hits—at 39 and in the sunset years of his marvelous career.

In table 5.1, the double-asterisked game marks Johnson's only no-hitter, coming against the Boston Red Sox, always a tough opponent for the strikeout king. He came into this game ailing, the grippe having played a number on him, adding to growing worries over his pitching arm, which was not responding to either treatment or rest as much as he had hoped. Before this particular tilt got started, Johnson had told manager Clark Griffith that he would start but would see how he felt during his first inning of action. In Johnson's mind the game was an inning-by-inning proposition.

Table 5.1. The 1-0 Record

1-0 Wins			1-0 Losses		
Date	Team	Opposing Pitcher	Date	Team	Opposing Pitcher
09/07/1907	Bos	Morgan	08/14/1907	StL	Pelty
08/14/1908	Chi	White	08/24/1908	Det	Donovan
10/07/1908	NY	Warhop	09/18/1908	Chi	Walsh
06/11/1909	Det	Killian	05/07/1909	Phl	Coombs
08/04/1909	Clv	Joss	05/10/1909	Chi	White (11)
08/17/1909	Phl	Bender (12)	07/31/1909	Chi	Burns
05/14/1910	Clv	Joss	08/29/1909	Chi	Walsh
08/04/1911	Chi	White	07/17/1910	Det	Willett
04/15/1912	NY	Quinn	08/23/1910	Chi	Walsh
05/10/1913	Chi	Benz	09/06/1912	Bos	Wood
06/06/1913	StL	Leverenz	05/30/1913	Bos	Collins
07/03/1913	Bos	Collins (15)	08/28/1913	Bos	Collins (11)
09/05/1913	NY	Ford (10)	09/29/1913	Phl	Wyckoff
05/29/1914	Bos	Rankin	06/01/1914	Bos	R. Johnson
07/06/1914	Bos	R. Johnson	05/19/1915	Det	Dubuc
09/18/1914	StL	Hoch	06/01/1916	Bos	Ruth
04/28/1915	Phl	Wyckoff	07/03/1916	NY	Caldwell
09/08/1915	NY	Shawkey	09/17/1916	StL	Sisler
06/07/1917	Chi	Russell	05/07/1917	Bos	Ruth
08/06/1917	StL	Plank	05/04/1918	Phl	Perry (11)
05/11/1918	Clv	Bagby Sr.	06/02/1918	Clv	Bagby Sr.
05/15/1918	Chi	Williams (18)	07/29/1918	Chi	Benz (13)
07/25/1918	StL	Sothoron (15)	06/25/1919	Bos	Jones
04/23/1919	Phl	Perry (13)*	07/21/1922	Clv	Morton
06/13/1919	Clv	Morton	09/02/1922	Bos	Piercy
06/29/1919	Phl	Naylor	06/07/1926	Det	Wells
07/03/1919	NY	Shore			
07/24/1919	Phl	Kinney			
07/01/1920	Bos**	Harper			
09/14/1921	StL	Davis			
06/18/1922	Chi	Faber			
06/28/1922	NY	Hoyt			
08/24/1922	Chi	Blankenship			
07/30/1923	Det	Dauss			
09/26/1923	Chi	Thurston			
04/13/1926	Phl	Rommel* (15)			

*Season opening game.
**No-hitter.

The first inning of the historic contest came and went without incident and Johnson said he'd try another. He did, and that also went well. So did the middle innings and quite suddenly, so it seemed, the seventh frame was underway and the Red Sox were still hitless. About this time the stands began buzzing with each out, and as the ninth inning approached even the concessionaires stopped things cold to see if the big fellow could wind it up in no-hit fashion.

In the Boston ninth, manager Ed Barrow, later to become the architect of Yankee fortunes in the 1920's, sent a pair of lefty pinch hitters to face Johnson, but the big fellow, by now in full battle mode, dispatched both in a moment's notice, on strikes of course. That left one to go. And the last of the Bostons standing was no grocery boy. Harry Hooper, the last of the famed Boston outfield of yore: Speaker, Hooper, and Lewis. Hooper was a tough out, en route to the Hall of Fame. And he really nailed one that had first baseman Joe Judge in hot pursuit. Fielding Hooper's rifle shot well behind the bag in an acrobatic stop that was a minor miracle in itself, he turned and threw to Johnson, covering first, a hair's breadth ahead of Hooper's arrival at first. It was the 27th out in a real test of mettle and skill, and celebrations afterward showed Boston's appreciation of Johnson's feat.

The game's lone run had been driven home by Bucky Harris, enjoying his first full major league season and later to become Washington's "Boy Manager." By then, Walter Johnson had learned to survive on a diet of meager Washington run-rations. His 1-0 games and many more 2-1 and 2-0 victories hardened him for this no-hit occasion. Among his more memorable 1-0 victories stood extra-inning efforts with Philadelphia's "Jittery Joe" Perry; one was a season opener at Washington in 1919 that meandered through 13 innings when, finally, pinch runner Mike Menosky scored on Eddie Foster's hit to give Washington, and Johnson, its first victory of the first WW I postwar season.

Two or three other Johnson games vie for attention. One of them, the 18-inning Washington-Chicago game of May 15, 1918, will be up for review in the chapter on 1-0 marathons. Another is the celebrated face-off between Smoky Joe Wood and Johnson in 1912. This highly promoted game turned out to be everything it was advertised to be, with Boston finally winning out 1-0 over the Senators. Still another occurred on August 28, 1913, when Ray Collins, 19 and 8 for the 1913 season, tangled with Johnson at Boston's still brand-new Fenway Park. Earlier in the 1913 season the very capable Collins had beaten Johnson in game 2 of a Washington double bill, 1-0. It was the first of three remarkable 1-0 games between the two in 1913. Another 1-0 tilt that was finally resolved at Fenway in the 15th inning on July 3 preceded the 1-0, August 28 clash. The two locked horns for 10 innings before a run found its way home to bring to naught a magnificent Johnson effort that featured 26 consecutive outs before Steve Yerkes singled with one out in the 11th inning. He scampered all the way to third while the usually reliable Clyde Milan was hunting down the Yerkes single that went through his legs. Moments later he came home with the winning tally on another single. In what many felt was Johnson's greatest game, even better than his no-hitter, he had walked none, struck out 10 and saw his 14-game winning streak come to an end.

There is still one other classic, a game that ended without a decision after 12 innings of play. On May 11, 1919, spitballer Jack Quinn and Johnson confronted one another at the Polo Grounds. They battled through 12 innings without a score, one probably as deserving of victory as the other. In this one, Johnson retired *28* Highlanders in a row between a single in the first inning and a walk in the 10th, enough for a complete game no-hitter plus one. But not on this day. Despite his two-hit, nine-strikeout effort, Johnson was denied victory. It was another typical Johnson experience on the mound at the behest of his willing, but oft-unable Senators. Chalking up 417 career victories, he never complained. He just kept on working—working his way toward Cooperstown to be named with the very first class so honored.

Old Low and Away: Grover Alexander

Essentially laid back, and *way* laid back when not quite up to sobriety standards, Grover Cleveland Alexander nonetheless knew a thing or two about pitching and did it so well that, despite the many bedevilments that plagued him, he made it to baseball's Hall of Fame, among the first honored. The centerpiece of his pitching was to keep his pitches at the edge of the strike zone down around the knees. The farther outside and low he could keep his deliveries and still get strikes, the better. Eventually he was tagged with the nickname Old Low and Away by a teammate of his during his St. Louis Cardinals days. That fellow was Jesse Haines, a Hall of Fame compadre who was the pitcher Alexander replaced in the famous 1926 World Series game featuring Tony Lazzeri at bat. What followed even left Haines speechless, as Ol' Pete struck out Lazzeri with the bases loaded, but not before the Yankee second baseman hit the most remembered long drive foul in baseball history.

So it was that Old Low and Away made his way through a score of big league years, beginning and ending at Philadelphia's Baker Bowl and in between stopping by at Chicago and St. Louis. Those ballparks, each a hitter's delight, make his achievements that much more impressive. Further, more than half of his career was spent with less-than-decent ball clubs behind him. All things considered, this fellow's accomplishments were far above the norm, so far, in fact, that he has left behind a number of records, some of them in the "untouchable" class. One of those latter is his National League record of 90 career shutouts, which makes him the Johnson of the National League.

Grover Cleveland Alexander. His 90 shutouts lead National Leaguers.

Almost one in five of those 90 were complete-game 1-0 victories. The complete 17 and 8 ledger appears in table 5.2 (there were also two 11-inning, 0-0 ties).

Four of Alex's 17 1-0 games were pitched during 1916, the midpoint of three 30-win seasons. During those three years he won 94 of his 373 career victories, 36 of which were shutouts, and of those 36, eight were 1-0 games. His

Table 5.2.   Grover Alexander's 1-0 Games

	1-0 Wins			1-0 Losses	
Date	Team	Opposing Pitcher	Date	Team	Opposing Pitcher
09/07/1911	Bos	Cy Young	09/16/1912	Cinc	Benton
05/01/1913	NY	Tesreau	05/16/1914	StL	Doak
08/05/1913	StL	Sallee	08/05/1915	Pit	Adams
08/14/1913	Cinc	Ames	08/26/1919	Bos	Oeschger
09/12/1914	NY	Marquard	07/17/1920	Bos	Watson
07/21/1915	Chi	Adams	07/08/1921	NY	Nehf
05/26/1916	Brk	Smith	09/06/1921	StL	Bailey
07/07/1916	StL	Meadows	06/28/1923	StL	Toney
08/02/1916	Chi	Prendergast			
08/09/1916	Cinc	Schultz			
05/10/1917	StL	Meadows			
07/06/1917	Cinc	Regan			
09/13/1917	Brk	Pfeffer			
08/31/1919	StL	Woodward			
07/01/1920	Cinc	Luque			
08/28/1920	Brk	Grimes			
07/21/1922	Brk	Ruether			

16 shutout conquests tied the major league mark set by George Bradley in the National League's first season of play, 40 years earlier. No one since has come within shouting distance.

Pete Alexander was not prone to give up many runs, and these figures substantiate that contention: his career 2.58 ERA was aided by his lowest single season mark in 1915 of 1.22, followed by 1.55 (in 1916), 1.83 (in 1917), 1.72 (in 1918), and 1.91 (in 1919). During the WWI season of 1918 his army hitch prevented a full season with the Cubs, but with his 3-1 record came a 1.73 ERA.

Among the more stingy afternoons offered by Mr. Alexander was the second game of a doubleheader that wound up getting called by darkness. That 10-inning standstill followed a 1-0 game won by Tom Seaton (previously hailed in this book) at Boston on September 5, 1913. The second game, a 0-0 tie, went 10 innings, thus winding up 19 innings and 38 at-bats with but a single tally to show for the effort of both squads. There were 19 hits in the two games, only one of them a double. In Alexander's nightcap he struck out four and issued one pass while 16 Braves bit the dust via grounders. That was rather typical of an Alexander outing, his offerings often turning into grounders because hitters had trouble getting the business end of their warclubs on his offerings. Old Low and Away, a control pitcher to his last day, hit his spots and often got the strike call, even though his catchers had to stretch a bit pulling the ball into the strike zone.

Some years later, on August 28, 1920, Alex was doing the same things that still had senior circuit hitters gnashing their teeth. In Brooklyn, the 30-something hurler, wearing the Cub uniform, throttled Wilbert Robinson's pennant-bound ball club, allowing a few hits but nothing more than a single. He walked only one hitter and struck out only one. The rest of the time most of his outs were spread around the infielders, who picked up more than 15 assists. The 1-0 victory over Hall of Famer Burleigh Grimes raised his 1920 record at that point to 22 and 11. The victory was one of his seven shutouts. Three of those were 1-0 games.

Two seasons later, still a Cub, Alexander took on the Dodgers once again, this time paired with Dutch Ruether, a capable lefty who that season was a 21-game winner. At the hands of Alexander, however, he sustained one of his 12 losses. This 1-0 victory for the old warrior, by now 35, was to be his last one in the 1-0 category. It came on a day when the Cubs were looking for a lift, having been exposed to an 11-run manhandling the day before. They got it, assisting their ace with 15 outs via the grounder-to-first route. Shortstop Charlie Hollocher logged nine assists himself in that effort, which, again, was simply the result of ol' Alex doing his thing. And with that kind of support there was no need for the Bruin hurler to work extra hard at the strikeout game—he registered none. After only slightly more than an hour this one was over. And that was another of the Alexander trademarks: keep on firing to the right places and those kinds of things happen. The boxscore appears in table 5.3.

Table 5.3.   Chicago (NL) vs. Brooklyn 1922

Chicago	AB	R	H	A	Brooklyn	AB	R	H	A
Maisel, rf	4	0	0	0	Olson, 2b	4	0	1	3
Hollocher, ss	4	1	3	9	Myers, cf	3	0	0	2
Terry, 2b	2	0	1	2	T. Griffith, rf	4	0	1	2
R. Grimes, 1b	4	0	1	15	Wheat, lf	4	0	1	0
Friberg, cf	2	0	0	0	Mitchell, 1b	3	0	0	0
Miller, lf	3	0	0	0	High, 3b	2	0	1	3
Krug, 2b	3	0	0	1	Ward, ss	3	0	0	1
O'Farrell, c	3	0	0	0	DeBerry, c	2	0	0	1
Alexander (WP)	3	0	1	2	Ruether (LP)	3	0	0	1
Totals	**28**	**1**	**6**	**15**	**Totals**	**28**	**0**	**4**	**9**

2bh: R. Grimes.
SB: Ward.
Sac. H: Terry (2), Myers.
DP, R. Grimes and Hollocher, Alexander, Hollocher and R. Grimes; Myers and Olson.
LOB, Brooklyn 4, Chicago 6.
BB: Ruether 1, Alexander 2; SO: Ruether 5.

Umpires: Sentelle and O'Day.
Game time: 1 hour, 12 minutes.

Chicago	000	000	000	1-6-0
Brooklyn	000	000	000	0-4-0

Bert Blyleven: The Dutchman

Whatever took the Hall of Fame Electors so long to bestow their honors on this native Dutchman is one of those baseball mysteries that will continue on into the mists of time. He retired in 1992, and it took them a decade beyond his eligibility for election to proclaim him fit for membership in baseball's Hall of Halls, and that just doesn't stack up with his numbers. Checking through the credentials of the likes of Tom Seaver, Steve Carlton, Robin Roberts, and Early Wynn, just to mention four among others for comparison, we find overall similarities that suggest his are no more lacking in luster than any of those named. It's just that they are all different kinds of titans.

In any case, one of the things Bert Blyleven did better than most was to throw 1-0 winners. He sits up there in the rarified air of the mighty ones, just behind Grover "Pete" Alexander, with a 15-6 record that glistens among his 60 career shutouts. Table 5.4 shows what that record looks like.

Table 5.4. Bert Blyleven's 1-0 Games

1-0 Wins			1-0 Losses		
Date	Team	Opposing Pitcher	Date	Team	Opposing Pitcher
05/12/1971	Bos	Culp	05/02/71	Bos	Culp
09/15/1971	Mil	Lockwood	09/27/72	Oak	Holtzman, SP Locker, WP
09/29/1971	Cal	Wright	05/15/74	Chi (AL)	Bahnsen
09/22/1972	Cal	Messersmith	09/19/75	Cal	Pactwa, WP Brewer, SV
05/29/1973	Mil	Slaton	07/02/76	Chi (AL)	Brett
06/21/1973	Cal	Wright	09/20/76	Cal	Ryan
09/25/1974	Oak	Abbott			
08/27/1975	Mil	Travers			
06/21/1976	Oak	P. Mitchell			
06/26/1976	Chi (AL)	Brett			
08/05/1976	Cal	Ross			
09/25/1976	KC	Hassler			
04/26/1978	NY (AL)	Myrick			
09/26/1984	Sea	Beattie			
07/18/1989	Tor	Key			

1-0 games:	Won 15, Lost 6
Career W/L:	287/250
Career low ERA:	2.66 (1974)
Shutout ranking:	9th (1960)
No-hit game:	vs. California (Hartzell), September 22, 1977, 6-0

In 1971 Bert Blyleven turned 20, a sturdy, 6'3" 210-pounder who could throw his snappy curveball past just about any American League hitter. He had been a long time developing it, having thrown baseballs from an early age forward. The Blyleven curveball soon became one of the sharpest breaking pitches in baseball history, rating raves to match Tommy Bridges, Sal Maglie, or Sandy Koufax. During his time with the Twins, the Dutchman, as he was often called, needed all the help he could get from his deliveries. Twins teams backing him were into the residue years of the great Minnesota ball clubs of the 1960's. They finished first in the AL West during Blyleven's debut year, but quickly settled into middle-of-the-pack finishes in the 1970's. That made it difficult, if not improbable, to post years with big won-loss records of the 20-5 or 25-11 sort. Blyleven's 1970 record was 10-9, barely nosing over the .500 mark, and in 1971 he won 16 and lost 15, again, just a tad over the break-even level.

There were no 1-0 skirmishes during his opening big league season, but in 1971, when Minnesota was heading south in the standings, he managed a 4 and 1 mark, establishing his proficiency in the tight, oft nerve-wracking atmosphere of 1-0 baseball. And it was in that year that he found himself in two September starts that show just how different 1-0 games can be—and offering proof positive that it takes a united team effort to bring about a winner in the low-scoring games. A great catch here, a terrific throw there, or a smart backup play along the way often enable both team and pitcher to bring home a victory.

At County Stadium in Milwaukee, Blyleven faced the Brewers' Skip Lockwood on September 15. The season's dog days had caused bats to be a little slower, pitchers' arms just a little more weary, and legs just a tad heavier. These were the season's days that were meant for drama just the same, as pennant races came very sharply into view. On this fair, late summer evening, the pitchers were in command, and, going into the late innings, retiring one hitter after another. In the top of the ninth Skip Lockwood retired Rod Carew and Tony Oliva, both dangerous with a bat in their hands, on infield grounders. That brought up Harmon Killebrew with that lethal home-run club of his. Lockwood made him his sixth free pass of the game. Sudsville fans must have thought: better a walk for this fellow than extra bases. The next hitter, Steve Braun, finishing his rookie year, hadn't had much success with Lockwood, though he did coax the Brewer hurler for a walk in the seventh stanza. But in the ninth it was a different story. Braun lashed a triple to right, scoring Killebrew, and the Twins had suddenly crafted a 1-0 lead. Now it was up to Big Bert to hold it, and he did—not with his patented strikeout pitches but with three fly balls that squelched the Brewers in 1-2-3 order, raising his season mark to 13 and 15 at that point.

Before closing out the season at home against the California Angels, Blyleven opened a twin bill at Kansas City, beating the Royals 7 to 2. That raised his season's record to an even .500 at 15 and 15. He would get one last chance to wind up the season just ahead of the even-up mark.

Skipper Bill Rigney penciled Bert into the starter's slot for the second-to-last game of the season at Metropolitan Stadium on September 29. His opposing number would also be a break-even pitcher, Clyde Wright, who at 16 and 16 was also eager to finish up the 1971 wars above .500.

Both pitchers came to the ballpark with good stuff, allowing but a single run between them. Fortunately for Bert Blyleven, that run would belong to Minnesota. Though Minnesota had but three hits off Wright's slants, one of them was enough by itself to turn this 0-0 contest into a Twins winner. The blow that won it all came off the bat of Warren Renick, a sometime ballplayer known more for his baseball smarts than his playing ability. Renick had played in precious few ball games in a short-lived major league career, but on this day was assigned to the left-field spot, batting seventh in Rigney's order. With two out in the second inning he faced Wright for the first time. Whaling away at Wright's fast one, he caught it with sufficient authority to reach the cheap seats, and Minnesota took a 1-0 lead. Suffice it to say that, although the Halos put Blyleven in two or three serious scoring jams and raked his offerings for 10 hits, the Twins and Blyleven survived it all and came away with a taut 1-0 victory. The pitchers' readings now looked like this: Blyleven, 16 and 15; Wright, 16 and 17.

Bert Blyleven found the 1-0 oasis once again five seasons later, when in three 1976 successive starts he was involved in two winners and a 1-0 heartbreaker. In this 1-0 triad he beat Oakland on June 21 for his 100th career victory, a milestone with the added gloss of a one-hitter (there were four in his career), and then added another on June 26, defeating the White Sox, the victories coming in Texas Ranger togs. Six days later his July 2 start was not so satisfying. This time he ran up against Chicago White Sox pitcher Bart Johnson and once again gave up 10 hits in a route-going performance. In this one it was a first-inning run that spelled doom, the Rangers all but helpless at the hands of the Pale Hose right-hander, managing but five harmless singles in the game. In his next start against Detroit he went through seven scoreless frames before yielding a Tiger marker in the eighth inning of a 2-1 loss. Thus, in the span of two 10-inning wins, and losses to Chicago and Detroit by one run each, he had surrendered a paltry two runs in 36 innings of work.

Bert Blyleven threw his intimidating curveballs for 22 seasons in the majors, all but three of them in the American League. Those three seasons were spent as a Pittsburgh Pirate. During one of them, his first, he was paired with Skip Lockwood of the Mets in an early season game on April 26, 1978, finally prevailing in a 1-0 white-knuckler. The game was Blyleven's second start as a National Leaguer. He had lost on his first try in St. Louis.

Giving up six scattered safeties along the way in an 11-inning ball game, he was definitely on the mark, allowing but one extra base blow, a double by Lee Mazzilli, and whiffing eight. Playing in New York, the Pirates led off the 11th inning, sending Eddie Ott, Blyleven's battery mate, to the plate to get things started. Stout and powerful Eddie wasted no time in getting things started—as well as ended—by lofting a four-bagger into Shea Stadium's seats, giving the Pirates a 1-0 lead. Blyleaven took care of business in the Mets' 11th, inducing three grounders after an inning-opening walk to Bruce Boisclair. His pitching and Ott's game-winning blow provided the big Dutchman with his first NL victory.

Blyleven's last 1-0 victory in a renaissance year with California during the 1989 season occurred in a game against Toronto's Jimmy Key. Wally Joyner, the Angels first baseman that evening at the Skydome, gave Blyleven the run he needed for a one-swat victory. It was one of his five shutouts in a fine 17 and 5 season, just a couple seasons removed from the end of his 22-year career. Though it took a little time in coming, the Blyleven career wound up where it belonged—in the hallowed halls of Cooperstown.

Christy Mathewson: Big Six

This gentleman was the baseball idol of the early 1900s and remains one of the game's storied ball players. He was also a pretty fair country pitcher. Our concern with him here is the 1-0 ball games he pitched, though it takes some self-discipline to resist going on and on about his many victories and Hall of Fame exploits. On then, to his 14 and 11, 1-0 record.

Table 5.5.   Christy Mathewson's 1-0 Games

1-0 Wins			1-0 Losses		
Date	Team	Opposing Pitcher	Date	Team	Opposing Pitcher
05/24/1901	Cinc	Phillips	05/28/1901	StL	J. Powell
07/08/1902	Chi	Rhoads	07/05/1902	StL	O'Neill
06/13/1905	Chi	M. Brown	06/18/1903	Chi	Weimer
08/10/1905	Chi	Reulbach	07/29/1904	Brk	Cronin
07/05/1906	Bos	Pfeffer	09/23/1905	Chi	Lundgren
04/22/1907	Bos	Flaherty	09/14/1906	Brk	McIntire
05/03/1907	Brk	Stricklett	09/03/1907	Brk	Pastorius
07/20/1907	Chi	Lundgren	09/09/1907	Bos	I. Young
08/27/1907	StL	Karger	07/17/1908	Chi	M. Brown
05/29/1908	Brk	Rucker	05/27/1913	Bos	Tyler
07/29/1908	StL	Sallee	09/19/1913	StL	Sallee
09/08/1908	Brk	Rucker			
08/21/1909	Cinc	Rowan			
08/26/1913	Cinc	G. Johnson			

Christy Mathewson, the idol of young and aspiring ballplayers in baseball's earlier days.

Among Christy Mathewson's 79 career shutouts there were 14 1-0 victories. One of the foundation pieces of John McGraw's mighty New York Giants, Mathewson contributed those shutouts and 1-0 victories during a New York hegemony in the National League in the first part of the 20th century. In an era known for its small-ball style of play, games were regularly won by a single run in low-scoring contests featuring bunts, hit-and-run plays, "hit-'em-where-they-ain't" place hitters, and base stealing. That was the world of baseball that Christy Mathewson lived in, and he knew better than anyone else that it was invariably up to him to come out of those 2-1 and 3-2 skirmishes on top. Why? Simply because a league lead or a contending position was usually on the line when

McGraw gave him the ball. Others helped, of course: Iron Man Joe McGin-nity, Red Ames, and Rube Marquard came along through the years. But it was Mathewson who was the bell cow. McGraw's teams, as well as McGraw himself, looked to Big Six right on down to the day he left in 1916 to finish his career with the Cincinnati Reds. And he was most assuredly up to the pressure. No, he didn't win every time out, but he did win enough in regular season play—373 times—and in World Series competition to establish not only himself but his Giants as "the team to beat."

Some numbers may be helpful here. In 1-0, 0-1, 2-0, 0-2, 2-1, and 1-2 games, Mathewson's log totaled some 82 decisions (there were also five 1-1 ties), 15 of them coming in 1907 alone. Forty-four times in his career he brought the Giants home a winner with scores of 1-0 (14), 2-0 (12), or 2-1 (18). You might well imagine the number of squeeze bunts, backhanded stabs, clutch strikeouts, and plays at the plate that were part of the quickened pulse beat of those games.

Mathewson, nicknamed Big Six after New York City's most famous fire engine, usually put out the big and dangerous fires. He was introduced to 1-0 games very early on in his career. In two consecutive 1901 starts he was exposed to winning and to losing these white-knucklers. On May 24, the 21-year-old Mathewson edged Cincinnati's William "Whoa Bill" Phillips, and his 1901 record at that point was 8 and 0, including four one-run victories. Then, just four days later, St. Louis' Jack Powell splashed some cold water on the young phenom's success with a 1-0 loss after his first career 1-0 victory. There would be 10 more of those kinds of losses before his career was over, but there would also be 14 of the W variety, enough for a fourth place spot on the all-time list.

During the early 1900s the team that bedeviled and hounded the Giants most was Frank Selee's Cubs. During their annual 22-game schedule, these two clubs battled each other as though every game would depend on every pitch, base hit, and stolen base. They baited one another mercilessly. And they played championship baseball.

Over his 16-season career Mathewson appeared against the hated rivals 78 times, about four to five times a season. His record was 39 and 39 with two ties, showing just how difficult the Cubs were. Against no other National League rival was Mathewson's competition as difficult. The oddsmakers were at 50-50 on most days the Cubs and Giants met. During that time there were six 1-0 games, and those too resulted in an even 3-3 break. Among those six, two of them showcased always crucial and always magnificent duels with Mordecai Brown, the Cubs' three-fingered wonder. What was the result? One and one! However, in one of those two conflicts the great Mathewson threw the book—and a no-hitter—at the Cubs and their ace, Brown, also referred to often as Miner. The game occurred at the Cubs' old West Side Park on June 13, 1905. The two staff aces attracted better than 9,000 for this game and for those who appreciated "inside baseball," which was a term coined to capture the very essence of the many low-scoring games of the era, this one was an epitome of sorts. Brown gave up five scattered hits, two walks, and was called for a balk, holding the scrappy Giants scoreless through eight innings. On this occasion Mathewson was better. He allowed nary a hit and walked none. He would have entered a perfect game into the record book had it not been for two Giant errors. His pitching on this day was about as close to perfection as he would ever get. As wondrous as his pitching was that day, he had yet to win the ball game, but finally, in the top of the ninth, the Giants pushed across the run he needed. When that happened, Cubs fans began heading for the exits. They knew the young sensation would find a way to shut down their Bruins on this occasion. He did, and without a hit. The box score appears in table 5.6.

1916 was the last year of Christy Mathewson's awesome career. It was a year divided between New York and Cincinnati, but baseball fans will recall that John McGraw provided for Mathewson during his last days as a starting pitcher by trading him to Cincinnati, where, by agreement between the two clubs, he became the Reds' manager. During the early part of the 1916 season Mathewson had a hand in New York's astonishing 17-game winning streak, made more significant by the fact that it was achieved on the road. On May 29 Mathewson took the hill on the heels of New York's 16th straight. That afternoon he added number 17 to the victory skein, a well-pitched 3-0 shutout over Dick Rudolph

Table 5.6.   New York (NL) vs. Chicago (NL), June 13, 1905

New York (NL)	R	H	PO	A	Chicago (NL)	R	H	PO	A
Donlin, cf	0	1	3	0	Slagle, cf	0	0	3	0
Browne, rf	0	1	1	1	Schulte, lf	0	0	1	0
McGann, 1b	1	1	14	0	Maloney, rf	0	0	5	0
Mertes, lf	0	1	3	0	Chance, 1b	0	0	8	0
Dahlen, ss	0	1	2	3	Tinker, ss	0	0	3	4
Devlin, 3b	0	0	0	1	Evers, 2b	0	0	2	2
Gilbert, 2b	0	0	1	5	Casey, 2b	0	0	1	2
Bowerman, c	0	0	3	0	Kling, c	0	0	4	2
Mathewson (WP)	0	0	0	4	Brown (LP)	0	0	0	0
Totals	**1**	**5**	**27**	**14**	**Totals**	**0**	**0**	**27**	**10**

DP: Browne and McGann.
SB: Schulte, Dahlen.
LOB: Chicago 1; New York 4.
Game time: 1 hour, 25 minutes.
Umpires: Bausewine, Emsley.
Attendance: 9,000.

New York	000	000	001	1-5-2
Chicago	000	000	000	0-0-2

and the Boston Braves. It was the 79th and final shutout of his brilliant Hall of Fame career.

There was, nonetheless, some unfinished business. Mathewson appeared only once as a player for Cincinnati's Red Legs. That appearance came in a specially arranged match-up (some called it contrived, rather than arranged) between himself and Mordecai Brown. The much ballyhooed game wound up with a final score of 10-8, the Mathewsons over the Browns. I'm sure that if there had been a rematch the score might have been something like 15 to 11, with Brown winning the game. After all, wasn't that the very nature of Mathewson and Brown ball games? But it did end a magnificent career on a winning note for Christy Mathewson.

Dean Chance: Career Year Extraordinaire

When a high school hurler wins 51 of the 52 games he pitches, throws 17 no-hitters, and leads his team to a state baseball championship, it's not only noticed—it's bound to bring a major league visit. The young man with a blazing heater who did all these things at West Salem Northwestern High in Ohio was Dean Chance. It didn't take very long before Baltimore came calling, and Paul Richards' eyes must have lit up at the very thought of a young stud like Chance joining his pitching staff. But there was a problem. Though Dean Chance did sign with Baltimore, he never wore an Orioles uniform. He had signed at a time when the American League was ready to expand, and when it came time to fill the rosters of teams in Washington and Los Angeles the young man was plucked from the O's by the new Angels franchise.

In the chapter on 1-0 masterpieces during the regular season, Dean Chance's career in general, and his 1964 Cy Young season in particular, were reviewed in brief. Our focus in this chapter will be on two games occurring later in his career. By June of 1967 he had won 12 1-0 games, an average of two each season. Toiling for his new team, the Minnesota Twins, Chance, after a 7-2 start, came to his June 23 date with the Chicago White Sox with a very respectable 9-5 record. Then, in a night game at home, he led the Twins to a sterling 1-0 victory, fueled by Harmon Killebrew's 22nd homer of the season. The victory also brought about Joel Horlen's first defeat of the season. Horlen had been victorious eight straight times before running into the Chance buzzsaw. This well-pitched game, played before 30,000 Minnesota diehards, saw a pitcher's duel from the start. Tommy Agee's double was about all the Sox could muster, and Killebrew's one-shot run-maker was Minnesota's only respectable scoring effort. Other than that, all eyes were glued on the mound where both pitchers were spinning their net of futility around opposing (and, no doubt, frustrated) hitters. The win for Chance

Dean Chance, whose 1964 season was one of the better 20th-century individual seasons. *Brace Photo*.

raised his season record to 10 and 5 en route to a 20 and 14 record, punctuated by league-leading numbers in games started (39), complete games (18), and innings pitched (283.2).

By 1971 Dean Chance was with his fifth and final ball club, never having fully recovered from his arm injury sustained during the season in Minnesota that was marked by a too-early return to action after a holdout. During these years, 1969 and 1970, he had done what all pitchers do when the end is in sight for one reason or another. They pace themselves, often adding pitches never needed before, trying to get by, sometimes on smoke and mirrors. Anything to forestall the time when big league owners let them know their services are no longer needed.

For the 1971 season Chance had hooked up with the Tigers. He had a decent spring training and headed north with the club expecting spot assignments and, if all went well, a shot at pitching in the starting rotation. The '71 Detroit club was a solid unit that ultimately finished second behind Baltimore's AL East champions. Headed by Mickey Lolich, Joe Coleman, the other Niekro, Joe, and reliever Freddy Scherman, the pitching staff was a shade more than reliable, and with the addition of Chance might just make for an interesting season, provided his health stood up.

It was far from interesting for Dean Chance, however. In his first six games through May 17's loss to Boston by a 3-2 score, the Tigers, usually a good-hitting team, managed but six runs in his six starts. That was a recipe for a losing record, and the record came to 0 and 6. Then came his seventh start, this time against Washington's Jerry Janeski. It had the earmarks of another low-scoring loss as the Tigers managed only five hits. But they did manage to get a pair of doubles, one from Dalton Jones and another from shortstop Eddie Brinkman, to score a run. It was the only one of the game.

Chance took no chances. He took matters into his own hands, throwing flames when he had to, hitting spots, mixing pitches, all in all throwing a pretty canny ball game. Sensing a duel from yesteryear, he reached back for just enough to emerge on top in a masterful exhibition. It was his 16th and final 1-0 game, and one of his 33 career shutouts. Further, it was his last winning game in a starting role. He won only three more games for the Tigers, each in a relief role.

In a cast of characters starring in 1-0 games Dean Chance's name is probably one of the last names fans look for. But the fellow seemed to have an uncanny knack for involvement in low-scoring games. Including 2-1 and 3-2 games on the list of his engagements that tried managers' souls, the numbers just kept climbing. In the short span of nine seasons in an 11-year career he fashioned 33 shutouts and won 13 times (he won an additional three with relief help) in games that featured a minimum of scoring, that is to say, 1-0. The Chance ledger is tallied in table 5.7.

Table 5.7. Dean Chance's 1-0 Games

	1-0 Wins			1-0 Losses	
Date	Team	Opposing Pitcher	Date	Team	Opposing Pitcher
08/10/1961	Minn	Kaat	08/22/1964	Clv	Siebert
06/21/1963	Wash	Rudolph	08/12/1966	Chi	John
06/02/1964	Bos	Lamabe	06/01/1968	Chi	Wood
07/11/1964	Chi	Talbot	09/13/1969	KC	Drabowsky
07/15/1964	Det	Regan	04/18/1971	Bos	Siebert
08/05/1964	Balt	Bunker			
08/18/1964	Det	Aguirre			
09/25/1964	Minn	Kaat			
05/03/1965	Bos	Stephenson			
08/31/1965	NY	Stafford			
08/23/1966	NY	Peterson			
05/16/1967	Chi	Buzhardt			
06/23/1967	Chi	Horlen			
06/24/1968	Chi*	Priddy			
08/19/1968	NY	Bahnsen			
05/21/1971	Wash	Janeski			

Won thirteen 1-0 complete games.
Won three 1-0 games with relief help.
Lost five 1-0 games.
Total record: W16, L5.

Ed Walsh: Struttin', Standin' Still

Standing 6'2", a 200-pounder and as handsome as a movie star, Ed Walsh stood tall. His pitching, while his arm lasted, was every bit as outsized as the man himself. Between August 27, 1906, when he bested Jack Coombs of Connie Mack's Athletics 1-0, and September 19, 1912, when he won his 13th and final 1-0 game (only seven seasons, all told), he ran a reign of terror among American League hitters. Not only did he run up some implausible pitching numbers, he also played his position with more grace and effectiveness than any other hurler to this date. It was a show of shows while it lasted.

Except for Adrian "Addie" Joss, a personal friend, he beat his Hall of Fame brothers Walter Johnson and Cy Young each time he met them, scoring a perfect 3-0 record against the Big Train and pinning a loss on the venerable one, Cy Young, the only time the two ventured into 1-0 territory, on June 20, 1908. There were 21 confrontations in total between Walsh and American League teams. He won 13 of them, lost 7, and tied once with Jack Coombs in a 16-inning contest that went unresolved in a 0-0 affair. The complete record appears in table 5.8.

Table 5.8.   Ed Walsh's 1-0 Games

1-0 Wins			1-0 Losses		
Date	Team	Opposing Pitcher	Date	Team	Opposing Pitcher
08/27/1906	Phl	Coombs	09/23/1906	NY	Hogg
04/19/1907	StL	Jacobson	09/24/1908	NY	Lake
05/31/1908	Det	Willett	10/02/1908	Clv	Joss
06/20/1908	Bos	Young	05/16/1909	Phl	Coombs
09/13/1908	Clv	Berger	06/09/1910	Wash	Walker
09/18/1908	Wash	Johnson	07/29/1910	Det	Summers
06/11/1909	NY	Lake	09/13/1910	StL	Nelson
08/29/1909	Wash	Johnson			
06/06/1910	Bos	Hall			
08/11/1910	Bos	C. Smith			
08/23/1910	Wash	Johnson			
07/17/1912	Bos	O'Brien			
09/09/1912	Phl	Houck			

It was one of the Chicago sportswriters who allowed that Big Ed could "strut while standing still," so self-assured and confident did he appear, whether in White Sox togs or in one of the tailored suits from his extensive wardrobe. There were those still around, when his 1908 season seemed an impossibility, who had seen 19th-century hurlers pitch as many as 500 innings in a season, with huge won-loss records, something in the 50 and 20 range. But by the time Ed Walsh came along in 1908 and offered up some 464 innings of work, with 40 notches in the win column, folks sat up and took notice. By that time, his 1908 campaign was already extraordinary, and from today's vantage point it is absolutely incredible. All of that in his monster season makes his "struttin' while standin' still" a little more understandable. During that year alone there were six 1-0 games. He won four of them, and he went on to pitch brilliantly, with patented spitter and fastball in tow, during one of the American League's tightest pennant chases. Four teams were involved right down to the last four games of the season. One of those games, already discussed earlier in this book, came as late in the season as October 2, the famous Joss-Walsh, 1-0 game won by Cleveland's Naps behind the Joss perfecto.

During Walsh's Sox years the great Connie Mack teams, with Hall of Fame hurlers like Rube Waddell in the earlier years, Chief Bender, Eddie Plank, and Jack Coombs during the 1910's, and further accompanied by their $100,000 infield, played in some fantastic low-scoring games. Every so often they were the cause of those into-the-sunset, extra-inning games that wound up with 1-0 or 2-1 scores, or ties. One of those nail-biters was played at old Shibe Park on August 27, 1906, a day when the clouds hung low over Philadelphia. Scheduled pitching opponents were young Jack Coombs, a curveball artist, and Ed Walsh, fast becoming the ace of manager Fielder Jones' White Sox pitching corps. They were pennant bound, but not without struggles like this one.

In the fourth inning of this game leadoff hitter Ed Hahn, the Sox's nimble right fielder, got on and scored the lead run in the game, and through six innings the score stayed that way with Walsh enjoying one of his best days of the season. He allowed a single to Topsy Hartsel and that was the sum and substance of the Mackmen's offense. But as the sixth ended the clouds overhead opened up and the rains came. Unable to resume play, umpires Connolly and Evans declared a halt and the game went into the books as a six-inning White Sox victory. Ed Walsh had won his first 1-0 game.[2]

These two stalwarts met two more times. The first of these two occurred in 1909, when on May 9 in Chicago the teams played 13 innings in a Coombs 1-0 victory. The other such occurrence was an August 4, 1910, match that went 16 innings without a score, another 0-0 ball game. Accordingly, in the three games Walsh and Coombs allowed only two runs between them in 35 innings in the only tie and 1-0 games they hurled against one another. In the 16-inning marathon Coombs hurled nine consecutive hitless innings as well.

In the last of three Johnson-Walsh 1-0 encounters, played in the nation's capital on August 23, 1910, Big Ed bested the Big Train 1-0 when Sox outfielders Paul "Molly" Meloan and Patsy Dougherty blasted successive triples in the top of the sixth for the game's only run. Washington's Charlie Conway, cleanup hitter and left fielder, playing in one of the two games of his major league career, was cited for two fine catches that prevented serious damage to Washington's fortunes, but the Senators lost one of their many 1-0 games (3 of the 26 were in Walsh games) behind Sir Walter anyway.

To conclude this Ed Walsh review, here are a few capsules about his 1-0 games:

- Ed Walsh joined the White Sox in 1903 but didn't establish himself as a starter until the 1905 season. Between 1906 and 1912, a short span of seven seasons, he won 168 games, right at 24 per season.
- On April 19, 1907, Fielder Jones stole home in a White Sox win over the St. Louis Browns. He was on the front end of a double steal. In gaining the 1-0 victory, Ed Walsh tied the record for most fielding assists by a pitcher in a nine-inning game, 11.
- On June 20, 1908, Walsh dueled Cy Young at South Side Park and beat him, 1-0. Not only did he win 40 games in this unbelievable season, but he was the club leader in wins and saves, 1907, 1908, and 1911.
- On June 11, 1909, the Yankees fell victim to the Walsh spitter and the White Sox in New York, losing 1-0.
- On August 29, 1909, Walsh's two-hitter subdued the Senators in Chicago. Washington had two hits, both singles, one by Jack Lelivett and the other by Germany Schaefer.

- On June 6, 1910, Big Ed's one-hitter whipped the Red Sox. Outfielder Duffy Lewis' single was the only Boston hit. In August he struck out 15 Red Sox while putting together a streak of 35.2 consecutive scoreless innings during an eight day span from August 4 through 11.
- In his last 1-0 game, on September 19, 1912, Ed Walsh held the Athletics hitless for seven innings before yielding three hits, closing it out with his 13th career victory at the 1-0 score.

Guy White: "Doc"

From 1903 through the 1912 season, Doc White and Ed Walsh were teammates, the one-two punch of the Chicago White Sox. Though their style, careers, and successes during the American League's first years differed, they had one thing in common: each won 13 1-0 victories. Guy White, better known as Doc because of his dental degree and practice, was a deadball-era Renaissance man, a multitalented person who not only did many things but did them exceedingly well. Everything from musical composition and performance to gardening, from teaching to professional baseball management—to mention but a few of his endeavors, each of them done well and with his own flair—were part and parcel of a life devoted to good things and positive enterprise.

Our interest here, nonetheless, is in his pitching prowess, and he is not lacking in achievement in this regard, either. Fresh off the college campus, he signed a Philadelphia Phillies' contract in 1901 and went right to work, chalking up a 14-13 record. The next season he won his first shutout game, a June victory over the Chicago Cubs. It was during that season that he was engaged in his first 1-0 ball games, losing two, one to Cincinnati and the other to Hall of Fame pitcher Jack Chesbro and the Pittsburgh Pirates.

Between the 1902 and 1903 seasons, White took advantage of the warfare between the two major leagues and signed, just ahead of their truce, with the Comiskey White Sox. He spent the rest of his major league career with the South Siders, finishing up in 1913 with 189 victories, a career 2.39 ERA, and over 3,000 innings pitched. For a frail, 145-pound athlete, that's quite a work load, which topped out at 300 innings pitched during his first Chicago season in 1903. His career 1-0 record appears in table 5.9.

From among a number of exceptional shutout performances, Guy White's September 1904 Whitewash Run is probably the best remembered. This extraordinary run of consecutive scoreless innings began at South Side Park on the 12th against Cleveland's Addie Joss, a 1-0 masterpiece that opened a set of three Pale Hose victories. Four days later we find him at Sportsmans Park, St. Louis, crafting another shutout, this one against the Browns' able lefty, Ed Siever. Carrying a no-hitter into the eighth inning, White finally settled for a one-hit, 1-0 shutout. Tom Jones, who got that one hit—a triple—was thrown out on a gem

Table 5.9.   Doc White's 1-0 Games

1-0 Wins			1-0 Losses		
Date	Team	Opposing Pitcher	Date	Team	Opposing Pitcher
09/06/1903	Clv	Glendon	07/31/1902	Cinc	Poole
08/11/1904	NY (AL)	Powell	08/09/1902	Pit	Chesbro
09/12/1904	Clv	Joss	06/16/1903	NY (AL)	Griffith
09/16/1904	StL	Siever	08/23/1904	NY (AL)	Chesbro
04/17/1905	StL	Howell	07/09/1905	Det	Mullin
07/02/1905	Det	Killian	08/14/1908	Wash	Johnson
06/01/1907	Det	Siever	04/20/1910	Clv	Joss
06/26/1907	StL	Pelty	07/14/1910	Bos	Collins
07/07/1908	Wash	Burns	08/13/1910	NY (AL)	Ford
08/29/1908	NY (AL)	Chesbro	04/29/1911	StL	Hamilton
04/27/1909	StL	Waddell	08/04/1911	Wash	Johnson
05/10/1909	Wash	Johnson			
04/30/1910	Det	Summers			

Won 13, lost 11.
One 0-0 tie, one 17-inning 1-1 tie.

of an infield play that disposed of his scoring threat at the plate. Three more shutouts followed the first two 1-0 games, running his consecutive scoreless inning skein to 45, establishing an American League record that still stands, and a major league standard that was finally broken when Don Drysdale extended White's mark from 45 to 58 in 1968. Those five shutouts, plus another 40 during his career, make up the 45 that rank him at 29th in the baseball record book.

During the championship year of 1906 the crafty southpaw contributed a career-high seven shutouts in an 18-6 season, his best won-loss percentage season. One would expect a couple of those shutouts to be 1-0 masterpieces, but the closest he came was an 0-0 tie with an old nemesis, Jack Chesbro, whom he eventually got around to beating in a 1-0 game. The win came during the 1908 season in the top half of a New York double bill.

Addie Joss and Jack Chesbro weren't the only Hall of Fame hurlers he dueled. White was also matched in 1909 with Rube Waddell. In one of those baseball oddities, played at South Side Park, the Browns and White Sox met for an April 25 to 27 three-game set. The Sox took the first two by identical 1-0 scores. On April 27 Guy White and Rube Waddell went at it. The result was another 1-0 victory for the White Sox. In the three games the two teams were able to come up with only 18 hits.

And then there was Walter Johnson, who took on virtually all comers in his 20-year career. Guy White and baseball's Big Guy met three times in 1-0 engagements, Johnson prevailing twice and White once, in the midst of another of his streaks, the sequence opening up with the St. Louis game of April 27 the first in line. In White's next outing he went the route through an 11-inning ballgame, battling Walter Johnson as the two blanked their opponents through ten frames of whitewash baseball. Then, in the 11th with two out, White, a threat with a bat in his hands, singled and was subsequently driven home with a pair of one-baggers by Ed Hahn and Mike Welday.

A week later the two were paired once again, and this time they made a real day of it, completely shutting down their opposition in a 17-inning ball game that wasn't decided one way or another because it was called when darkness made it impossible to play any further. This time the score was tied at one apiece. From the eighth inning on, the slight lefty allowed one measly hit, a single, in what amounted to a 10-inning one-hitter. His assignment prior to the 17-inning tie resulted in a 4-0 blanking of the Tigers, again in Chicago. The four games combined, one with St. Louis, one with Detroit, and two with Johnson and company, added up to 45 more successive scoreless innings.

Table 5.10.   Washington vs. Chicago, August 4, 1911

Washington	AB	R	H	PO	A	Chicago (AL)	AB	R	H	PO	A
Milan, cf	4	1	1	0	0	McConnell, 2b	4	0	2	1	1
Schaefer, 1b	4	0	2	15	1	Lord, 3b	4	0	0	3	3
Elberfeld, 2b	4	0	0	1	5	Callahan, lf	4	0	0	4	0
Gessler, rf	4	0	0	0	0	McIntire, rf	4	0	1	2	0
C. Walker, lf	4	0	0	5	0	Bodie, cf	3	0	0	1	1
McBride, ss	4	0	0	2	5	Zeider, 1b	3	0	1	8	0
Conroy, 3b	4	0	1	2	4	Collins, 1b	1	0	0	3	1
Street, c	4	0	1	7	0	Tannehill, ss	3	0	1	6	6
Johnson (WP)	4	0	0	1	4	Payne, c	4	0	0	4	0
						White (LP)	4	0	0	0	2
Totals	**36**	**1**	**5**	**33**	**19**	**Totals**	**34**	**0**	**5**	**32**	**15**

E: McConnell, Tannehill.
2bh: Schaefer, Conroy, Milan.
SH: Lord, Tannehill, Schaefer, Gessner.
SB: Callahan, Zeider, Schaefer.
DP: Bodie, McConnell and Zeider; Tannehill unassisted, 2; Conroy and Schaefer; McBride, Elberfeld and Schaefer.
LOB: Washington 7; Chicago 6.
BB: Johnson 3; White 2.
K: Johnson 4; White 1.
LP: White 1.
Game time: 1 hour, 55 minutes.
Umpires: Connolly, Parker.

Washington	000	000	000	01	1-5-0
Chicago	000	000	000	00	0-5-2

Guy White didn't close out his 1-0 career record in a blaze of glory. He managed but one victory in his last six 1-0 games, losing five times by the very frustrating 1-0 score, his only win coming in that 1910–11 stretch over the Detroit Native American Ed Summers in April of the 1910 season. His last brush with a 1-0 game was his fourth pairing with Walter Johnson, who defeated him on August 4 in game 1 of a doubleheader in Chicago. Johnson's win and White's loss gave them identical 12-9 records as of the August 4 Washington victory. As though one run in 11 innings was not feature enough for this game, the fielding gems of the day, which served to keep the game in a scoreless state, were hailed as exceptional. The box score of the White-Johnson encounter is shown in table 5.10.

Cy Young: The Cyclone

When it comes to baseball numbers, Cy Young's got 'em. So one would expect that his 1-0 games would be of the same order as his 511 victories or 7,356 innings pitched, both of which lead the major league charts by a wide margin. With regard to 1-0 victories, though others exceed him, he does have one distinction: that of establishing the consecutive victory number when, between 1892 and 1903, he ran off nine consecutive victories over National and American League foes. It took until August 1, 1903, for an opponent to subdue him in one of these 1-0 contests, and that one was achieved when the Boston Red Sox were at Washington in that famed first World Series season. His opponent that day, Howard "Highball" Wilson, threw his only shutout in a 7-18 season. It was one of those days when the downtrodden rise up against the mighty ones, as Wilson achieved the only shutout of his very short career.

Should you wonder about Denton True Young's original baseball nickname (his boyhood "handle" was Dent), Reed Browning, Young's biographer, gives us this account in *Cy Young: A Baseball Life*:

> It happened innocently enough. Eager to impress his new manager and teammates, who had some doubts about the awkward-looking hayseed in his blue overalls, Dent fired some of his fast balls against a fence at Pastime Park, home grounds of the Canton (Ohio) nine. "I threw the ball so hard," he later explained, "I tore a couple of boards off the grandstand. One of the fellows said the stand looked like a cyclone struck it." The name stuck, and by late April a Canton newspaper account not only referred to Young twice as "the Cyclone" but even listed him as "Cyclone, p" in the box score. The abbreviation of "Cyclone Young" to "Cy Young" lay two years into the future.[3]

The cyclone that struck the major league record book so devastated it that its effect is still felt today, a century after many of the Young entries had been

Cy Young. His heater was the equal of Rube Waddell's, and that was mighty quick.

made. His exploits, including his 79 shutouts, of which 13 were 1-0 victories, pointed inevitably to one destination: Cooperstown. The Cyclone arrived with the second contingent of players that included Nap Lajoie, Tris Speaker, and himself in 1937. Cy Young's 1-0 record appears in table 5.11.

Cy Young's exploits in the world of 1-0 include the first perfect game pitched in the history of the American League. That this particular game was a no-hitter thrown against a strong Philadelphia Athletics batting order is probably wonder enough. After some nearly 20,000 baseball games to this date, there have been only a little more than 200 no-hitters thrown, still few enough—and rare enough—to merit a separate listing in baseball's encyclopedias. Add to that a perfect game (only 22 of those) and you get a sense of the distinction—indeed

Table 5.11. Cy Young's 1-0 Games

1-0 Wins			1-0 Losses		
Date	Team	Opposing Pitcher	Date	Team	Opposing Pitcher
05/06/1892	Balt	Healy	08/01/1903	Wash	Wilson
04/24/1894	Cinc	Parrott	09/10/1904	Phl	Plank
08/14/1894	Wash	Mercer	05/26/1905	Chi (AL)	Altrock
06/14/1895	NY (NL)	Clarke	06/20/1908	Chi (AL)	Walsh
07/16/1895	Balt	Esper	09/12/1908	NY (AL)	Manning
09/24/1900	Pitt	Waddell	09/17/1908	Clv	Joss
06/23/1903	Det	Donovan	09/07/1911	Phl	Alexander
06/28/1903	StL	Donahue			
07/01/1903	Chi (AL)	Flaherty			
05/11/1904	Det	Killian			
10/08/1904*	NY (AL)	Powell			
09/19/1905	Wash	Townsend			
09/22/1911	Pitt	Adams			

*7-inning game.
Won 13, lost 7.
Two 0-0 ties.
Two 1-1 ties.

magnitude—of his achievement on May 11, 1904 (at age 37, no less). Add still another ingredient to this marvelous afternoon, the inimitable Rube Waddell, and we come up with one of the more outstanding contests in the game's storied history. The score of that oft-told game was, by the by, 1 to 0.

It wasn't Young's only no-hitter. Though of lesser stature, the no-hitter he threw on July 25, 1890, was, for Young and those 600 in attendance, just as thrilling. It was, in fact, a send-off game, his last before signing with the Cleveland Spiders to pitch "in fast company," as the big leagues were then known. Against the McKeesport team on that day he struck out 18, but, victimized by Canton errors behind him, he gave up a run in the ninth inning. The final score was 4 to 1 and evened his 1890 record at 15 and 15. The no-hitter was a dramatic ending to his brief minor league career and within a month he was attired in Cleveland livery.

We'll encounter the Cyclone again further on when he is paired with the strangest of baseball stablemates, Virgil Trucks. A few of Cy Young's more memorable moments of 1-0 baseball follow:

• While still in the National League, Cy Young encountered Rube Waddell for the first time in1900, defeating the Hall of Fame lefty twice, initially by a 3-0 count, and Waddell's Pittsburgh team 1-0 on September 24. The two were to meet up again in the American League, where they encountered each other on September 9, 1907, this time playing to a 0-0 tie in Boston against the Athletics.

- On September 10, 1904, Cy matched pitches with Connie Mack's great left-hander Eddie Plank and was bested by him by a 1-0 score in 13 innings of superb baseball. It was one of Plank's four victories over Young in ten match-ups. In this late-season game there were no free passes issued by either pitcher.
- The Old Master defeated Babe Adams in his last season, 1911, as a Boston Rustler (soon to be, Braves) hurler, on September 22. In that game he walked none, struck out three, and spaced nine hits, one of them a single by Honus Wagner, in what was also to be his last 1-0 effort. There were only 1,208 in attendance, slightly more than twice as many as the 600 fans who were in attendance at his last minor league game 22 years earlier.

Notes

1. Henry Thomas, *Walter Johnson: Baseball's Big Train* (Lincoln: University of Nebraska Press, 2001), 139.

2. In order to get credit for a shutout victory a pitcher has to pitch nine or more innings. For this reason, the Walsh victory goes into the win column, but not as a pitcher's shutout victory.

3. Reed Browning, *Cy Young: A Baseball Life* (Boston: University of Massachusetts Press, 2000), 8.

CHAPTER 6

1-0 Marathons

Some call them doughnuts. Others call them goose eggs. A nine-inning (or more) 1-0 ball game has at least 17 of those zeroes on the scoreboard. Only once is there a numeral on the scoreboard other than a zero, and that is the number one. This book, through the many games reviewed in various settings and with a variety of heroes and games, certainly has its share of goose eggs. But they pale in number, as well as in probability, as compared with "the marathons." Here we have a shutout breed in the *rara avis* category.

When a ball game heads into extra-inning territory a variety of things *unor-dinary* begin to happen. These may include pitchers appearing as base runners or even as pinch hitters; special plays at work, for example, the squeeze bunt; specialists whose forte is chasing down fly balls or throwing a ball from the out-field like a rifle shot; and still many others. All of this and more comes into play when a ball game can be won with a single score. And each additional inning beyond the required nine heightens the drama when each pitch, each out, and each player's savvy is called into play. That's baseball drama. Doing things right at such moments is more often than not the difference between winning and losing. And losing in extra innings, if only by a single run, is no badge of honor. Indeed, there is a heavy weight that hangs on a ball club that often takes some time to dispel. One exception to that "rule" might possibly be the game played on July 2, 1963, a game that will be recognized alone by its two Hall of Fame pitchers, Juan Marichal and Warren Spahn. Another Hall of Famer in this game was Willie Mays and mention of his name probably gives away the extraordinary nature of one of the most famous One Swat homers in baseball history. It is this game that serves as a departure point for an excursus into the believe-me-if-you-dare wonderland of extra-inning marathons.

Warren Spahn and Juan Marichal: The Ol' Timer and the Young Pup

The elder statesman who is paired with the rising young star emerges from the baseball wars victorious more often than one might suspect. With youth, boundless strength, stamina, and a determination to prove oneself, one would think the youngster would win out; but he's often defeated by the wiles of the veteran. But on July 2, 1963, the young fellow *did* win out, besting one of the greatest left-handers in the game's annals in a 16-inning confrontation that wasn't over until the clock passed the midnight hour.

Sixteen innings is a long time to play ball. There are many games that last between 10 and 12 innings, and even though it seems a long time to get to the final out that winds up the game, they do go by with relative dispatch. Then come the games that require 15 or more innings to complete. Beyond 15 innings there's no room for errors or bone-headed plays. Managers pull out all kinds of strategic stops.

The City by the Bay in the golden west hosted such a thriller, including 16 innings and a walkoff homer for good measure. A meager crowd of around 16,000, at least for the first nine or ten innings, was on hand to watch this exceptional slice of baseball history take place. In the lineups were the likes of McCovey, Cepeda, Mays, Marichal, Spahn, Mathews, and Aaron, all of whom were eventually honored with Hall of Fame status. That would have made for a festive evening's entertainment. But 16 innings worth?

And so Spahn, the elder warrior (by now 42), and Marichal, the Dominican young pup at 25, went at it, splashing goose eggs on the San Francisco scoreboard. Through nine innings in a scoreless tilt, the two of them gave up but five hits, were rendered the disservice of two errors, and generated all the zeroes the scoreboard people could muster.

Three more innings went by during which Marichal and Spahn clamped down even harder, allowing only a bunt single between them. Then, in the bottom of the 13th, Ernie Bowman singled to lead off for the Giants. At last, something to work with! Manager Alvin Dark, a heady ballplayer himself during a better-than-average playing career, must have been thinking about several options here. One of them was *not* to see Bowman wasted by that magic Spahn move to first base, but sure enough, Spahn fired to first-baseman Norm Larker, who, after a run-down play, victimized Bowman. The inning produced another pair of zeroes.

In the bottom of the 14th the Giants had the old master in a spot of trouble once again. They sent leadoff hitter Harvey Kuenn to hit for the seventh time that lengthening evening, and he hit, doubling to put the Giants in a good spot for a game-ending score. That brought up the ever dangerous Willie Mays, and the two

Juan Marichal insisted that he could pitch as long as Warren Spahn did, and he did, winning their titanic 1-0 duel in 1963 on a Willie Mays homer.

managers went through the expected moves which resulted in Mays' second intentional base on balls of the game. That put runners on first and second with another
of those Giants named Willie (McCovey by name) coming up. There was to be
no playing with fire with this fellow, so Mr. Spahn treated him with kid gloves,
nibbling the corners. McCovey popped one of those straight up, and catcher Del
Crandall caught it for an out. With one away, spray hitter Felipe Alou hit one to
center that wasn't far enough away for Kuenn to venture anything risky, so the runners stayed put. Orlando Cepeda, another one of those who could ruin a pitcher's
game with one swing, shot an inning-ending grounder at shortstop Dennis Menke,
who bobbled it to load up the bases. But the ancient one then got out of the whole
mess with a flyout to end the inning. Score after 14 innings: 28 goose eggs.

After that excitement it would come as no surprise that both teams would
go down in order in the 15th. And they did.

But it all came down around Warren Spahn's shoulders when, with one out
in the 16th, Willie Mays launched a bomb that lit up what remained of the San
Francisco evening, touching off a celebration that signaled a Giant conquest by
that minimalist of victory margins, 1 to 0. Jim Kaplan recalls that amazing night:[1]

> Nearly two games worth of action took just four hours and ten min-
> utes. The fans stood and cheered—for Mays, for Marichal, for Spahn
> and for themselves. . . .
>
> Spahn's fateful screwball was the last pitch of an unforgettable
> night of baseball, even if it is one that Spahn tried forever to forget.
> "That pitch probably bothered him more than any he ever threw,"
> said his son Greg. "For years he said that if he had one pitch he'd like
> to take back, that was it."
>
> But the game cemented Spahn's greatness forever. There he was,
> the ageless marvel, astounding the fates and fans alike, matching wits
> and wisdom with the greatest young pitcher of his time. On July 2,
> 1962, Spahn and Marichal merged as mirrored pitchers, doppelhang-
> ers, future friends and authors of baseball's greatest pitching duel.
> What a pity they'll never meet again.

Ben Sheets & Co. vs. the Angels:
17 Frames in Haloland

Along about the ninth inning of this interleague game, the big news was all
about the magnificent effort Ben Sheets, Milwaukee's starter, was putting together. He had retired the first 20 batters he faced before yielding a single to
California's Vladimir Guerrero, and by the time 27 Angels had been retired
in regulation play he had thrown a one-hitter, only to be removed as the two
clubs went into extra innings. Quite an evening's work. One could hardly call

a workout like that fruitless, but it was merely a slice of the greater story that night: Milwaukee's 1-0, 17-inning victory set the record for both extra-inning interleague games and 1-0 extra-inning games in the interleague setting. Scott Podsednik's two-bagger that won the game for the Brewers got the big print and Sheets' one-hit exhibition got the what's-left comments. Not that Big Ben Sheets minded. He was, after all, a significant part of a record setter and it turned out to be his best ball game in his 12-14 2004 season.

Zeroes were the order of the evening in beautiful Anaheim, the home of the Angels. Venezuelan Kelvim Escobar wasn't all that bad, either, throwing eight goose eggs at the scoreboard before leaving the game without a decision à la Sheets. In half the innings he worked, Escobar retired the side in order and fanned 11. The two starters certainly earned their keep. But the fates decreed another kind of game, one with not merely 18 zeroes and a 1-0 outcome, much to the dismay of the 37,589 Halo faithful, but a game that was marked up as an agonizing defeat. Their rally monkeys, a very real part of baseball in the land of the Halos, seemed powerless in the face of six Milwaukee hurlers. The last of them, Danny Kolb, picked up his 16th save behind reliever Matt Kinney's third win. The order of business being what it is in these latter days, neither reliever went more than an inning, though both added numbers to the plus side of their season ledger. The evening *did* do one thing for Ben Sheets: it lowered his ERA and that, at season's end, was a very respectable 2.70.

These long ball games are not bereft of scoring opportunities. At one time or another a scoring opportunity presents itself, but some strange happenstance forces itself on the flow of the game, outs are made, sometimes astonishing even the players themselves, and the game moves on to still another inning. Those things are especially significant in scoreless ball games.

In this one, there were the usual what-ifs that haunted the Angels afterward. In several innings runners were on base with less than two outs; but a pop up here, a thrown-out base thief there, or a hard-hit ball with two outs and the runner moving, and, alas, the outs look very ordinary in the scorebook as the third out is recorded.

Garnering but four hits all evening, leaving the few runners they did have on base, and giving up the deciding run in inning number 17, the Halos wound up in the loss column and the Brewers in the victory column. That's baseball.

Phils vs. Expos:
A Nail-Biter in Canada

In this series of marathon games, another 17-inning contest begs attention, a September 21, 1981, tilt that pitted the Philadelphia Phils against the Expos at Montreal's Olympic Park. A bases-loaded ground ball by Andre Dawson with one out in the bottom of the 17th gave the Expos the run they needed to win in a game that marked the strikeout, by the legendary lefty Steve Carlton, that broke Bob Gibson's National League record with number 3,118. Neither Carlton, who hurled the first 10 frames, nor Ray Burris, the Montreal starter, were around at the end of the game. Bryn Smith, Phillie reliever, was credited with the 1-0 victory. Dawson's hard shot at Mike Schmidt, the Phils' Hall of Fame third-sacker, was converted into a play at the plate that was very close but ruled in favor of Expo base runner Rodney Scott. That call won it for the folks across the border.

Five stars with Cooperstown plaques appeared in this game: Mike Schmidt, Steve Carlton, and Ryne Sandberg of the Phils, and Andre Dawson and catcher Gary Carter of the Expos. There are those who feel that Pete Rose and Tim Raines, then with Montreal, ought to be in the Hall as well. Time will tell.

Carl Hubbell vs. the Cards: Three for the Price of Two at the Polo Grounds

There was baseball aplenty for Giants' fans on July 2, 1933. On that midsummer day New Yorkers sat in on 27 innings in a doubleheader matching the Giants with the fast-moving Cardinals who had won the first two of a five-game set that had them within a couple of games of the frontrunning Giants. A doubleheader win for the Cards in this engagement would bring the New York margin to a half-game lead over St. Louis in a very tight pennant race. Though there remained a half season of play, the twin bill stood out as the matchup of the day, of no small import to either ball club.

Manager Bill Terry slated his ace to open up the proceedings, with Roy Parmelee assigned to the second of two in this early July encounter. Carl Hubbell—of screwball fame, with the pitch that, as many avowed, looked like Christy Mathewson's famed fadeaway—was on his way to an MVP season, posting an imposing 23 victories and 10 shutouts.

In the games preceding the Sunday doubleheader the Cards defeated the Giants behind Tex Carleton 3-2, then won again as Diz Dean threw a 1-0 gem at the Terrymen. That trimmed the Giant lead to one and a half games. Freddie Fitzsimmons got a game back with his 11-1 win. Two wins on Sunday would cut the lead to a half game, so the Giants had their challenge directly in front of them, as did the Redbirds.

It would be unfair to exclude the Cardinals from an A rating for this monumental twin bill. Tex Carleton, who went 16 innings in the first game without

"The Meal Ticket," Carl Hubbell.

allowing a run, and the inimitable Dizzy Dean, who worked the second game in a losing but valiant 1-0 game, provided the Cardinals with more than enough pitching.

To get directly to the point of Hubbell's 18-inning master stroke of pitching brilliance, here is a paragraph from the *New York Times*, July 3 edition, that sums things nicely: "But it was Hubbell who commanded the center of the stage.

The tall, somber left-hander rose to his greatest heights, surpassing even his brilliant no-hit classic of 1928. He pitched perfect ball in twelve of the eighteen innings yesterday, with not a man reaching first base."

The Giants won this game by virtue of a Hughie Critz base hit, a single, the lowliest of all safe blows, that scored outfielder JoJo Moore with one out. Critz is not now, nor was he during the height of his major league career, a household name. In 1933 Mel Ott or Bill Terry would have been recognized immediately as an expected hero. Not so Critz.

But the Giant second baseman did have his moments in a 12-year career. This was one of the special moments he enjoyed. It isn't often a player can drive home the winning run in an 18-inning game, and Critz did it.

Carl Hubbell's mastery on this day manifested itself in the form of 12 out-in-order innings in this 18-frame marathon. Further, in his six-hit effort, he struck out 12 and walked nary an opposing batsman. Of the six hits mentioned above only two reached the outfield, and Hubbell saw to it that no Cardinal runner reached third base. An added fillip: no one to this very day has gone 18 innings in a single 1-0 game, and the way the game is played in these modern times, it seems safe to say that it won't happen again.

King Carl, as you might expect, resides these days in Cooperstown for a number of reasons. Two of the most compelling were his 24-game winning streak over two seasons, his stellar career record, and that 18-inning gem in the summer of 1933. The latter achievement, incidentally, ranks as one of baseball's five-star, single-game achievements.

Walter Johnson and Claude "Lefty" Williams: A Capital Marathon

On May 15, 1918, the White Sox and host Washington Senators played an 18-inning game in less than three hours—2:50 to be exact. Walter Johnson was one of the pitchers. But unlike the Hubbell game just reviewed, the opposing pitcher in this elongated tilt also went the entire 18 innings. That pitcher was the stylish little southpaw Lefty Williams, who was on his way to a great career until he became enmeshed in the Black Sox scandal. On this particular day at Griffith Stadium he was master of all he surveyed—at least until an 18th-inning wild pitch proved to be his undoing in a 1-0 loss to the Johnson-led Senators. He had spaced eight hits, walked only two, and caused 22 of 51 possible outs to be retrieved as outfield fly balls, almost half.

On the other hand, Walter Johnson's forte this day seemed to be inducing grounders, 17 of them, as he kept White Sox hitters at bay. And it was a Walter

Johnson hit in the 18th that put Eddie Ainsmith in scoring position at third base, from which Ainsmith scored on the Williams wild pitch.

Claude Williams spent 1918 working in Uncle Sam's naval shipyards. He played in only 15 games with a 6-4 record. But two of his victories were shutouts, and combined with his 18-inning stint against Washington, he logged a 2.73 ERA for the season. Not bad for a part-time worker.

This 18-inning wonder put both hurlers into the record book, as they were the last pitchers *in the same game* to complete all 18 innings. That record will be around for a while, as we seem to have left the closing of baseball games to a corps of pitchers whose specialty is finishing up what others started.

The respected sabermetrician and baseball analyst Bill James would probably label the work of Hubbell, Williams, and Johnson—and many another pitcher's log in years gone by—as an abuse of human talent and pitching health. That may be open to question, but there are grounds for substantiation. Nonetheless the present change in strategy and the pitcher's workload have brought about a situation in which even a complete, nine-inning day is considered about all a pitcher can handle. The workload of 19th-century hurlers, which was modified through the years, yet significantly higher through the 1970s than it is these days, no longer exists.

Pitching gurus today shudder at the thought of an Ed Walsh, 400-plus-inning season (Walsh in 1908 pitched 464 innings). That's not about to happen any time soon. And yet, in earlier days pitchers turned in as many as 500 to 600 innings in a single season. But in the longest 1-0 game on record, played in 1968, two teams used 13 pitchers in their 24-inning game, a Houston vs. New York marathon that will be reviewed later in this chapter. In the 19th century, 13 pitchers would staff at least three teams. Today, 13 pitchers make up a single pitching staff.

Indeed, beyond wartime restrictions, things were different in 1918. The Senators put Walter Johnson to work big time. He was worth more to Washington than most of a 21st-century pitching staff all by himself. For him, the 18-inning affair with the White Sox was "just another day at the office," and he was ready soon afterward for another ball game, this one against Detroit—in which, by the by, he went the distance for a 4-0 shutout victory against Ty Cobb's Tigers.

Vida Blue & Co. vs. Rudy May & Co.: Left-Coast Scoring Woes

As we move on toward the longest of the 1-0 marathons, a pause is in order for a look at two games, the first a 19-inning, record-breaking tiff staged in 1946, and the second another 18-stanza tilt in San Francisco. The first of these games set a record for scoreless ties at the 19-inning mark and had to be replayed later in the season. So, on September 20, 1946, the same two contenders, Cincinnati's Reds and the Brooklyn Dodgers, went at it again at Ebbets Field. The second time around the teams added another four innings to the scoreless fix they found themselves in before a Dixie Walker home run spelled defeat for the Reds. Walker was also a star player in the 19-inning tie on September 11. The People's Cherce cut down Dain Clay at the plate with a ninth-inning laser, preventing a go-ahead run. But the Dodgers were unable to cut loose a tally either, so the game went on, inning after inning, until darkness was the winner, not the Reds or Dodgers. That's what caused the replay. The next time around Brooklyn's boys won it, 5 to 3.

The second of these two extra-inning contests was played at San Francisco's Pacific Bell Park, the teams laboring well into the San Francisco night before one of them, the Arizona Diamondbacks, pushed across a tally in the top of the 18th to win. The marathon took almost six hours to complete, and the write-ups following this game seemed to concern themselves as much about the time consumed and the concessions sold as the game itself. Finally, in the top of the 18th, an Erubiel Durazo two-bagger scored Steve Finley with the go-ahead run. Miguel Batista, who pitched from the 14th through the 17th frame, got the win. Ryan Vogelsong, the last of the Giants relievers, was tabbed for the loss. A person would expect a parade of pitchers in a 19-inning game played in the year 2001. There were 14 of them, seven for each ball club. Almost 40,000 had made their way through the turnstiles to see their Giants beat the Diamondbacks. Alas, that didn't happen for them. You can rest assured that only a small percentage of those 40,000 were on hand as catcher Benito Santiago flied out to end the game.

We come now to a very big event in this little triad of marathon ball games. This one consumed 20 innings before yielding a single score as the Oakland A's edged their California rivals, the Angels, 1-zip. The date of this one was July 9, 1971.

Two youngsters were at the helm of their ships. One of them, Vida Blue, 21 and midway through the best season in his entire career, contributed 11 near-faultless innings while fanning 17, walking no one, giving up seven hits, and was in utter command of the evening's entertainment. Stepping into the void left by the young southpaw's absence were Rollie Fingers, with another set of zeroes through his seven-inning outing, Bob Locker, and finally Darold Knowles, who got credit for the win. They accounted for the remainder of the game in a smothering series of relief innings.

California's pitching on this occasion was equally impressive. Rudy May soldiered through the first 12 frames, whiffing 13 before turning over the Halos' fate to the bullpen. The veteran Eddie Fisher worked the first follow-up innings and Mel Queen added another two before faltering in the bottom of the 20th, eventually absorbing the California defeat. The seven pitchers on this spectacular evening got through 100-plus outs before allowing a run. The two portsiders who charted the course for this game left behind a stiff challenge for the pitchers who followed, and by dint of their cumulative excellence all seven of them showed once again what superb pitching looks like, all tied up in a neat 20-inning bow.

Gaylord Perry and Mel Queen: 21 Innings at the Cradle of Professional Baseball

Cincinnati, hard by the banks of the Ohio, was the cradle of professionalism among baseball enthusiasts. Just a century before a September 1, 1967, clash in many, many extra innings, the descendants of the original Reds, known then as the Red Stockings, took five hours and 40 minutes before bowing to the San Francisco Giants, 1-0. To spend that much time playing 21 innings in 1867 would probably have been unheard of. Further, the two rivals would not have gone their separate ways afterward. There would have been a meal of banqueting proportions awaiting them, with conversation and a keg or two of Cincinnati beer to wash down the delicacies prepared for the players and for the Queen City's good burghers.

The conventions and conduct of leisure-time sports like base ball (19th-century spelling), played in bucolic settings at parks and open fields, were far different in those times. But it didn't take long for much of that to change and the Cincinnati ball clubs of the late 1860s were in the vanguard of the game's transformation from genteel competition among friendly rivals to more demanding, highly competitive contests played by skilled ballplayers who were paid to play—and win.

The Red Stockings of Harry Wright, the game's pioneer professional, played 18 games in 1867. They won 17. That was, principally, because of paid players, such as Harry Wright's brother George, Andy Leonard, Cal McVey, Charlie Sweasy, and others who put their signatures to professional contracts.

The Reds' lineup a century later bore few similarities to the 1867 juggernaut, but there were still nine players in it, this time with names like Pete Rose, Vada Pinson, Johnny Bench, and pitcher Melvin Douglas Queen. One hundred years later these Cincinnatians played not 18, but 162 games in places like Los Angeles and Houston. They won 87 of those engagements, while struggling through 18 extra-inning games, two of which may be classified as authentic marathons. They lost both of them, unfortunately, but Reds fans would doubtless say that their boys went down in a valiant effort and the 18-inning, 2-1 loss to the Phillies in one of them was probably due to a couple of bad calls by every fan's favorite whipping boys, the umps. For the other loss, a bitter 1-0 pill their Reds were made to swallow, there was no getting away from the fact that a bases-loaded walk was the culprit. In this instance, there was simply no escape or excuse. That loss, to San Francisco, is the one we'll explore. The September 1 San Francisco–Cincinnati game was the 135th played in 1967. The National League race was all but decided already at that early date, as the Cardinals were winging their way to the pennant. But behind the front-running Birds, the Reds were making a determined effort to bring the season to a close with second-place money in their pockets. San Francisco, at 71-64 in the standings, was in hot pursuit of the Reds, who owned a 73-62 mark at game time. There was still the last month of the season to make things happen. The four-game series between the Giants and Reds was, consequently, an important one.

For Reds fans the series started out well with a victory, as strong-armed Jim Maloney dealt the Friscos a 3-1 loss. The win positioned the Reds three games up in the race for second place. Next up came Mel Queen, whose last assignment resulted in his 12th win of the season. He would face a formidable opponent in Gaylord Perry who, several days before, had shut down the Dodgers and Don Sutton, 7-0, in a matchup that featured two future Hall-of-Famers. Perry outlasted Queen, both leaving the game in a scoreless tie, with Perry at work for 16 innings before being lifted in favor of the Giants' relief corps. Ted Abernathy relieved Queen, plastering more zeroes on the scoreboard.

The two teams battled through 13 innings on even keel, but the Giants put up the first real scoring threat an inning later when Jim Ray Hart singled to lead off the 14th. The first out came moments later when Hal Lanier forced Hart at second. Dick Groat slashed a double to left and Lanier headed for home without a pause as he was waved on. The play at the plate was a close one, but a perfectly played relay from left fielder Pete Rose to shortstop Leo Cardenas to Johnny Bench nipped Lanier at the plate. The play forestalled a Giant lead—but not for long.

Though it took another seven innings, the Giants at last put the Reds away. In the 21st inning Willie McCovey led off with a strikeout. Up came Hart once again with another single to start a San Francisco uprising. Hart motored to third on Ollie Brown's double, which was followed by an intentional pass to Hal Lanier. That loaded the sacks. Bob Lee, who came on in the 19th to pitch for the Reds, then issued the base on balls that forced in what turned out to be the winning run. Subsequently, two Giants force outs ended the inning and the game went into the bottom of the 21st. Due up were three solid hitters, fully capable of tying or winning the contest. The three were Pete Rose, Vada Pinson, and pinch hitter Bruce Edwards. All three, however, succumbed to the slants of Frisco's fine reliever, Frank Linzey, who picked up the win.

The victory was a momentum builder for the Giants, who took the next two games, winning the series three games out of four. The Giants moved on to win nine of their next 10 games and wound up salting away the second spot in the 1967 standings.

We began the story of this marathon 21-inning game with a look at Cincinnati baseball a century earlier, to the month, and its pioneering success in professional baseball. Following the 17-1 season in 1867 there came three more years of domination (by the end of the 1870 season Cincinnati had played a schedule of 74 games, winning 68 of them) before professionals throughout the eastern states organized themselves into an 11-team association in 1871, the National Association of Professional Base Ball Players (NAPPBP). It was to be expected that Cincinnati's pros would be among the entries in the new professional league. But that didn't happen. Discontent with some of the 1870 losses and a drop-off in support caused the Cincinnatians to wait until they could reorganize on more solid ground. That finally came to pass with the demise of the NAPPBP and the onset of the National League in 1876, going strong in 1967 and still stronger in a new millennium.

For professionals losing is never acceptable. It was so just as soon as the whole baseball enterprise turned professional, was so in 1967 when San Francisco won on a walk, and is still so today. Cincinnati and all the others have learned to live with that . . . and the game goes on.

Orel Hershiser and Dennis Martinez: A 21-Inning Marathon with the Dodgers and Expos

On August 23, 1989, the two geographical extremes of the National League met to do battle at Montreal's Stade Olympique. More than 20,000 Canadians turned out to see their Expos take on Orel Hershiser and the Los Angeles Dodgers. The temperature reached into the 70s (F) on a warmish day in the Canadian metropolis. Only a year before the game played on this evening, the roof of the stadium was made fully retractable, and on the occasion of the Expos-Dodgers game it was opened to a pleasant Montreal evening. Little did those in attendance at the start know that they were in for a long, long evening of baseball. So long, as a matter of fact, that they would be witness to the runner-up game in the 1-0 marathon category: a 22-inning game.

It seems that record-setting baseball events often favor the visitors. That was the case for the Dodgers on this date. In the Dodgers' 22nd Rick Dempsey, LA's veteran catcher, caught hold of a Dennis Martinez heater that wound up in the Expos seats to give the Angelinos a one-run lead. Dempsey picked on one of the very best pitchers in the short-lived history of the Expos franchise, the Hispanic they called El Presidente, to pound out only the second of two Dodger extra base hits, adding 18 singles to their hit total during the previous 21 innings. Getting good wood on that many Montreal offerings, amounting to almost a hit each inning, one would expect that it was about time for one of those safeties to go farther than singles territory. This one surely did, winding up over the left-field fence. Dempsey's home run trot, in need of practice, was not as much noticed as the single marker it put up on the board, piercing the Montreal evening with bad news and foreboding.

Sure enough, reliever John Wetteland turned back the Expos' Tim Wallach and Mike Fitzgerald, leaving a last gasp hope in the hands of Rex Hudler, who manfully poked a single through the Los Angeles defense. With so fragile a hope at stake it could hardly have been that Hudler would venture into stolen base mode, but he did have a stab at it, only to be thrown out by the Expos tormentor, Rick Dempsey. Side out—game over—Los Angeles wins in 22.

In a 22-inning game there are more than a few pitchers. These kinds of things have been known to use up entire pitching staffs save the next game's starter. In this one the Dodgers trotted out five including Wetteland, who spared still others with a six-inning stretch. The intermediaries were Howell, Pena, and Crews. Montreal sent six to the hill, including the last one, El Presidente, who usually presided over games from the other end of things with the opening frame. His fine 13-3 record prior to Mr. Dempsey's effronteries was sullied a bit, dropping his record to 13-4 in a 16-victory season.

There was a comic moment in the evening's proceedings. It was reported as follows on a website named *Wanna-Be Sports Guy*:

> During the game, the Expos' mascot, Youppi! provided comic relief. He was ejected by the umpires in the 11th inning for dancing on top of the Dodger dugout. Youppi! was allowed to return if he agreed to stay in the Expos dugout. Youppi! put on a pair of pajamas in the 13th inning and pretended to sleep on top of the Expos dugout. No wonder Youppi! was tired. The epic game lasted over six hours and ended close to 2:00 a.m.

That kind of comedy might have been welcome, but not after Dempsey's shot that was heard round the Canadian provinces. The 1-0 victory might have thrilled Californians, but it was less than sensational for the Canucks, whose time had not yet fully arrived. Even then it didn't come to Montreal but to Toronto, where the Blue Jays won the World Series in 1992.

Of the 17 extra-inning games played by the Expos in 1989, the 22-inning loss to Los Angeles had to be the most disappointing. The Expos were also in-

Table 6.1. Longest 1-0 Marathons

Date	Winner	Loser	Innings Played	Starting Pitchers
April 15, 1968	Houston (NL)	New York (NL)	24	Don Wilson, Houston Tom Seaver, New York
August 23, 1989	Los Angeles (NL)	Montreal (NL)	22	Orel Hershiser, Los Angeles Pascual Perez, Montreal
September 1, 1967	San Francisco (NL)	Cincinnati (NL)	21	Gaylord Perry, San Francisco Mel Queen, Cincinnati
July 9, 1971	Oakland (AL)	California (AL)	20	Vida Blue, Oakland Rudy May, California

volved in six 1-0 games, winning three of them for a break-even record in those games. After the loss to the Dodgers, they were eight and eight, adding one last extra-inning victory to their 1989 record, moving it to nine and eight.

Before turning to the longest 1-0 game of them all, table 6.1 lists the four longest 1-0 marathons in order of their length in innings.

Tom Seaver and Don Wilson: A Record 24 Innings at the Astrodome

Throughout the pages of this book we have been dealing with one of baseball's exceptional events. As long as the game is played, one run in a nine-inning game will be something to savor as one of the more noteworthy feats. Reporting on games such as those in this chapter, or other versions of the 1-0 classics, invariably brings a few comparisons with the rarities of the past, the record book's entries, or references to "the last time this happened."

And when one comes to those games that go on and on, extra innings mounting into the wee hours of another day, the thing becomes even more treasured because of its rarity and the many elements that went into the makeup of such a feat.

We have, in the longest 1-0 game ever played, something that commands respect even beyond the extraordinary. This game has become the great standard

"Tom Terrific" Seaver, ace of the Miracle Mets pitching corps in 1969, a Hall of Fame pitcher who won 311 games. *Brace Photo.*

bearer for 1-0 games. The only thing that will make it number two on the 1-0 list, ahead of strong challengers like the Koufax-Hendley game or the Addie Joss-Ed Walsh game would be a longer 1-0 game. Until that happens the Astrodome Affair will remain first. The Houston Astros opened the 2000 season at The Ballpark at Union Station, now Minute Maid Park, a very modern, state-of-the-art ballpark. But before Minute Maid Park, the Astrodome was home to the Houston nine. It was *more* than state of the art, capable of hosting better than 42,000 fans, and history-making as the first domed stadium to house major league baseball. The Astrodome had its share of grand moments through its 35-year history, one of which was Nolan Ryan's fifth no-hitter. But it was never more historic than on a two-day period of time in 1968, when one baseball event took two days to complete. That event was the longest 1-0 tilt in the game's history.

Clocked at six hours and six minutes, this incredible monster of a game started on April 15 and wound up on the 16th, long after most Houstonians had hit the hay. In the process it consumed 24 innings, sending home the 1,000 (or so) diehards who stayed on to the very end. Unlike the ending at the Alamo, this wearied ending had a much happier outcome. The Astros prevailed, though with a big assist from their adversaries, the New York Mets, scoring the winning marker at 1:37 a.m. on April 16, 1968.

Here are some salient issues that you might have missed about this remarkable game.

- 1968 became known as the Year of the Pitcher. So dominant was pitching throughout the 1960s, that after 1968 some significant changes were made to the mound and the strike zone. This game certainly got that special year off to a roaring start.
- The Mets played in seven shutout games in April 1968 alone. Tom Seaver, who started and went 10 innings in this marathon, had a 1-1 record at April's end and had given up but eight runs in 36.1 innings.
- The Astros, finishing last in this season (the Mets escaped the cellar by one game), won only 9 of 25 shutout games in 1968. Among the nine victories were two 1-0 games won by Don Wilson, who started for the Astros in this two-day ball game.
- The New Yorkers played in 45 shutout games in 1968. 13 of them resulted in 1-0 scores; they won seven and lost six. Tom Terrific (Seaver) won two of them, losing none. The Mets' shutout record was 24 and 21, a whopping 28 percent of their 162-game schedule, nearly three out of every 10 games they played.
- Consider the case of Mets' right-hander Jim McAndrew. In 1968 he had a less than eye-opening record of 4 and 7, but if you were to check his ERA numbers for the season (2.28), it would cause you to wonder just what was going on when he was pitching. In '68 he became the first hurler in history to lose four shutout games at the start of a major league career. Some of his games that season included July 21, lost 2-0; August 4, lost 2-0; August 10, lost 1-0; August 17, lost 1-0; August 26, won, 1-0; August 31, lost 2-0; and September 11, won 1-0.

The 1968 NL record of 1-0 and shutout (SHO) games appears in table 6.2. Numbers in bold indicate high league totals. The teams are listed in the order of their 1968 finish.

Table 6.2.   1968 National League 1-0 and Shutout Games

Team	1-0 Wins	1-0 Losses	SHO Wins	SHO Losses
St. Louis	8	5	29	15
San Francisco	6	1	19	17
Chicago	4	7	11	17
Cincinnati	0	4	15	13
Atlanta	3	3	16	18
Pittsburgh	1	6	19	23
Los Angeles	5	6	20	19
Philadelphia	5	3	12	14
New York	7	6	24	21
Houston	3	4	9	16

Before bidding this record breaker and all the other marathon 1-0 games *adieu* a word or two is in order about the Met's infielder, Al Weis, who bobbled the ball that allowed the winning run to be scored in the 24th inning. Those who recognize his name, especially in connection with this game, also know that his error on the Bob Aspromonte grounder was uncharacteristic of this usually sure-handed infielder. Weis was a 10-year man in the bigs, principally *because* of his brilliant fielding. During his time, which was divided between Chicago (AL) and New York (NL), the slender shortstop also enjoyed a few games in which his base knocks were instrumental in victories, especially for the Mets. He was one of the 1969 Miracle Mets, and on July 28 and 29 of that season he had a couple game-winning hits that beat Chicago in the tight NL race. And in the famed 1969 World Series he was a thorn in the side of the Baltimore Orioles, getting key hits and RBIs in two of their four Series victories. All of this from a good-field, no-hit infielder, no less.

Interestingly, the Mets, in ninth place, and the Astros, in 10th, brought up the rear in the 1968 pennant race. Nonetheless, their April 15 extravaganza of 24 innings of zeroes in an unprecedented exhibition of scoreless baseball hit the record books, as no other teams in baseball ever did.

Note

1. Jim Kaplan, unpublished manuscript, p. 6.

CHAPTER 7

Strange Bedfellows

If Cy Young and Virgil "Fire" Trucks have not before been mentioned in the same breath, we're going to change all that right here. The connecting link I'm suggesting is a pair of threesomes illustrative of the pitching arts. They happened a half century apart and seem to be about the only plausible connection between two very dissimilar careers and two quite dissimilar persons. Here are some features they share: They were both flamethrowers; both were, on most occasions, personable people; and both carried on their business in a most professional way that was evidenced by overall success. Beyond those generalities they were both sturdy, powerfully armed individuals who could actually throw a ball through a fence. The earlier of the two, Denton True Young, actually did. The later one, Virgil Trucks, was probably able to.

Regarding the threesomes: Cy Young was the first *and last* to pitch three consecutive 1-0 baseball games, and Virgil Trucks was the first *and last* pitcher to make it through three games in one season that had the element of a no-hitter about them.

Cy Young, 1903

One June 23, June 28, and July 1 of 1903, Cy Young downed the Tigers at Navin Field, St. Louis at old Sportsmans Park, and the White Sox at Chicago's South Side Park in three successive starts. Each time the score was 1-0. Virgil Trucks' mighty three events included three 1-0 games during the 1952 season during which he no-hit the Senators on May 15, one-hit the Senators on July 22 (a fuller explanation of this one follows), and no-hit the New York Yankees on August 25. That is the bare bones sum and substance of the two hurlers' awesome threesome that brings them together in this story of 1-0 games and 1-0 pitchers.

We'll start with Cy Young, a baseball immortal claimed by the Cleveland Spiders and the Boston Red Sox. Young's terrific triad was forged in the midst of a piping-hot pennant race that as late as July had several teams in close pursuit of the league's championship. Though the teams he finessed—Detroit, St. Louis, and Chicago—were not among those frontrunners, every game was important. Heading on to the season's midpoint, understood to be the 4th of July holiday break, Boston, at 41 and 23, four games up on Philadelphia, at 37 and 27, followed by Cleveland and New York, all saw themselves as potential pennant winners. The great divide had not yet come in this 1903 race. A thing or two should also be said about 1903 to put the race for league laurels into even sharper perspective.

Baseball historians who discuss the 1903 season usually begin by pointing out the new peace between the two leagues. For years, going back as far as 1882 at least, there had been confrontations and outright war between the National League magnates and those who challenged their hegemony. New leagues, player unions, and franchise replacements were but a few of a number of irritants that caused bitterness, disputes, and an eye-for-an-eye struggle that seethed unabated for more than a score of years. Though the game went on, it did have its distracting features that caused incessant feuding. And when the American League appeared in 1901, with the audacity to proclaim itself a major league, outright warfare began. Players jumped teams, some of them signing more than one contract, as baseball hell broke loose. By 1903 both leagues and the players with them were sufficiently frazzled as to create an atmosphere of negotiation, bargaining, and finally peace so as to start the 1903 season with a newfound respect and predisposition to get on with the *real* business, playing ball.

Cy Young was a part of that entire scenario, having signed his first professional contract back in the 1890s. He was well aware that what was going on could ruin everything for everyone unless brought under amicable control. His contract aggravations with Cleveland and St. Louis were part and parcel of the whole unruly mess of the 1890s. And when, finally, the Boston club of the American League settled with him he was ready to spend the second half of his history-making career at peace with the world of baseball and his part in it. The new Boston club in a fledgling league opened its history with a second-place finish and got better and better until, in 1903, it was a pennant winner, repeating as champs in 1904. And it was the very year that the NL's Pittsburgh owner, Barney Dreyfuss, agreed with Boston's CEOs, Somers and Killilea, to stage what has become known ever since as the World Series. There were no small consequences to the aura of peace that descended on professional baseball. Keen competition for baseball's spoils and individual performances of record-breaking stature were products—on a continuing basis—throughout the early 1900, a superstar among the league's stars.

Cy Young's trifecta of 1-0 victories around the end of June 1903 was a prime factor in Boston's July surge that helped distance itself from the rest of the AL, resulting finally in an eye-popping 14-1/2-game gap between it and the second-place Athletics. With Cy Young in the vanguard they simply blew away the rest of the league.

Cy Young's 1-0 victories were part of an 11-game winning streak between May 24 and July 29. Over a period of seven successive games he surrendered but three runs, all in one game against Clark Griffith and the Highlanders (Yankees). Here are those seven games:

- May 24 at Chicago (Flaherty), 7-0
- May 30 vs Washington (Patten), 4-0
- June 3 at New York (Griffith), 9-3
- June 13 at St. Louis (Powell), 7-0
- June 23 at Detroit (Donovan), 1-0
- June 28 at St. Louis (Donahue), 1-0

At the close of the day on June 13 the Americans (aka Pilgrims), dubbed the Red Sox in an earlier year, were just a half game ahead of the American League. On this day Cy Young and his teammates downed one of the better AL pitchers, Jack "Red" Powell, 7-0, at Boston's Huntington Avenue Grounds. The shutout was Young's third of the season, enabling the club to maintain its grip on first place, however precariously.

That game was followed by a furlough amounting to 10 days because of the death of the famed hurler's father-in-law. Afterward, manager Jimmy Collins assigned him a June 23 start in Detroit, by which time the team's first-place advantage had shriveled to a tie for the league's leadership. Though he was well rested for this engagement, the veteran hurler had his work cut out for him, facing "Wild Bill" Donovan, another of the junior circuit's fine pitchers.

Cy Young proved equal to the task, shutting down the hard-hitting Tigers, 1-0, doling out seven hits, none of them particularly threatening, while closing out another shutout. One of the fielding gems of the game was a double play that Cy initiated, fielding a difficult nubber, and then firing a bullet to shortstop Parent, giving Parent enough time to relay the ball to first for the double play. The Boston club had just enough punch that day to push a run across in the top of the eighth. Bill Donovan pitched a tough nine innings; it's just that Big Cy went him one better.

By the time Boston got to St. Louis on its road trip the AL standings showed a two-and-a-half game bulge favoring the Americans. So Young went to work in the Mound City hoping to increase the Boston lead. And that he did. This time

The 1901 American League entry, the Boston Pilgrims, were spearheaded by Cy Young (standing behind manager Jimmy Collins, seated center). Cy's favorite catcher, Lou Criger, is seated to manager Collins's right.

his 1-0 effort occurred as the first game of a doubleheader before the largest St. Louis gathering of the 1903 season to date, around 20,000. The veteran Red Donahue and Young hooked up in one of those airtight duels, neither budging an inch. Young's moment of trial came in the bottom of the ninth, when the Browns put runners on first and third, but Cy and company. settled down and retired the Browns without any further damage to win the contest. They also won the nightcap via the shutout route, ending the day three games up on the A's.

By the time the calendar had run through the month of June, Cy Young had put together three straight shutouts, the last two of the 1-0 variety, and 21 consecutive scoreless innings. He was pitching as well as he had done in his entire career and both leagues were abuzz with comments about his stellar work. Was a third straight 1-0 in the cards? The pesky White Sox, at home in their South Side Park den, were next in line to see about pouring some cold water on Cy Young's heat.

There were around 3,000 on hand to see the White Sox' young southpaw, Pat Flaherty, try to get some revenge for a 7-0 beating he took from Cy Young earlier in May, and through nine innings he was masterful in taming the Chicago offense, swift afoot with its base-to-base, single run offense. It appeared that all Flaherty would need was a single marker to take down Boston's invaders. Alas, for South Side followers, Boston got that run.

In the July 2, 1903, issue of the *Chicago Interocean* Jack Tanner explains the errorless proceedings this way:

> Cyrus Young, the grand old man of baseball, was at his best yesterday, and as a result Boston shut out the White Sox in a ten inning game by a score of 1-0.
>
> It was a perfectly played game on both sides, and the lion's share of the credit for the Bostonian's timely triumph justly belongs to the aforesaid Mr. Young.
>
> He walked out on the South Side lot smiling a smile that never faded, and cheerfully complaining of a sore arm. But before he had tossed a dozen balls over the plate Comiskey of Chicago, who is passing wise, sized up the situation in a nutshell when he said: "Old Cy is all right and so is Pat Flaherty. This is going to be a pitcher's battle, and I wouldn't be surprised if it does not prove an extra-inning affair. The team that scores the first run will have the edge, and, in my opinion, win the game."
>
> The "Old Roman" proved a true prophet. It was a heart-breaking duel between Young, the veteran, and Pat Flaherty, the young left-hander, from start to finish, and in the final inning it was Young's scratch two-bagger to left field which scored the lonely run that won the victory for the New Englanders.

It was a grand game to look at. Both teams played spectacular ball in the field and gave the rival pitchers superb support, the infield work of the visitors being simply perfect.

It was a day of grand ball playing, with Jones, Green, Holmes, and Tannehill figuring as star performers, and Ferris, LaChance, Criger and Parent carrying off first honors for Boston.

The line score of the July 1, 1903, game follows:

Boston	000	000	000	1	1-7-0
Chicago	000	000	000	0	0-6-0

2bh: Young
3bh: Criger
DP: Young, Parent and Lachance (2); Magoon, Tannehill and Isbell
SH: Young
K: Flaherty 2, Young 1
BB: Flaherty 2, Young 0
Game time: 1:50
Umpires: White and Winters

On July 23, three weeks later, Cy Young won the last game of his 11-game winning streak. The Boston team had maintained a two- to three-game edge in the standings throughout that time, and by the time Young threw his next shutout in mid-September, his seventh and final in 1903, the thin edge had exploded into a 10-game advantage. Mr. All-Time Winner had done his best work when it was needed most.

Before turning to the Virgil Trucks account in this "Strange Bedfellows" story, a comparison of some of the 1903 and 1952 figures will be helpful to establish the singularity of their numbers, as well as their superiority, as the case may be. These are listed in table 7.1.

Virgil Trucks, 1952

Gregory Wolf has penned a summary review of the Virgil Trucks baseball story that can be found through the Society for American Baseball Research (SABR). In his review he got around to the topic Virgil Trucks is best known for: his 1952 season with the Detroit Tigers. Here is that very helpful paragraph: "Trucks' 1952 season is one of the most incongruous and surprising ones imaginable. The Tigers

Table 7.1. Cy Young and Virgil Trucks Stats

	Cy Young, 1903	Virgil Trucks, 1952
1-0 wins	3	3*
1-0 losses	1	0
Season record	28-7	5-19
K	176	129
BB	37	82
IP	341.2	197.0
ERA	2.08	3.97
Career shutouts	76	33
Similar Pitcher Records	*For Young:*	*For Trucks:*
	Alexander	Reynolds
	Keefe	Bridges
	Galvin	Stieb

*On August 7, 1952, Virgil Trucks dueled Satchel Paige in a 0-0 game, eventually won by St. Louis in the 12th inning. Trucks was relieved in that game after the ninth inning. WP, Paige; LP, White; no decision, Trucks.

suffered through the worst season in franchise history. . . . Deeper research reveals that all those losses weren't his fault; the Tigers scored 0, 1, or 2 runs in 15 of his starts. Among his five wins were two no-hitters, a one-hitter, a two hitter in 7 and 2/3 innings, and a six-hitter. After his first no-hitter, Trucks remarked, "Before my arm trouble, I depended mostly on my fastball. Now I am using curves and sliders . . . but my fastball has (also) returned."

For the baseball purist Virgil Trucks, known more familiarly as Fire to baseball players and fans, achieved a more illustrious threesome than Cy Young did in 1903. His two no-hitters in one season is a record he shares with only three other no-hit pitchers or among the 250 plus no-hitters hurled in major league history, and in the larger picture among some 200,000 major league games played. And except for a leadoff single, stroked on Trucks' first pitch in the July 22 game with the Washington Senators, he might have become the only pitcher to throw three no-hitters in a single season. That the Fates had provided such a mystery-laden and inept cast as company to a shutout is worth pondering, to say nothing of no-hit games happening with a man at the helm who was on his way to an otherwise undistinguished and heartbreaking season. There is no analogy apt enough to convey the enormity enacted in Detroit and other environs in the form of some of the game's more spectacular events as they unfolded during that one 1952 season.

The first of these three occurred early in the 1952 season, when hopes, paradoxically, are still rather bright; but the inner foreboding that comes with playing on a second-tier ball club lingers in Detroit. Tigers players already knew that it would be a long trek to the end of the season, realizing that a win here

Virgil "Fire" Trucks, shown here warming up at Comiskey Park, Chicago, where he was to become a 20-game winner in 1953. *Provided personally by Virgil Trucks.*

and there would be something to savor. So they were still savoring Art Houtteman's victory over the visiting Washington Senators as they checked into Briggs Stadium for a May 15 game with the Senators. Already a fixture in last place, they had somehow managed to get away with their sixth win in 24 tries. Maybe, just maybe they could take two in a row.

Fire Trucks, who hadn't started a game since May 4, was slated to go against Bob Porterfield in this one. He was hopeful of nailing down—any way he could—his first victory of the year.

Through the first six innings the Senators were retired in order three times, while three of them, each in a different inning, became a base runner. Trucks hit both Eddie Yost and Jim Busby with errant missiles and Gil Coats reached on an error. There were no hits, and the Tigers seemed toothless themselves, putting runners on base via the free pass twice plus a George Kell single in the sixth, the game's first hit. Porterfield and Trucks kept their base runners far from threatening a score.

In the last three innings, aside from catcher Clyde Klutz's base on balls, there were no Senators cluttering the base paths, and much to even his own amazement, Mr. Trucks had set down the Senators without a hit in nine innings of a pretty fair pitching exhibition. As for the Tigers, George Kell, with a single in the sixth, Vic Wertz, with a double in the seventh, and Trucks, with a one-base shot in the eighth, put runners on base, but to no avail. Bob Porterfield had smothered any hopes Detroit's faithful (there were only 2,215 of them) might have had to see their favorites cross home plate.

On to the bottom of the ninth. George Kell grounded out and Pat Mullin lofted a lazy fly ball to Jim Busby in center field. Vic Wertz then became the only Tiger between prolonging the game and extra innings. He did neither. Big Vic hoisted a bomb into the upper deck and with one swish of his bludgeon brought victory to "The Corner." The one-swat win was, of course, only part of the story. There was this most unlikely and quite unexpected factor, a no-hit ball game, that was the other and greater part of this story.

There is more to be said about this game, and we're going to let Virgil Trucks himself do the honors. In a 2012 correspondence with the author, the old Tiger, now 95, graciously took the time to share his thoughts about his no-hitters:

> Regarding the May 15 no-no against Washington, I thought we would never get a run this day. It was quite a pitcher's battle. We didn't get a hit until the seventh inning. When we went into the ninth inning I had a no-hitter completed. In the bottom of the ninth with two outs, two strikes and two balls on Vic Wertz he hit the next pitch into the upper deck in Detroit for a home run and the no-hitter.
>
> I was so excited I jumped up to go to home plate to greet Wertz and I hit my head on the dugout (ceiling) so hard I saw stars. But I got there to greet him at home plate. And the rest of the team was there, too.

Here's what Virg had to say about his second no-hitter on August 25th at Yankee Stadium:

> This was my most memorable game. In the early part of the game, the third inning, I think, Phil Rizzuto hit a ground ball to Johnny Pesky, our shortstop. He hesitated in his throw to first and the

umpire, Bill Grieve, called him safe while the whole infield thought he was out. When the inning was over I looked at the scoreboard and it showed an error. When I went back to pitch it changed to a hit.

No one thinks of a no-hitter at that stage of the game. So the innings go on with one hit on the scoreboard. But then we [the Tigers in the dugout] heard that the other writers in the pressbox were arguing with John Drebinger [*New York Times* and Hall of Fame sportswriter], the official scorekeeper that day, that the Pesky play was an error. So in the bottom of the seventh inning Drebinger called our dugout to talk to Pesky and John said the ball was rolling around in his glove. That caused the delay to first [base].

So the call was reversed to an error. It was announced on the PA system what transpired. I still had two innings to pitch.

The eighth inning there were three routine, easy outs and in the ninth inning Mantle led off—I struck him out. Then Joe Collins popped up to the catcher. Then Hank Bauer hit a line shot to second and was out at first. HOORAY!

By the time Trucks' New York no-hitter became history, the two teams were well established in their 1952 season's direction: the Yanks of Casey Stengel were on their way to a pennant, subsequently squeaking by the Dodgers in the 1952 World Series, and the Tigers were burrowed, out of sight, in the AL basement. That had some bearing—but not much—on the meaning or significance of this game, though it is worth pointing out that sports scribe Drebinger alertly went the extra mile to determine what was probably the most crucial decision of this game, the Pesky play. And with regard to this special chapter on Cy Young and Virgil Trucks, and their threesome of exceptional feats, you might well know that the comparisons would not have been made at all.

But there remains a third part of this little trinity of events. That would have to do with the Trucks one-hitter, pitched on Tuesday evening, July 22, at Briggs Stadium against, once again, the Washington Senators. The bad news about this game was its first pitch. In the batter's box stood one of the premier leadoff hitters the game has known, a fellow who not only worked deep into the count (and as a result was often given a free pass to first base) but hit with enough consistency to command a great deal of respect. Eddie Yost was his name, and before almost 19,000 fans got settled in their seats the game was underway and Virgil Trucks was ready to deliver his first pitch to him. Before that pitch even got to home plate Trucks thought: Oh-oh—I've grooved one.[1] Eddie Yost's eyes lit up and he hopped on that pitch, sending a line drive through the Detroit infield for a Senator hit, which turned out to be their only safe blow of the evening, as Trucks then retired 27 consecutive hitters to make it a no-hitter—of sorts—and lead the Tigers to a 1-0 victory. The *New York Times* carried a Universal Press release the next day, commenting on the fastballer's work, as follows:

DETROIT, July 22 (UP), Virgil Trucks, who tossed a no-hitter against Washington on May 15, stopped the Senators with one hit tonight as Detroit squeezed out a 1-0 victory before 18,706 fans at Briggs Stadium. . . .

It was only the fourth victory of the season for the 33-year-old right-hander, against eleven losses, but it was his third brilliant performance of the season. One other victory was a two-hitter against Philadelphia, in which Billy Hitchcock collected the first base hit in the seventh inning.

The only offensive fireworks of the evening were ignited in the bottom half of the first evening when Walt Dropo, hitting safely in his 11th straight game (he would get another safety during his next game), singled home Johnny Groth, who led off the Tigers' inning with a walk. That little "scoring spree" gave way to a pitcher's duel between Washington's Walt Masterson, who allowed only two hits after the first inning, and the maestro of the evening, Virgil Trucks, who none. The line score of this game follows.

Washington	000	000	000	0-1-1
Detroit	100	000	00x	1-4-0

WP, Trucks; LP, Masterson

As if that were not enough of the Trucks 1-0 saga in 1952, there remains one other game to report on, the 12-inning, 1-0 loss suffered by Trucks, this time at the hands of his friend Satch Paige. The game was played on August 6 in St. Louis and featured a Trucks six-hitter in nine innings of the 12-inning affair. Trucks was lifted for pinch hitter Juhnny Pesky and replaced by reliever Hal White, who surrendered the game's only run in the bottom of the 12th. Paige went the distance, the only time in his belated major league career that he pitched a complete, extra-inning game. Trucks's 1952 victory record is summarized in table 7.2.

Table 7.2. Virgil Trucks's 1952 Victory Record

Date	Opponent	Score	Hits	K	BB
May 15	Washington	1-0	0	7	1
May 21	Philadelphia	5-1	2	5	4
June 24	Boston	7-1	6	7	4
July 22	Washington	1-0	1	10	3
August 25	New York (AL)	1-0	0	8	1

Note

1. From a letter sent by Trucks to the author, February 23, 2012.

CHAPTER 8

In These Latter Days

For today's average fan, the 1-0 game still has its fascination. In its own way it commands attention, just as other kinds of games, like the 15-12 game or the 20-0 game or the pursuit of perfection with its nine innings, no hits, no runs, no errors, no base runners. We may prioritize the list of the kind of games we like best differently, but each list will probably have the 1-0 game in it.

During the span of years between 2006 and 2010 there have been refinements in the way pitchers have been handled, the roles they have played, the kinds of pitches thrown, and their training regimens. All these and more have been a part of the diminishment of the power game with its long home runs, big scores, and bloated hitting statistics. The so-called steroid days of the 1985–2005 era are behind us, it seems. There have, so far, been no significant rule changes like those after the Year of the Pitcher in 1968, which shriveled up the strike zone and altered the height of the pitcher's mound. Consequently, the game has evolved according to its own good pace and pleasure. Precision pitching has momentarily taken command, and the number of scoreless games, no-hit games, shutouts, and 1-0 games has risen.

I have often felt that there have been too many interpretations, too much conjecture, too many Bill Jameses and perhaps too many numbers with respect to discussing and analyzing what goes on in a baseball game. But that is an established, entrenched, if you will, part of baseball. And it's not all bad. Numbers do tell stories and do help establish standards, and to that end we follow up with a few tables of numbers that illustrate some of the 2006-2010 achievements.

Table 8.1 lists the 1-0 games for each of the 30 major league teams for the years 2006–2010. They are listed in alphabetical order. Boldface numbers indicate "mosts."

Baseball conversations lately don't get too far without the Year of the Pitcher cropping up. With 1968 as a comparison point, and pitching greats

Table 8.1.   1-0 Games, 2006–2010

Team (AL)	2006	2007	2008	2009	2010	Total
Anaheim	12	9	10	13	9	53
Baltimore	9	9	4	3	7	32
Boston	6	13	16	11	9	55
Chicago	11	9	10	11	11	52
Cleveland	13	9	13	6	4	45
Detroit	16	9	2	9	5	41
Kansas City	5	6	8	9	3	31
Minnesota	6	8	10	7	13	44
New York	8	5	11	8	8	40
Oakland	11	9	7	10	17	54
Seattle	6	12	4	10	10	42
Tampa Bay	7	2	12	5	12	38
Texas	8	6	8	11	8	41
Toronto	6	9	13	10	11	49
Total						**378**

Team (NL)	2006	2007	2008	2009	2010	Total
Atlanta	6	6	7	10	9	38
Arizona	9	12	9	12	3	45
Chicago	7	10	8	8	14	45
Cincinnati	10	7	6	12	9	44
Colorado	8	7	8	7	12	42
Florida	6	4	8	5	17	40
Houston	12	6	13	13	10	54
Los Angeles	10	6	11	9	16	52
Milwaukee	8	6	10	8	7	39
New York	12	10	12	12	19	65
Philadelphia	6	5	11	9	21	52
Pittsburgh	10	5	7	7	6	35
St. Louis	9	8	7	11	16	51
San Diego	11	20	6	9	20	66
San Francisco	9	10	12	18	17	66
Washington	3	6	8	3	5	25
Total						**495**

from that year as discussion pivot points, you just knew that something special was afoot in 2010. Before that season was half over special articles appeared touting the domination of not one or two but many pitchers. The bombast of seasons past faded into the mists, with low-scoring games or even no-scoring games the hot topic. New names appeared in sports headlines, and those names often belonged to pitchers who had just thrown the latest 1-0 or no-hit or low-scoring game.

Table 8.1 gives some indication as to the high numbers of 1-0 games. In 2010 alone there were 87 1-0 games in the National League and 157 in the American League. That adds up to a total of 244, and this says nothing about the greater shutout total. It's indicative of the rise in domination and prominence of major league pitching.

Table 8.2 examines some of the 1968 and 2010 numbers beside one another. Keep in mind that in 1968 there were 20 ML teams and in 2010, 30. We're admittedly nearing apples and oranges territory in this comparison table. Nonetheless there are several sets of numbers that warrant a closer look. Tossing complete games in big numbers, such as the numbers of the deadball era convey, or in other eras or years, is usually the sign of dominating pitchers. Without pushing that general truth farther than it will hold up, we note a significant difference between the 1968 and 2010 numbers. The difference in the way pitchers were used in 1968 and 2010 readily explains the numbers involved. In 1968 pitchers were left, as often as possible, to finish what they started. In 2010 specialists were hurried into ball games when situations or pitch counts warranted it or "fresh arms" were needed. Thus, Bob Gibson, in 1968, completed 28 of his 38 starts. Roy Halladay, the Phillies' fine pitcher, completed 9 of his 33 starts in 2010—the NL high for the season. Barring anything unfortunate between now and his retirement, Halladay will wind up in the same place as Gibson: Cooperstown. The comparative numbers just don't hold up simply because the strategy and style of using pitchers in 2010 was different than it was in 1968. To make the statistics more comparable one would be cautioned to use numbers within eras rather than between them. Consequently, spikes in numbers within an era are more significant and deserve closer scrutiny.

Table 8.2. 1968 and 2010 Stats

	1968	2010
1-0 games (AL and NL)	155	244
Average/team (AL and NL)	7.75	8.13
Shutouts (AL and NL)	339	329
Complete games (NL)	471	72
Complete games (AL)	426	93
Strikeouts (NL)	9,501	19,092
Strikeouts (AL)	9,639	15,214
Home runs (NL)	891	2,404
Home runs (AL)	1,104	2,209
ERA (NL)	2.99	4.02
ERA (AL)	2.98	4.14

There is yet another variable: defense. At the turn of the millennial century major league teams once again began emphasizing the defensive part of the game. The "glove man," a catchall term that characterizes a player's ability to get to a batted ball, handle it cleanly, and throw it to the right base, has reappeared to become the pitcher's number one resource in limiting offensive output. Increasingly, major league teams have been on the hunt for high-quality defensive players and have been unafraid to put them out there alongside the sluggers and contact hitters. Flashback names like Ozzie Smith, Al Gionfriddo, Al Kaline, Keith Hernandez, and Brooks Robinson are the kind of infielders and outfielders that conjure the defensive wizardry sought during this era. It's made a difference, a big difference, in a pitcher's potential for throwing the low-hit, low-scoring games this era has featured. Shutouts, 1-0 games, and no-hitters have become part of the fan's expectation. That would have been fantasy during the 1995–2005 era.

Were 1968 and 2010 Years of the Pitcher? Indeed, they were, culminating a trend that saw a steady rise in pitching domination within a ten-year period of time, or an era. There may be a plateau of years before another trend suggests that something extraordinary, or at least out of the ordinary, is under way.

Table 8.3 highlights the difference that great pitching and defensive play made during the decade of the 2000s. The table was adapted from the original by Tom Verducci, *Sports Illustrated*'s able baseball man, for their May 10, 2011, issue. You will undoubtedly note the rise from 2000 to 2010 in low-scoring games, documenting the upswing in outstanding pitching and defense. You will also see the decline in high-scoring baseball games.

We've thus far had a detailed and somewhat lengthy review of recent history, numbers, strategy review, and background information. That's the grunt work. Now comes the fun part: a look at some of the more interesting 1-0 games during the 2006–2010 era. Regular season and championship games showcasing the 30 major league franchises are included in this sampling of 1-0 excellence selected for your perusal.

Table 8.3.   The Rise of Pitching and Defense, 2000–2010

Year	No. of Games with No Score	No. of Games with 10 or More Runs
2010	329	330
2008	271	386
2006	260	415
2004	251	433
2002	275	384
2000	204	571

New York (NL) vs. Chicago (NL), July 26, 2006

Chicago	000	000	000	0	0-4-0
New York	000	000	000	1	1-7-0

WP, John Maine; LP, Mark Prior

In many respects the "Chicago Heat" pitchers Kerry Wood and Mark Prior were alike, particularly in their heaters and their willingness to exceed accepted work loads. In the early 2000s they regularly exceeded what is deemed to be acceptable pitch counts. And they paid the price. Both of them wound up on the disabled list (DL) and struggled to get back to their blow-'em-away starts. Prior's start on July 26, 2006, came just a few days after he was once again recalled for duty from the DL. He started for the Cubs against the Mets' John Maine and had a pretty fair showing, with five-plus innings of no-hit ball to his credit. Holding the Mets without a run, Prior got the Cubs to the halfway point in this game at even keel, but it was as far as he could go according to manager Dusty Baker. The first of five relievers took over, holding the Mets at bay until the bottom of the tenth, when a bases-loaded single by veteran Jose Valentin drove home the winning run with two away.

The Prior-Wood situation recalls an article by Bill James for a book written by himself and Rob Neyer, *The Neyer/James Guide to Pitchers.*[1]

It's a discussion about overextending the stamina and capabilities of pitchers entitled "Abuse and Durability." There are some keen and perceptive concepts to grapple with in this chapter, well worth reading for the insights presented. The number of Priors in baseball's world is numerous, far too numerous. However, the games go on, as the New York-Cub tilt illustrates.

Cleveland vs. Seattle, July 28, 2006

Seattle	000	000	000	0-5-1
Cleveland	000	001	00x	1-6-1

WP, Jeremy Sowers; LP, Felix Hernandez

Jeremy Sowers was one of those thousands of young major leaguers who had a day or two in the sun and subsequently faded away, out of the limelight and into public life in some other capacity. At first blush that looks like a sad, if not cruel beginning for a young man. But these things have a way of sorting themselves out and perhaps later than sooner, the wannabes of the baseball world find their way. But not many of them get their first shot in the bigs as full-blown heroes of the day. It happens on occasion, of course, and in the case of southpaw Sowers, that first big splash had Cleveland fans wondering if perhaps there was another Herb Score or Sam McDowell on the way. There was, alas, no McDowell or Score incarnation, but for a couple of games Jeremy Sowers looked every bit the kind of major league stuff that would be around for a while. Called up from the Buffalo training grounds in midseason of 2006, the young lad found a groove shortly after his arrival and threw an impressive shutout on June 20, then followed up with another shutout his next time out, this one over the Seattle Mariners at The Jake, as Clevelanders call their home park, Jacobs Field.

In this Friday evening clash he was paired with the young Seattle phenom Felix Hernandez, who would become a Cy Young Award winner in 2010. On this night, however, Sowers had the better of it, shutting down Ichiro Suzuki and company in a complete-game five-hitter that netted a tight, 1-0 victory. As interesting as Sowers's first innings of play with the Indians were, Shin-Soo Choo's were just as exciting, for the South Korean, who had donned an Indians' uniform just a couple days beforehand after a trade had brought him to Cleveland, picked on a Hernandez offering in the sixth inning and clubbed it for a home run that provided Sowers and his new Tribe teammates with a victory. It was Choo's first hit as an Indian, his first major league home run, and the first time he had won a game with a homer. When Choo, formerly a southpaw pitcher but converted to an outfielder, returned to his position he received a standing O and a number of signs greeted him, one of which pictured a locomotive and said, "Choo-Choo." For a couple of beginners like Sowers and Choo it was quite an evening.

When a game comes down to a one-run margin, especially a low-scoring game, there is usually a defensive play or two that makes it possible. Such a play came right off the bat in the opening inning when the human hit machine, Ichiro, singled and advanced to second on a Jose Lopez groundout. The play of the game then followed as left fielder Todd Hollandsworth threw out the fleet-footed Ichiro trying to score from second on Adrian Beltre's single.

Jeremy Sowers extended his scoreless-innings streak four more innings in his next start at Boston to max out at 22 consecutive scoreless innings. It was the high point of a short career that ended, at least for him, all too soon. But there was that well-pitched 1-0 game, and as the lyrics of the old song averred, "They Can't Take That Away from Me!"

Boston vs. Oakland, June 7, 2007

Boston	100	000	000	1-4-1
Oakland	000	000	000	0-1-1

WP, Curt Schilling; LP, Joe Blanton

Between 2006 and 2010, the five-year era under scrutiny in this chapter, the Boston Red Sox won 11 1-0 games and lost four. The most impressive of those 11 victories was Curt Schilling's victory at Oakland's McAfee Stadium with 31,211 Oakland rooters on hand. Schilling brought his best game to the park on this day, allowing one hit, a sharp single to right by Shannon Stewart with two out in the ninth. The burly Boston right-hander had come close to a no-hitter before, but never this close. The hit came on a pitch Schilling called himself after shaking off Jason Varitek, Boston's catcher. This is what he said about it: "We get two outs, and I was sure, and I had a plan, and I shook Tek off. And I get a big 'What if?' for the rest of my life!" Big Papi, Boston's David Ortiz, put the one run Schilling needed on the board with a four-ply shot in the first inning. That's not much of a cushion, but the way Schilling was hurling on this sunny day in Oakland, one run was more than enough.

Curt Schilling threw 20 shutouts during his career, but he had to wait to the last year of his illustrious career to throw this 1-0 masterpiece. He retired in 2009.

Cincinnati vs. Cleveland, June 16, 2007

Cleveland	000	000	000	000	0-7-0
Cincinnati	000	000	000	001	1-6-0

WP, Marcus McBeth; LP, Aaron Fultz

Bragging rights for the state of Ohio were on the line at the Great American Ball Park, one of America's latter-day additions to 21st-century baseball architecture. The home town nine, the great-granddaddys of professional baseball, won an old-fashioned extra-inning struggle in interleague play with a 12th-inning run, courtesy of an Alex Gonzalez single. The game would have made baseball pioneer Harry Wright proud. Great pitching, great and sometimes sensational fielding, and equally matched ball clubs, at least on this day, were features in an afternoon of entertaining play.

Starting pitchers Harang and Sabathia couldn't have been much better, neither of them minded to give up a run. Sabathia went nine innings, doling out three scattered hits, and winning pitcher Aaron Harang, the big (6'7" and 270 solid pounds) Cincinnati right-hander, went seven stanzas, walking two and fanning 10. Both of them gave way to relief specialists, and as things turned out, Cincinnati's were a shade better, the victory going to Marcus McBeth, who logged his first big league win. Josh Hamilton turned in the play of the game on a perfect zinger to home plate that nailed pinch runner Jason Michaels in the 10th inning. Of such plays winners are made. The youngster, reliever McBeth, said this about the Hamilton throw: "You try to stay even keeled, but I'm backing up home plate when he threw that guy out, and I was shouting and pumping my fist," McBeth said. "Right man, right spot, right time." The old Red Stockings would have loved it!

Detroit vs. Minnesota, July 17, 2007

Detroit	000	001	000	1-5-0	
Minnesota	000	000	000	0-3-1	

WP, Billy Buckner; LP, Yasuhiko Yabuta

With a little help from his reliever friends, Nate Robertson put his sixth victory into the 2007 win column. En route to his victory, the 30-year-old southpaw allowed three harmless singles before giving way to Macay McBride and closer Todd Jones, who picked up his 24th save of the season. The Tigers scored in the sixth inning, benefiting from Minnesota lapses in the form of an error and a wild pitch that put Brandon Inge in scoring position. Mags Ordonez took note of that and poked a run-scoring single to left, putting the Bengals out in front 1-0. Three remaining innings of scoreless ball followed and the score remained at its 1-0 margin.

Save for that wobbly sixth inning, the Twins got an excellent game from Matt Garza, who, like Robertson, gave up three hits, walked one, and struck out three. With any offense at all the Twins might well have scored a run or two, but Tiger pitching on this day was pretty stingy. That makes for tough afternoons resulting in less-than-satisfying outcomes. That was Minnesota's fate as they fell to their 44th loss of the season.

As for the two starting hurlers, Robertson went on to a 9 and 13 season, his win over Minnesota turning out to be his best effort of the season. Matt Garza finished his pitching for the Twins at the end of the 2007 season, moving on to the Tampa Bay Rays, where, in 2010, he became one of the six no-hit pitchers of that Pitcher's Year season.

Minnesota vs. Texas, August 19, 2007

Texas	000	000	000	0-2-0	
Minnesota	010	000	00x	1-4-1	

WP, Johan Santana; LP, Kevin Millwood

During the 2007 season the Minnesota Twins played in six 1-0 games, tying Cleveland for the most in the major leagues. They began with an 11-inning squeaker on April 26 at the Metrodome against Kansas City and wound up with a brilliantly pitched game, again at the Metrodome, with their ace Johan Santana at the helm. This time Texas was the victim, garnering but two hits and going down for the KO count 17 times in eight innings, a franchise record. Santana racked up 17 of those and Joe Nathan, with his 27th save, got two more to make the final tally 19. There was only one inning in which there was no Texas whiff, and in six of their at-bats they went down in order. Next to a no-hitter, that's about as dominating as it gets. The Rangers found another Alamo on this encounter, only it was at a place named the Metrodome.

Right fielder Mike Cuddyer, a seven-year Twinkie vet, saw to it that Santana got the run he needed to win this game. He led off the second inning with a homer, and that ended the scoring for the day. Aside from that clout Kevin Millwood was pretty much in command of the Twins, pitching with Santana-like efficiency. He only surrendered four hits in his seven-inning stint and found a way to keep Minnesota away from home plate—except for that Cuddyer blast.

Three different winners and three different losers comprised the 1-0 sextet for the Twins in '07, but none of them had the stamp of authority that Johan Santana's did. On August 19, he had it.

Arizona vs. Kansas City, June 13, 2008

Kansas City	000	000	000	0	0-7-0	
Arizona	000	000	000	1	1-5-0	

WP, Billy Buckner; LP, Yasuhiko Yabuta

The major leagues began interleague scheduling in 1997. That has brought teams to major league cities who in some cases had been seen only on TV. When the Kansas City Royals journeyed to Phoenix to play at Chase Field, it was their second appearance there. In a June night game during the 2008 season, Royals ace Zack Greinke was paired with Doug Davis, and the two of them put on quite an exhibition, as each starter went seven innings without allowing a run. From the eighth inning on, both managers went to their bullpens and both teams' relievers continued pasting doughnuts on the score board. The game went into extra innings—but only one. In the bottom of the 10th first baseman Chad Tracy put the wood to a Yasuhiko Yabuta pitch that ended the game on the spot. Tracy's one swat, the blow that is every pitcher's worst nightmare, won this errorless pitching duel, tagging the loss on the Nipponese right-hander Yabuta. Tracy's comment about his walkoff dinger? "Now that I've done it, I don't think there's any better feeling in baseball than winning the game with a home run."

Anaheim vs. Los Angeles, June 28, 2008

Anaheim	000	000	000	0-5-2
Los Angeles	000	010	00x	1-0-2

WP, Chad Billingsley; LP, Jered Weaver

It's one of those improbable things: win a game without a hit. Yet it does happen. Case in point: the Dodgers' victory over the Angels at Dodger Stadium on June 28, 2008. Only the fourth time in the game's history, this no-hitter has to be encased in parentheses because it didn't go a full nine innings since the home team won the game. The combined effort was, therefore, not considered a no-hitter.

But what an effort! Jered Weaver went six innings and reliever Jose Arredondo, two. Before a packed house of 55,784, Weaver K'd six and pitched near-perfect ball during his six-inning stint. But there was one fatal glitch: Weaver's error put leadoff hitter Matt Kemp on base to start the fifth inning. Kemp then stole second base and a throwing error allowed him to move over to third base. A sacrifice fly then scored Kemp with an unearned run. It was the run that beat Weaver and the Angels. There was no angelic reprieve in this one.

The Dodgers didn't need a hit to win this game. But that was possible only because Chad Billingsley pitched a pretty fair ball game himself. It wasn't a no-no, but Billingsley throttled the Angels' attack enough to post his seventh win.

Philadelphia vs. San Diego, August 15, 2008

Philadelphia	000	000	100	1-6-0
San Diego	000	000	000	0-4-1

WP, Jamie Moyer; LP, Greg Maddux

The Phils' left fielder, Pat Burrell, homered in the seventh inning at PetCo Park to give the ballplayers from the City of Brotherly Love a 1-0 victory. But to hear Burrell talk about it, his homer played second fiddle to the match-up of elderly warriors Jamie Moyer, who got the victory, and Greg Maddux, who is on his way to the land of baseball immortals. Moyer, at 45 and with some seasons yet to go, and Maddux, at 42, mixed 'em up like youngsters, giving up eight hits between them, and frisking about as though they had just visited the fountain of youth.

Home run hitters thrive on pitching mistakes, and Burrell's four-bagger was the result of a Maddux fastball that missed its intended location. Instead, the mistake, momentarily, was right down the middle and Burrell made the kind of contact that told all who were on hand: "This one's a goner!" Those things happen, though rarely, even to Hall of Fame pitchers, and this time they cost the "Mad Professor," as he was often known, another victory.

Though the ball game went up in smoke at that moment, it shouldn't detract from what was going on in the middle of the diamond. For those who appreciate the finer points of baseball and the acumen of the pitchers who are such a huge part of the game's skills and rhythm, this pairing of elder statesmen was worth the price of two admissions. For you old timers, it was like watching an afternoon of Ted Lyons against Red Ruffing in the early 1940's.

Colorado vs. Los Angeles, September 14, 2008

Los Angeles	000	000	000	0	0-8-0
Colorado	000	000	000	1	1-6-0

WP, Manuel Corpas; LP, Hong-Chih Kuo

This game marked the first time in the 14-year history of the Colorado Rockies (to that point) that a ball game had gone scoreless through nine innings.

Greg Maddux, "The Professor," 300-game winner and control artist extraordinaire.

It was the rarest of rare treats for fans in the Mile High City, as they watched their Rockies win out in the 10th inning of an old-fashioned nail-biter. Troy Tulowitzki singled home the winning tally with a line shot down the right-field foul line, putting an end to a four-game winning streak of the Dodgers and, more importantly for Colorado, an end to their seven-game losing streak.

Everybody's old nemesis, Greg Maddux, hurled seven masterful innings for Joe Torre's Dodgers, leaving the game after seven smothering innings of goose eggs. Of his work Rockies' manager Clint Hurdle observed that going

Ageless Jamie Moyer, who was pitching shutouts in his late 40s.

through it as a player is like sitting in the dentist's chair. It looked to the Dodger skipper as though Maddux was throwing half a baseball, and he readily recognized that Maddux could do things with a baseball that were very special.

Maddux's best outing in a number of seasons was nearly matched by Colorado's Aaron Cook who, à la Maddux, toured his eight-inning hitch without giving up a run. Two relievers for each club took the game into an extra inning, the win going to the Panamanian Manny Corpas and the loss to the Taiwanese specialist Hong-Chih Kuo. The Dodgers had won the first three games of this four-game series before Tulowitzki's line drive rescued the Rockies in the 10th frame.

New York vs. Baltimore, September 20, 2008

Baltimore	000	000	000	0-6-1
New York	000	000	001	1-4-0

WP, Mariano Rivera; LP, Jim Miller

It had been over two years since the Yankees last won a 1-0 game at Yankee Stadium. This one came as the Yanks were about to close down the stadium. The next game would be the last before moving into baseball's latest state-of-the-art ballpark, due for inauguration in 2009. Consequently, the last games in the venerable park loomed important not just for the pennant race but for historical moments as well.

The 1-0 victory on September 28, their third win in four 1-0 games for the 2008 season, served as an opening salvo to the closing ceremonies of the next night, which also resulted in a victory led by the great Yankee veteran Andy Pettitte. History had been served, Yankee style!

For this clash between the Bronx Bombers and Baltimore Orioles, New York manager Joe Girardi sent the husky right-hander from Mexico, Alfredo Aceves, to the hill to do battle with Brian Burres. Both pitched exceptionally well, Aceves going six sharp innings and Burres matching the big Yankee right-hander pitch for pitch. The game finally came down to the ninth, when, in the top of that frame, Yankee managers of the past 15 seasons or so had usually called on the premier reliever the game has known, Mariano Rivera. And he did his 1-2-3 thing on a pair of pop-ups and a strikeout. A last-inning run on a single by Robinson Cano was all it took to give Rivera the victory. The sure-fire Hall-of-Famer had won the second-to-last Yankee Stadium victory, and, much to the chagrin of the rest of the league, he would be around to help open up the new stadium.

Milwaukee vs. Pittsburgh, April 29, 2009

Pittsburgh	000	000	000	0-2-0
Milwaukee	000	000	10x	1-6-1

WP, Yovani Gallardo; LP, Ian Snell

In this game's postgame interview Brewer manager Ken Macha said, "I'll be fast. Hitting? Gallardo. Pitching? Gallardo. Any questions?" That pretty well summed up a 1-0 conquest of the Pirates at Miller Park in Milwaukee. The 23-year-old Mexican right-hander had just gone eight innings, whiffing 11, walking only one Pirates hitter, and allowing only two hits. But wait. There's more. Gallardo's moon shot was his second game winner in three weeks, the first coming off San Francisco's Randy Johnson. That's pitcher vs. pitcher. In his Pittsburgh victory his homer came off Ian Snell, the Pirates' starter, breaking a scoreless tie. Then he went to work making the run stand up, pitching a scoreless eighth before giving way to reliever Carlos Villanueva, who tacked down the victory with his second save of the young season.

The two Brewers youngsters collaborated on another 1-0 victory just a month later when they took down the St. Louis Cardinals, again at Miller Park. This time the winner was Villanueva, in a 10th inning victory. A pretty impressive pair.

Philadelphia at Florida, May 28, 2010

Philadelphia	001	000	000	1-7-0
Florida	000	000	000	0-0-1

WP, Roy Halladay; LP, Josh Johnson

There are those pitchers who just get better as the years roll on. They seem to have more presence, more command, and even more stuff. Several greats, Hall-of-Famers all, come to mind: Cy Young, Herb Pennock, Carl Hubbell, and Greg Maddux, among others. Now Roy Halladay's name can be added to that exclusive and distinguished list. In his 33rd year, the man tossed the 20th perfecto in the game's lengthening history. Shutouts and 1-0 victories, especially no-hitters, are all rare and exceptional achievements. But not allowing a person to reach first base over nine innings? Well, the total number of 20 tells you something about its rarity, as well as its extraordinary nature.

This was Halladay's contribution to baseball lore at Sun Life Stadium when the Phils scored an unearned run in the third inning of a 1-0 victory over the Florida Marlins. The fact that the run was unearned takes nothing away from Josh Johnson's marvelous stint of seven innings, during which he issued but one walk and struck out six. He just chose the wrong day for a great outing. Johnson's counterpart, the aforementioned Halladay, picked that same day to be perfect, and there's no match for perfection.

In his second major league start as a Toronto Blue Jay in 1998, Roy Halladay took a no-hitter into the ninth inning against the Detroit Tigers when, with two out in the ninth frame, Tigers outfielder Bobby Higginson ruined his no-hit bid with a home run. That was a huge hurt to have to live with, but some dozen years later the times had come full circle, and on May 29, 2010, Halladay, the amiable fellow they call Doc, made up for that. Added below are a few bits of data that help dress up Doc's showcase achievement.

- The last Phils' pitcher to complete a perfect game was Senator Jim Bunning on Father's Day, 1964.
- 11 K's in this perfect game was a season high to this date for Halladay.
- Doc's pitch count topped out at 115, about 13 an inning.
- This perfect no-hitter was the Philadelphia franchises 10th no-hit game.
- Roy Halladay completed the 2010 season with only 30 bases on balls, his second Cy Young Award (the first was in 2003 as a Blue Jay), and yet another no-hitter, pitched in the National League Divisional Playoffs against Cincinnati.
- Halladay made a presentation of an appropriately engraved Swiss watch to every one of the players and support personnel in the Phils' clubhouse in appreciation for their support and assistance in his perfect game later in the season.
- Halladay's perfecto was only the sixth won on the road.
- Six perfect games, including Halladay's, have been won by a score of 1-0.
- Doc became the fifth Cy Young Award winner to throw a perfect game. The others are Catfish Hunter, Randy Johnson, David Cone, and Sandy Koufax.

St. Louis vs. Toronto, June 23, 2010

St. Louis	000	000	001	1-11-0	
Toronto	000	000	000	0-4-1	

WP, Chris Carpenter; LP, Kevin Gregg

Chris Carpenter had pitched against Toronto's Blue Jays only once before manager Tony LaRussa gave him the ball for the June 23 game at Rogers Centre. In his prior start he allowed only one hit. His effort on this June night in Canada wasn't quite as good, but splendid just the same. This time around the Blue Jays managed three hits, but were unable to dent the scoring column in their 1-0 loss. With the win Carpenter ran his record to nine wins against a single loss.

The big bats in the Cardinal lineup got their hits, but none of them were of the long-range variety nor did they come at just the right time. Albert Pujols and Randy Winn, a reserve outfielder in the lineup for this game, had four and three hits respectively, none of which brought home a Redbird run. That was left to Matt Holliday, who smacked a solid base hit to center field to bring home Winn with an eleventh hour tally to win the game.

In 1-0 ball games the loser really doesn't have a bad day. Toronto's Rickey Romero pitched well enough to win—but not against Chris Carpenter this time.

Kansas City vs. Washington, June 23, 2010

Kansas City	000	010	000	1-9-0
Washington	000	000	000	0-6-1

WP, Brian Bannister; LP, Stephen Strasburg

More than 30,000 turned out to see the Washington Nationals' young sensation, Stephen Strasburg. In his first two major league starts he stood at 2-0, having beaten Pittsburgh 5 to 2 and Cleveland 9 to 4, with 22 K's in those two games. He had fans daring to hope that Washington had another Big Train on its hands, and they had come in big numbers to see for themselves. Well, they saw plenty: six well-pitched innings, another bunch of strikeouts, nine in number, and no free passes. Visiting Kansas City did work him for nine hits, but garnered only one run. Unfortunately that run took him under, and the young phenom lost his first big-time game.

The run that beat Strasburg was manufactured by three singles, the final one by the veteran outfielder Jose Guillen. Nothing bombastic, just enough to bring home the only marker necessary to put the W behind the Royals' starter, Brian Bannister, and the L behind Strasburg's name.

The Strasburg story has yet to play out, but already there has been a record-setting start in major league ball, preceded by hype beyond all reason, however matched by his prowess, and then the heartbreak that goes with Tommy John surgery. Time will tell how well he does with rehab. One can only hope and pray that his future resembles, if only in part, that of his illustrious predecessor, Walter Johnson. That would be success and glory enough!

Tampa Bay vs. Arizona, June 25, 2010

Arizona	010	000	000	1-7-1
Tampa Bay	000	000	000	0-0-0

WP, Edwin Jackson; LP, Jeff Niemann

This interleague game was by no means perfect. The winning pitcher, Edwin Jackson, did, however, piece together a no-hit ball game. His pitcher's ledger shows that he faced 36 batsmen, nine over the perfect number of 27. There were eight free passes issued and an error behind him, but the big man from Germany (he is one of nearly 30 German-born big leaguers) came through it all with one of the six no-hitters in 2010. He registered only three perfect innings. In every other inning the Rays had men on base, and in the third, fourth, and sixth innings advanced runners as far as third only to have Jackson deny Tampa Bay either a hit, or a run. It was probably the gutsiest—and wildest—no-hitter of that or any other year.

The run the Diamondbacks needed to win this game came early and made it a one-swat affair. Adam LaRoche, the Arizona first baseman, smoked a long-distance shot, his 11th of the season, in the second inning to give Jackson a one-run lead. However shaky he might have been from that point on, Jackson had just enough power and poise to go the route, winding up with his fifth win of the season.

2010, the Year of the Pitcher, might also be called the Year of the No-Hitter. Joining Jackson that season were Ubaldo Jimenez on April 17, Dallas Braden on May 9; Roy Halladay with his perfect game on May 29; Matt Garza on July 26; and Halladay again on October 6.

Atlanta at San Francisco, October 7, 2010: 2010 NL Division Series Game 1

Atlanta	000	000	000	0-2-2
San Francisco	000	100	00x	1-5-0

WP, Tim Lincecum; LP, Derek Lowe

In Tim Lincecum the San Francisco Giants had a dominating, strikeout pitcher who let 'er rip each and every pitch. He was the heart and soul of the franchise. In fact they called him "The Franchise." So it was to be expected that manager Bruce Bochy would give the lanky right-hander the ball for game 1 of the divisional playoff sequence. Lincecum did not disappoint, going the route, striking out 14, and allowing just two hits, one of them a leadoff double by Atlanta's Omar Infante. Following the Infante two-bagger, there was a routine fly-out and then a pair of strikeouts that assured Giants' fans that their hero hadn't somehow lost it just when his mastery was needed most.

San Francisco broke through for the singleton that ultimately won the game in the fourth frame on a Cody Ross single that scored Buster Posey, who had also singled to lead off the inning. It wasn't a thunderous attack, but it turned the trick. What remained to be done was taken care of by The Franchise.

Before bringing this chapter on special 1-0 games to a close, we're going to present a listing of all the 1-0 games in championship play (see table 8.4, next page). Championship play at the major league level began with a three-game series in 1884 between New York of the American Association and Providence of the National League. Between that championship, won by the Providence Grays, and the 1905 World Series, there were, rather unbelievably, no 1-0 games. The one tilt that came closest was played in 1892 to a 0-0 tie, featuring Cy Young for Cleveland and Jack Stivetts for Boston. That game went 11 innings before it was called because of darkness.

All games in this listing have the same score, 1-0. Therefore scores are not listed. The list includes all 1-0 games in divisional and league championship series play. World Series games are listed in bold.

Note

1. Bill James and Rob Neyer, *The Neyer/James Guide to Pitchers* (New York: Simon & Schuster, 2004), 449-463.

Table 8.4.   1-0 Games in Championship Play

Date	Teams (Pitchers)
October 13, 1905, game 4	**New York NL (McGinnity), Philadelphia AL (Plank)**
October 12, 1906, game 4	**Chicago NL (M. Brown), Chicago AL (Altrock)**
September 5, 1918, game 1	**Boston AL (Ruth), Chicago NL (Vaughn)**
October 11, 1920, game 6	**Cleveland AL (Mails), Brooklyn NL (Smith)**
October 13, 1921, game 8	**New York NL (Nehf), New York AL (Hoyt)**
October 12, 1923, game 3	**New York NL (Nehf), New York AL (Jones)**
October 6, 1948, game 1	**Boston NL (Sain), Cleveland AL (Feller)**
October 5, 1949, game 1	**New York AL (Reynolds), Brooklyn NL (Newcombe)**
October 6, 1949, game 2	**Brooklyn NL (Roe), New York AL (Raschi)**
October 4, 1950, game 1	**New York AL, Philadelphia NL (Konstanty)**
October 9, 1956, game 6 (10)	**Brooklyn NL (Labine), New York AL (Turley)**
October 7, 1957, game 5	**Milwaukee NL (Burdette), New York AL (Ford)**
October 6, 1959, game 5	**Chicago AL (Shaw, WP, Donovan SV), Los Angeles NL (Koufax)**
October 16, 1962, game 7	**New York AL (Terry), San Francisco NL (Sanford)**
October 5, 1963, game 3	**Los Angeles NL (Drysdale), New York AL (Bouton)**
October 3, 1966, game 3	**Baltimore AL (Bunker), Los Angeles NL (Osteen)**
October 9, 1966, game 4	**Baltimore AL (McNally), Los Angeles NL (Drysdale)**
October 5, 1969 ALCS game 2 (11)	Baltimore AL (McNally), Minnesota AL (Boswell)
October 18, 1972, game 3	**Cincinnati NL (Billingham), Oakland AL (Carroll)**
October 8, 1974 ALCS game 3	Oakland AL (Blue), Baltimore AL (Palmer)
October 10, 1980 NLCS, game 3	Houston NL (Niekro SP, Smith, WP), Philadelphia NL (Christenson, SP: McGraw RP-LP)
October 7, 1981 NLDS, game 2 (11)	Houston NL (Niekro SP, Sambito RP-WP), Los Angeles NL (Reuss SP-ND, Stewart LP)
October 4, 1983, NLCS, game 1	Philadelphia NL (Carlton WP, Holland SV), Los Angeles NL (Reuss LP)
October 5, 1984 ALCS, game 3	Detroit AL (Wilcox WP, Hernandez SV), Kansas City AL (Leibrandt LP)
October 8, 1986 NLCS, game 1	Houston NL (Scott), New York NL (Gooden)

October 18, 1986, game 1 Boston AL (Hurst WP, Schiraldi SV), New York NL (Darling)

October 13, 1987 NLCS, game 6 St. Louis NL (Tudor WP), San Francisco NL (Dravecky LP)

October 10, 1991 NLCS, game 2 Atlanta NL (Avery WP, Pena SV), Pittsburgh NL (Smith LP)

October 14, 1991 NLCS, game 5 Pittsburgh (Smith WP, Mason SV), Atlanta NL (Glavine LP)

October 15, 1991 NLCS, game 6 (Atlanta NL (Avery WP, Pena SV); Pittsburgh NL (Drabeck LP)

October 27, 1991, game 7 (10) **Minnesota AL (Morris WP), Atlanta NL (Smoltz SP-ND, Pena LP)**

October 28, 1995, game 6 **Atlanta NL (Glavine SP-WP, Wohlers SV), Cleveland AL (Martinez SP-ND, Poole RP-LP)**

October 24, 1996, game 5 **New York AL (Pettitte WP, Wetteland SV); Atlanta NL (Smoltz LP)**

October 12, 1997, ALCS game 4 (11) Cleveland AL (Nagy SP-ND, Anderson RP, Mesa RP-WP), Baltimore AL (Mills LP)

October 15, 1999, NLCS game 3 Atlanta NL (Glavine WP, Rocker SV), New York NL (Leiter LP)

October 9, 2001, NLDS game 1 Arizona NL (Schilling WP), St. Louis NL (Morris LP)

October 10, 2001, NLDS game 2 Atlanta NL (Glavine WP, Smoltz SV), Houston NL (Mlicki LP)

October 13, 2001, ALDS game 3 New York AL (Mussina WP, Rivera SV), Oakland AL (Zito LP)

October 26, 2005, game 4 **Chicago AL (Garcia WP, Jenks SV); Houston NL (Backe SP-ND, Lidge RP-LP)**

October 7, 2010, NLDS, game 1 San Francisco NL (Lincecum WP), Atlanta NL (Lowe LP)

1-0 No-Hit Pitchers

Presented here are the pitchers who have thrown no-hit, 1-0 games through the 2010 season. Please note that perfect game pitchers have been presented in chapter 4. Of the 31 winning pitchers listed, 11 (those in bold) have been enshrined in baseball's Hall of Fame. (Bob Feller is listed twice.)

Date	Pitcher/Team	Opponent/League
August 20, 1880	**Pud Galvin**, Buffalo	Worcester (NL)
September 13, 1883	Hugh Daily, Cleveland	Philadelphia (NL)
August 29, 1885	Charles Ferguson, Cleveland	Providence (NL)
July 24, 1886	Adonis Terry, Brooklyn	St. Louis (AA)
June 13, 1905	**Christy Mathewson**, New York	Chicago (NL)
July 4, 1908	Hooks Wiltse, New York	Philadelphia (NL)
September 20, 1908	Frank Smith, Chicago	Philadelphia (AL)
April 20, 1910	**Addie Joss**, Cleveland	Chicago (AL)
May 2, 1917	Fred Toney, Cincinnati	Chicago (NL)
May 5, 1917	Ernie Koob, St. Louis	Chicago (AL)
July 1, 1920	**Walter Johnson**, Washington	Boston (AL)
April 16, 1940	**Bob Feller**, Cleveland	Chicago (AL)
May 5, 1944	Clyde Shoun, Cincinnati	Boston (NL)
April 30, 1946	**Bob Feller**, Cleveland	New York (AL)
July 12, 1951	Allie Reynolds, New York	Cleveland (AL)
May 5, 1952	Virgil Trucks, Detroit	Washington (AL)
August 25, 1952	Virgil Trucks, Detroit	New York (AL)
September 20, 1958	**Hoyt Wilhelm**, Baltimore	New York (AL)
August 18, 1960	Lew Burdette, Milwaukee	Philadelphia (NL)
April 28, 1961	**Warren Spahn**, Milwaukee	San Francisco (NL)
August 1, 1962	Bill Monbouquette, Boston	Chicago (AL)

(continued)

Date	Pitcher/Team	Opponent/League
August 26, 1962	Jack Kralick, Minnesota	Kansas City (AL)
June 15, 1963	**Juan Marichal**, San Francisco	Houston (NL)
September 17, 1968	**Gaylord Perry**, San Francisco	St. Louis (NL)
June 3, 1971	Ken Holtzman, Chicago	Cincinnati (NL)
June 1, 1975	**Nolan Ryan**, California	Baltimore (AL)
May 30, 1977	**Dennis Eckersley**, Cleveland	California (AL)
September 11, 1991	Kent Mercker (6 IP) Atlanta	San Diego (NL)
September 11, 1991	Mark Wohlers (2 IP) Atlanta	San Diego (NL)
September 11, 1991	Alejandro Pena (1 IP) Atlanta	San Diego (NL)
June 25, 1999	Jose Jimenez, St. Louis	Arizona (NL)
April 23, 2003	Kevin Millwood, Philadelphia	San Francisco (NL)
May 29, 2010	Roy Halladay, Philadelphia	Florida (NL)
June 25, 2010	Edwin Jackson, Arizona	Tampa Bay (AL)

APPENDIX B

Greatest at 1-0

This listing presents pitching greats who have amassed 10 or more career 1-0 victories. A total of 15 present Hall of Fame members, and one whose name will be added very soon, Greg Maddux, comprise this distinguished list. Highest stats are listed in bold.

Legend:

CW   Career wins
SHO   Shutout victories
1-0   Shutout wins by 1-0 score
% C   % of 1-0 wins to career wins
% SHO   % of 1-0 wins to shutout wins

Name	1-0	SHO	CW	% C	% SHO
Walter Johnson	**38**	**110**	417	9.1	34.5
Pete Alexander	17	90	373	4.6	18.9
Bert Blyleven	15	60	287	5.2	25.0
Christy Mathewson	14	79	373	3.8	17.7
Dean Chance	13	33	128	**10.2**	**40.6**
Ed Walsh	13	57	195	6.7	22.8
Guy White	13	45	189	6.8	28.9
Cy Young	13	76	**511**	2.5	17.1
Steve Carlton	12	55	329	3.6	21.8
Stan Coveleski	12	38	215	5.6	31.6
Gaylord Perry	12	53	314	3.8	22.6
Eddie Plank	12	69	326	3.6	17.4

(continued)

Name	1-0	SHO	CW	% C	% SHO
Ferguson Jenkins	11	49	284	3.9	22.4
Greg Maddux	11	35	355	3.1	31.4
Charles Nichols	11	48	361	3.0	22.9
Johnny Rucker	11	38	134	8.2	28.9
Nolan Ryan	11	61	324	3.4	18.0
Joe Bush	10	35	196	5.1	28.6
Paul Derringer	10	32	223	4.9	31.3
Bill Doak	10	34	169	5.9	29.4
Sandy Koufax	10	40	165	6.1	25.0
Dick Rudolph	10	27	121	8.3	37.0
Warren Spahn	10	63	363	2.8	15.9
Lefty Tyler	10	30	127	7.9	33.3
Virgil Trucks	10	33	177	5.6	30.3
Jim Vaughn	10	41	178	5.6	24.4

Brooklyn 1, Chicago 0: 1890

John Montgomery Ward stood out among 19th-century baseball players. He is a Hall-of-Famer for more than one reason. Not only was he a versatile great, he was also among the game's entrepreneurs, workers' rights leaders, and forward-looking people. He was the chief instigating and organizing force behind the Players League, and though it lasted only one season, it was what its name implied—and constituted a league of players that played the game at least a cut or two above the highest minor leagues of the day.

In Ward's league there were only two 1-0 games. One of them was an eight-inning no-hitter fired by Silver King of the Chicago Pirates who were led by Charley Comiskey. The account of the game was written up for Chicago's *Interocean*, one of the Windy City dailies, and appeared in its June 22 issue. The full account appears here because it helps to understand how late-19th-century sportswriters viewed ball games and, further, because it reveals the writing style that described sporting events in such deliciously quaint wording. Here's the article.

Brooklyn 1, Chicago 0

Brotherhood spectators have frequently been treated to the spectacle of a tea-store chromo pitcher stultifying the efforts of his talented colleagues. The thing was reversed yesterday. Mr. Charles King stood up in the middle of the diamond and tossed a game of ball that was apples of gold in pictures of silver, while a couple of big, strong men in the infield made monkeys of themselves and gave away the game.

For eight innings John Ward and his eight gentlemanly assistants poked at Mr. King's grape and canister, and for eight innings the Brooklyn base-hit column was as immaculate as Andean snow. The Eastern young men were fairly retired from the game without a single, solitary base-hit. It was an extraordinary feat, and the first instance of the kind during the present season.

And the Brooklyns won the game! It was awful. Mr. Darling did it, with his little wild throw. It may be stated as a general truth that Mr. Darling played ball as well as the dear old gentlewoman who conducted a *caravanairy*.[1] His play was of the tawny, old-gold variety. Then Boyle threw to first like a boy knocking *haws*.[2] The visitors only drew one muff—a muff by Bierbauer.

The skinny man Weyhing was nearly always there, too. He held the Buccaneers down to four scattering hits, inducing quite a bevy of them to abuse the air, and in many little ways showed that he deserved the patronage of the public.

Indeed, it was, all through, a game in which the pitchers played the star roles, shifted scenery, watched the stage door and played a xylophone solo between the acts. As for King, the visitors never had a chance to shake hands with him and only on four occasions did the home gang pass the time of day with Mr. Weyhing.

Outside of a fifty-foot[3] streak of red flame between the centerpiece and the rubber, there were three features.

In the first Johnny (Ward) got a base on balls. He stole second like a flash and repeated the act to third. It was so easy that he probably concluded that he would take a run in home while the folks were busy about household cares and things. At any rate, he was poising like Mercury on the ball of his foot, about ten feet from the bag, while Charles Farrell threw his everyday arm around like a man cutting corn. There was a spanking sound and Mr. Ward remarking that he believed it was getting warmer, walked to the bench and set down.

Mr. Ward was also pleasantly fooled in the fourth inning. He bunted, Boyle threw over Comiskey's head and Ward started for second. But Pfeffer had got the ball in some marvelous way and threw to the captain (Comiskey) in a shot. Again Mr. Ward sat down.

John [Ward] made a wonderfully good catch himself. In the sixth he boosted his frame a few yards in the air and pulled down a liner of Comiskey's that was traveling north like a sky-rocket. Then Ward fired the ball to first before he got half way down and fooled Mr. Ryan, who was playing off a few yards.

It will be a long time before as queer a game will be seen again. The one run that juts out above the wide space of nothingness and on the wrong side of the channel at that, was made in the simplest way in the world. Van Haltren hit an easy one to Darling. The short-stop got it quickly enough to hand it to Comiskey, almost, and like a crazy man. The runner reached second; third on Cook's sacrifice, home on Bierbauer's out from Duffy to Comiskey. There is the whole story in a nutshell.

Chicago	AB	R	H	A	Brooklyn	AB	R	H	A
Duffy, rf	3	0	0	1	Joyce, 3b	4	0	0	1
O'Neill, lf	4	0	1	0	Ward, ss	3	0	0	2
Ryan, cf	3	0	0	0	Van Haltren, rf	3	1	0	0
Comiskey, 1b	4	0	0	1	Cook, 1b	4	0	0	0
Pfeffer, 2b	4	0	0	3	Bierbauer, 2b	3	0	0	2
Darling, ss	3	0	1	0	McGeachy, cf	3	0	0	0
Farrell, c	2	0	1	2	Seery, lf	2	0	0	0
Boyle, 3b	3	0	0	3	Kinslow, c	3	0	0	2
King (LP)*	3	0	1	4	Weyhing (WP)	3	0	0	1
Totals	**29**	**0**	**4**	**14**	**Totals**	**28**	**1**	**0**	**8**

*King's no-hit game is not sanctioned as a no-hitter because a no-hit game is considered such only if the pitcher pitches at least nine innings. This was the Players League's only "no-hit" game, played on June 21, 1890.

Chicago	000	000	000	0-4-8
Brooklyn	000	000	10x	1-0-0

Notes

1. A canarvansairy is an inn suited for a caravan stopover.
2. Haws is a term used for a hawthorn tree or its fruit.
3. The fifty-foot distance referred to here is the distance between the pitcher's box and home plate as specified by Players League rules.

APPENDIX D

The Perfect 1-0 Loss

Throwing twelve perfect innings is a major league record that hasn't been broken since it was set by Harvey Haddix on May 25, 1959. It may be a long time before that record is either tied or broken. It was an evening in the life of Harvey Haddix that defined his career, one of those sublime yet heartbreaking moments never to be forgotten, for on that dank and damp Milwaukee evening "The Kitten" lost a ball game—and not just another ball game but a ball game that was earmarked for history, a 1-0 loss that came in the bottom of the 13th inning on a home run ball by Joe Adcock, the huge Braves' first baseman, with runners on first and second. That should have made the final count read Milwaukee 3,[1] Pittsburgh 0. But it didn't. After reviewing the play National League President Warren Giles ruled that because Adcock had passed base runner Hank Aaron on the base paths in running out his homer, his hit had to be ruled a double, thus permitting only one run on the play. So the official scoring made it a 1-0 ball game.

That is almost neither here nor there as compared to the extraordinary nature of Haddix's astounding feat. Imagine retiring 36 batters in a row.

Reviews and interviews about this game have been written and conducted by countless numbers of people. Google will list dozens of articles for you about this bittersweet game. And since it belongs in a book about 1-0 games, it just had to find a place somewhere along the line. Since the Haddix feat does not readily fit into the book's prior chapters, it finds its place here, accompanied by the boxscore of that singularly exceptional game at Milwaukee's County Stadium.

Pittsburgh	AB	R	H	A	Milwaukee	AB	R	H	A
Schofield, ss	6	0	3	4	O'Brien, 2b	3	0	0	5
Virdon, cf	6	0	1	0	Rice, ph	1	0	0	0
Burgess, c	5	0	0	0	Mantilla, 2b	1	1	0	2
Nelson, 1b	5	0	2	0	Mathews, 3b	4	0	0	3
Skinner, lf	5	0	1	0	Aaron, rf	4	0	0	0
Mazeroski, 2b	5	0	1	1	Adcock, 1b	5	0	1	3
Hoak, 3b	5	0	2	6	Covington, lf	4	0	0	0
Mejias, rf	3	0	1	0	Crandall, c	4	0	0	1
Stuart, ph	1	0	0	0	Pafko, cf	4	0	0	0
Chistopher, rf	1	0	0	0	Logan, ss	4	0	0	5
Haddix (LP)	5	0	1	2	Burdette (WP)	4	0	0	4
Totals	**47**	**0**	**12**	**13**	**Totals**	**38**	**1**	**1**	**23**

Pittsburgh	000	000	000	000	0		0-12-1
Milwaukee	000	000	000	000	1		1-1-0

Error: Hoak
2bh: Adcock
DP: Milwaukee 3
LOB: Pittsburgh 8; Milwaukee 1
SH: Mathews
K: Haddix 8; Burdette 2
BB: Haddix 1 (int.); Burdette 1
Time of Game: 2:54
Attendance: 19,194
Umpires: Smith, Dascoli, Secory, Dixon

Note

1. Aaron was ruled out on this play because he had discontinued running the bases and headed for the dugout. Only Mantilla's run, therefore, was allowed.

Other Venues, Other 1-0 Stars

The Negro Leagues, beginning in the early 20th century, and the Japanese Major Leagues, beginning in the mid-1930s, have had colorful histories, originating within a context of national and international baseball and providing outstanding ball, if not exactly of major league caliber then certainly very close to it. Out of those settings have come a number of 1-0 games, a few of them presented here to acknowledge both their origination and their stars, some of whom eventually found their way to major league baseball teams.

Negro Leagues 1-0 Games: I

On August 2, 1930, Kansas City's Muehlebach Field was the site of one of the Negro League's most sensational games. The pitchers in that game, Smokey Joe Williams (Hall of Fame, 1999) and Chet Brewer (Hall of Fame, 1990) struck out 46 batters in a 12-inning game won by the Homestead Grays of Pittsburgh. Williams, at the advanced baseball age of 44, struck out 27 and Brewer, 19. Another of Williams's more notable games was a 1-0 victory over the Philadelphia Phillies with Pete Alexander on the mound. In this barnstorming game played in the fall of 1915, he struck out 10.

Negro Leagues 1-0 Games: II

Negro League All-Star Games, a midseason feature (1933–1950), were played at Comiskey Park, Chicago, between Eastern and Western Division stars. The 1934 game was a pitcher's duel between Satchel Paige, the first Negro League pitcher inducted into the Hall of Fame (1971), and Willie Foster (Hall of Fame, 1991). The East team scored the winning tally on a double by Jud Wilson in the eighth inning. The box score follows:

East	AB	R	H
Cool Papa Bell, cf (Pittsburgh Crawfords)	3	1	0
Jimmie Crutchfield, rf (Crawfords)	3	0	0
W. G. Perkins, c (Crawfords)	1	0	0
Oscar Charleston, 1b (Crawfords)	4	0	0
Jud Wilson, 3b (Philadelphia Stars)	3	0	1
Josh Gibson, c (Crawfords)	4	0	2
Vic Harris, lf (Crawfords)	2	0	1
Dick Lundy, ss (Newark Dodgers	4	0	0
Chester Williams, 2b (Crawfords)	4	0	3
Slim Jones, p (Stars)	1	0	0
Harry Kincannon, p (Crawfords)	1	0	1
Satchel Paige (WP) (Crawfords)	2	0	0
Totals	**31**	**1**	**8**

West	AB	R	H
Willie Wells, ss (Chicago American Giants)	3	0	1
Alex Radcliffe, 3b (Amer. Giants)	4	0	0
Turkey Stearns, cf (Amer. Giants)	4	0	0
Mule Suttles, 1b (Amer. Giants)	4	0	3
Red Parnell, lf (Nashville Elite Giants)	3	0	0
Sam Bankhead, rf (Elite Giants)	3	0	1
Larry Brown, c (Amer. Giants)	3	0	1
Sammy T. Hughes, 2b (Elite Giants)	2	0	0
J. Patterson, 2b (Cleveland Red Sox)	1	0	0
Theodore Trent, p (Amer. Giants)	1	0	0
Chet Brewer, p (Amer. Giants)	1	0	0
Willie Foster (LP) (Amer. Giants)	1	0	1
Totals	**30**	**0**	**7**

East	000	000	010	1-8-1
West	000	000	000	0-7-1

Negro Leagues 1-0 Games: III

There are three 1-0 no-hitters recorded in Negro League play that have been registered against top-level Negro League competition through the years. The first was crafted by Frank Wickware of the Chicago American Giants against the Indianapolis ABC's on August 26, 1914. Smokey Joe Williams threw the second, pitching for the Lincoln Giants against the Brooklyn Royal Giants on May 9, 1919, in the first game of a doubleheader. The final of these noteworthy achievements occurred on June 28, 1925. This no-hitter was pitched by Andy Cooper of the Detroit Stars in a game against the Indianapolis ABC's.

Cooper, a Hall-of-Famer (2006), was a big, strong southpaw, the ace of the Detroit Stars pitching staff from 1920 to 1927, before he was traded to the Kansas City Monarchs for five players in 1928. With a variety of pitches, a good change of pace, and excellent control, his overall record was 116 and 57. His no-hit, 1-0 gem was his only shutout in an 11 and 2, 1925 season, during which he fashioned a sparkling 1.88 ERA.

Japanese Major League Baseball

Since the mid-1930s major league baseball, as it is known and understood in American settings, has been played in Japan. It is an enthusiastically supported sport, and since American visits by major league players in the 1930s, beginning with Lou Gehrig, Lefty O'Doul (O'Doul has been honored with membership in the Japanese Hall of Fame), and Babe Ruth, it has gradually risen in caliber and presentation to a near-par status with American major league baseball.

For a look at some superlative 1-0 games in its more recent history, here are pitching gems turned in by two Japanese Hall of Fame pitchers, Yutaka Enatsu and Masaichi Kaneda. The latter, a left-handed Korean, pitched a perfect game on August 21, 1957. Yutaka Enatsu is the only Japanese major leaguer to win his own no-hitter, a 1-0, 11-inning game in 1973 with a walkoff home run he himself hit. These two extraordinary games are presented below.

THE KANEDA PERFECTO ON JULY 21, 1957

During his Hall of Fame career Masaichi Kaneda owned most of the important pitching records in Japanese Major League (NML) history. Some of the more notable ones include most victories (400) in NML history, most innings pitched, and most strikeouts. Those and several others will no doubt stand for a long, long time.

Playing for one of Japan's lesser franchises and perennial losers, the Tokyo Kokutsetsu Swallows, Kaneda pitched a perfect game in 1957, winning it 1-0. It was the first no-hitter won by a lefty in NML history. In command throughout the game, his mix of breaking pitches and speeds held the Chunichi Dragons in check, as the Swallows eked out a run to win one of Kaneda's 28 victories in

1957, a season during which he earned the Eiji Sawamura Award, the equivalent of MLB's Cy Young Award.

ENATSU'S SAYANORA, AUGUST 30, 1973

Yutaka Enatsu was not merely one of the NML's best ballplayers, he was also one of its most colorful players. A charismatic, bigger-than-life individual, he was a flame-throwing pitcher with Lefty Grove–like strikeout numbers, and he achieved his star status both as a starter and as the NML's pioneer saver.

In 1973 he put up huge numbers for the Hanshin Tigers, winning 24 games in a career-high 39 starts. During that banner season, on August 30 he put together a 1-0 game that Japanese baseball fans consider to be one of the most thrilling games ever staged on Nipponese soil. The game went into extra innings,

The colorful NML pitcher Yutaka Enatsu.

tied 0-0 at the end of nine. The 10th frame came and went without a score. Nor was there anything doing in the 11th stanza. Yutaka Enatsu had gone through the Chunichi lineup without having given up a hit. Then he added the 12th. In the bottom of the 12th, however, Enatsu crushed a sayanora clout that won the game for Hanshin, 1-0. That blast brought the house down. It was one of the few sayanora (walk-off) home runs in NLB baseball history, and coming off the bat of a pitcher made it just that much more sensational. It was a feat that matched its creator's personality: BIG.

Selected Bibliography

Books

Alexander, Charles C. *Our Game: An American Baseball History.* New York: Holt, 1991.

Barzilla, Scott. *Checks and Balances: Comparative Disparity in Major League Baseball.* New York: Atria Books, 2002.

Benson, Michael. *Ballparks of America.* Jefferson, NC: McFarland, 1989.

Buckley, Bill, Jr., and Phil Pepe. *Unhittable.* Chicago: Triumph Books, 2004.

Coffey, Michael. *27 Men Out.* New York: Atria Books, 2004.

Craft, David. *Great Moments in Baseball.* New York: Friedman/Fairfax, 1997.

Dewey, Donald, and N. Acocella. *The Biographical History of Baseball.* New York: Carroll and Graf, 1995.

Dickey, Glenn. *The Great No-Hitters.* Radnor, PA: Chilton, 1976.

Enders, Eric. *Baseball's Greatest Games.* Minnetonka, MN: MLB Insiders Club, 2008.

Fimrite, Ron. *The World Series.* New York: Bishop Books, 1993.

Gillette, Gary, and Pete Palmer, eds. *The ESPN Baseball Encyclopedia*, 5th ed. New York: Sterling, 2008.

Guschov, Stephen. *The Red Stockings of Cincinnati.* Jefferson, NC: McFarland, 1998.

Honig, Donald. *Baseball When the Grass Was Real.* New York: Berkeley, 1975.

James, Bill. *The New Bill James Historical Abstract.* New York: Free Press, 2001.

James, Bill, and Rob Neyer. *The Neyer/James Guide To Pitchers.* New York: Simon and Schuster, 2004.

Lanigan, Ernest J. *The Baseball Cyclopedia.* New York: Baseball Magazine Company, 1922.

Lorimer, Lawrence. *Baseball Desk Reference.* New York: DK Publishers, 2001.

MacKay, Joe. *The Great Shutout Pitchers.* Jefferson, NC: McFarland, 2004.

Mackin, Bob. *Baseball's Most Unusual Records.* Vancouver: Greystone Books, 2004.

Mayer, Ronald A. *Perfect.* Jefferson, NC: McFarland, 1991.

McCollister, John. *The Best Baseball Games Ever Played.* New York: Citadel Press, 2002.

Nemec, David, and Scott Flatow. *Great Baseball Feats, Facts and Firsts (2010)*. New York: Signet, 2010.

Reichler, Joseph L., ed. *The Baseball Encyclopedia*, 7th ed. New York: Macmillan, 1988.

Selzer, Jack. *Baseball In the 19th Century: An Overview*. Cooperstown, NY: SABR, 1986.

Solomon, Burt. *The Baseball Timeline*. New York: DK Publishing, 2002.

Sugar, Bert Randolph, ed. *The Baseball Maniac's Almanac*, 2nd ed. New York: Skyhorse Publishing, 2010.

Thomas, Henry. *Walter Johnson: Baseball's Big Train*. Lincoln: University of Nebraska Press, 1995.

Wilbert, Warren N. *What Makes An Elite Pitcher?* Jefferson, NC: McFarland, 2003.

Circulars

Baseball America
Baseball Research Journal
ESPN: The Magazine
Inside Sports
National Pastime
Sports Illustrated
The Sporting News

Websites

baseball1.com
baseballalmanac.com
baseballhalloffame.com
baseballlibrary,com
baseball-reference.com
bleacherreport.com
cnnsi.com
efastball.com
fanhouse.com
foxsports.com
hardballtimes.com
joeposnanski.blogspot.com
majorleaguebaseball.com
nytimes.com
retrosheet.org
sabr.org
totalbaseball.com

Newspapers

Atlanta Constitution
Chicago Interocean
Chicago Tribune
Detroit News
Los Angeles Times
New York Times
St. Louis Post-Dispatch

Name Index

About the Author

Dr. Warren N. Wilbert, veteran Society for American Baseball Research (SABR) member and baseball historian, has written a number of baseball books and articles. Retired since 1993, he is the dean emeritus of Concordia Ann Arbor's School of Adult Learning.

Wilbert has written articles for SABR's *Baseball Research Journal* and *National Pastime*. His books include *Strategies for Teaching Christian Adults*, *The Chicago Cubs: Seasons at the Summit*, *The New York Yankees: Seasons of Glory*, *Rookies Rated*, *The Best of Baseball*, *What Makes an Elite Player?*, *A Cunning Kind of Play*, *The Arrival of the American League*, *The 1917 White Sox*, and *The Opening Pitch*.

Wilbert resides in Fort Wayne, Indiana, the home of professional baseball's first game in 1871 and its first shutout.